ANNA TRAPNEL'S REPORT AND PLEA

The Other Voice in Early Modern Europe:
The Toronto Series, 50

MEDIEVAL AND RENAISSANCE
TEXTS AND STUDIES

VOLUME 503

The Other Voice in
Early Modern Europe:
The Toronto Series

SERIES EDITORS Margaret L. King *and* Albert Rabil, Jr.
SERIES EDITOR, ENGLISH TEXTS Elizabeth H. Hageman

Previous Publications in the Series

The Other Voice in
Early Modern Europe:
The Toronto Series

SERIES EDITORS Margaret L. King *and* Albert Rabil, Jr.
SERIES EDITOR, ENGLISH TEXTS Elizabeth H. Hageman

Previous Publications in the Series

The Other Voice in Early Modern Europe: The Toronto Series

SERIES EDITORS Margaret L. King *and* Albert Rabil, Jr.
SERIES EDITOR, ENGLISH TEXTS Elizabeth H. Hageman

Previous Publications in the Series

The Other Voice in
Early Modern Europe:
The Toronto Series

SERIES EDITORS Margaret L. King *and* Albert Rabil, Jr.
SERIES EDITOR, ENGLISH TEXTS Elizabeth H. Hageman

Previous Publications in the Series

The Other Voice in
Early Modern Europe:
The Toronto Series

SERIES EDITORS Margaret L. King *and* Albert Rabil, Jr.
SERIES EDITOR, ENGLISH TEXTS Elizabeth H. Hageman

Previous Publications in the Series

ANNA TRAPNEL

Anna Trapnel's Report and Plea; or, A Narrative of Her Journey from London into Cornwall

~

Edited by

HILARY HINDS

Iter Press
Toronto, Ontario

Arizona Center for Medieval and Renaissance Studies
Tempe, Arizona

2016

Iter Press

Tel: 416/978–7074   Email: iter@utoronto.ca

Fax: 416/978–1668   Web: www.itergateway.org

Arizona Center for Medieval and Renaissance Studies

Tel: 480/965–5900   Email: mrts@acmrs.org

Fax: 480/965–1681   Web: acmrs.org

This project benefitted from a Scholarly Editions and Translations grant awarded by the National Endowment for the Humanities.

Library of Congress Cataloging-in-Publication Data

Names: Trapnel, Anna, author. | Hinds, Hilary, editor.

Title: Anna Trapnel's report and plea : or, a narrative of her journey from London into Cornwall / edited by Hilary Hinds.

Other titles: Narrative of her journey from London into Cornwall

Description: Toronto, Ontario : Iter Press, [2016] | Includes bibliographical references and index.

Identifiers: LCCN 2016027967 (print) | LCCN 2016032015 (ebook) | ISBN 9780866985581 (pbk. : alk. paper) | ISBN 9780866987264 ()

Subjects: LCSH: Trapnel, Anna, author. | Great Britain—Politics and government—1649–1660—Sources. | Sermons, English—17th century. | Baptist women—England—History—17th century. | Fifth Monarchy Men—Sources.

Classification: LCC DA420 .T728 2016 (print) | LCC DA420 (ebook) | DDC 942.06/3092 [B] --dc23

LC record available at https://lccn.loc.gov/2016027967

Cover illustration:

Anna Trapnel, after Richard Gaywood; line engraving, late 18th to early 19th century; © National Portrait Gallery, London, NPG D29220.

Cover design:

Maureen Morin, Information Technology Services, University of Toronto Libraries.

Typesetting and production:

Iter Press.

Contents

Cover illustration: "Anna Trapnel, after Richard Gaywood." Line engraving, late eighteenth to early nineteenth century. NPG D29220. © National Portrait Gallery, London. Reproduced with permission.

BDBR   Richard L. Greaves and Robert Zaller, eds. *Biographical Dictionary of British Radicals in the Seventeenth Century.* 3 vols. Brighton: Harvester, 1982–1984.

CCC   Great Britain. Public Record Office, Mary Anne Everett. *Calendar of the Proceedings of the Committee for Compounding, & c., 1643–1660.* 5 vols. London: H. M. Stationery Office, 1889.

CSPD   Great Britain. Public Record Office. *Calendar of State Papers, Domestic Series: The Commonwealth, 1649–1660.* 13 vols. London: Longman, Brown, Green, Longmans, & Robert, 1856–1872.

ODNB   *Oxford Dictionary of National Biography.* Oxford University Press, 2004. Online edition. http://www.oxforddnb.com/

OED   *Oxford English Dictionary.* Oxford University Press, 1989. Online edition. http://www.oed.com/

Sheppard William Sheppard, *The Whole Office of the Country Justice of Peace. Wherein is Plainly Set Down all their Power and Duty both in, and out of the Quarter Sessions,* 2nd edition. London, 1652.

Thurloe Thomas Birch, ed. *A Collection of the State Papers of John Thurloe, Esq., Secretary, First, to the Council of State, and Afterwards to the Two Protectors, Oliver and Richard Cromwell.* 7 vols. London: Woodward and Davis, 1742.

VCH   *The Victoria History of the Counties of England.* London and New York: Oxford University Press, 1911–.

VCV   College of Arms, Great Britain. *The Visitations of Cornwall, Comprising the Heralds' Visitations of 1530, 1573, & 1620. With additions by J. L. Vivian.* Exeter: William Pollard, 1887.

Acknowledgments

My first thanks go to Professor Elizabeth H. Hageman, who invited me to contribute this volume to the Other Voice in Early Modern Europe series. I am grateful to her not only for the invitation but also for her enthusiasm for the project and her meticulous and generous scrutiny of early drafts. I am also grateful to my anonymous reader for his/her enthusiastic comments and very helpful suggestions; the latter enabled me to make some invaluable improvements late in the day.

I am greatly indebted to the National Endowment for the Humanities for their financial support for this project, and to Professor Albert Rabil, general editor of this series, who gave so liberally of his time and expertise to secure this funding. The Faculty of Arts and Social Sciences at Lancaster University also supported the project with a small grant to fund a research assistant to transcribe the text. Dr. Jessica Dyson undertook this work, and I am grateful to her for the scholarly and professional manner in which she undertook it. Rose Deller, with her customary calm efficiency and acuity, provided invaluable assistance with the compilation of the bibliography and with proofing the manuscript.

The staffs of many libraries and archives have responded with great kindness and generosity to my requests for help. I would like in particular to thank Josef Keith of the Library of the Religious Society of Friends, London, and Colin Gale, archivist at Bethlem Museum of the Mind. I am grateful too to the staff of the Cornwall Records Office and the Royal Cornwall Museum, both in Truro; the Cornish Studies Library, Redruth; the Devon Records Office, Exeter; the British Library and Dr. Williams's Library, London; and Lancaster University Library.

A number of people—friends, colleagues, and strangers—have helped me to answer questions that arose as I edited the text; thanks go to John Appleby, Brian Austin, Simon Barker, Arthur Bradley, Rebecca Bullard, Andrew Dawson, Liz Oakley-Brown, Robert Poole, and Ian Thompson. Professor John O'Hagan, of Trinity College, Dublin, gave me more help than I deserved as I tried to work out what £150 in 1654 would be worth today; thanks also to Joan O'Hagan, Emer O'Hagan, and Sorcha O'Hagan for their contributions to the discussion. Meg Twycross was willing to be regularly distracted from her own work when I asked for help with deciphering seventeenth-century handwriting; I count myself fortunate to have such an enthusiast as a close colleague. I was also touched by the kindness of John and Jennie Keeler, the owners of Tregassow Manor, near Truro. I spent a very enjoyable morning with them at Tregassow, and I am grateful to them for sharing with me their very considerable knowledge of the history of their home.

Last, but never least, my thanks go to Jackie and Anna, who have been fellow travelers with me on this project for longer than should have been necessary. I am indebted to them for their patience and enthusiasm.

Introduction

The Other Voice

The work of Anna Trapnel (1620–after 1660) is a signal instance of "the other voice" in early modern England. Her rank, her gender, her religious beliefs and practices, the kinds of texts she wrote, the manner in which they were written, the reputation of the works and of their author—all of these situate Trapnel as "other" to almost all the centers of social, religious, political, and literary power in the mid-seventeenth century and beyond.

Anna Trapnel's background was not that of someone whose voice was likely to contribute to a national political debate. The daughter of a shipwright, she was brought up in the vicinity of the London shipyards in the hamlet of Poplar, part of the large parish of Stepney. This area lies to the east of the City of London, and so was at one remove from the civic and trading heart of the capital and the nation. While Trapnel was not brought up in poverty—she was literate, "trained up to my book and writing," as she put it, and of substantial enough means to be a willing tax-payer—her social origins nonetheless were unlikely to have led to any expectation that she might intervene in public life.[1] Without the unprecedented political turbulence of the 1640s and 1650s, the years of the English Civil Wars, the execution of the King, and the establishment of an English republic, her modest background probably would have led her to live as her mother had, largely within the bounds of her family, her local community, and her congregation. Women of her rank and milieu were expected to work, certainly, running their households and frequently contributing to their husbands' businesses. In those contexts, however, women's voices would have been exercised in the interests of family (the principal social and economic unit), in line with expectations regarding the proper behavior of their sex.

It was the incessant political and religious flux and uncertainty of the middle years of the seventeenth century that gave Trapnel both the desire and the means to speak and write for larger and more powerful audiences. Hers was a voice that insisted on its own significance to the unfolding events of the English Revolution of the 1640s and 1650s. However, because she was a woman, because she came from a modest family background, because she rejected the practices of the Church of England, because she railed against the political establishment, and because she frequently uttered prophecies while in a state of trance, it was a voice without the endorsement of official discourse, and indeed a voice actively castigated by those who held the reins of power. As a woman, a radical, and a prophet, she had no ready access to public religious and political debate.

---

1. Anna Trapnel, *The Cry of a Stone*, ed. Hilary Hinds (Arizona: Arizona Center for Medieval and Renaissance Studies, 2000), 6.

The Civil War was a war of words as much as it was an armed encounter between the armies of the King and of Parliament. The ideas at stake inhabited that composite early modern domain that was at once political and religious, seeking to determine just what the institutions and practices of a godly society would look like. These debates took place not only among the upper echelons of the ruling elites of aristocracy, Parliament, gentry, and the army but also within and between congregations, in the coalescing of new political groups, in petitions to Parliament, and in the medium of cheap popular print. The proliferating radical religious groups that rejected the ordinances and practices of the Church of England and formed their own dissenting congregations proved to be one particularly rich source of such debate, as their members argued their positions not only in rejection of the Church of England but also in contradistinction to other religious splinter groups. Trapnel's voice was exercised and honed in just such an environment. A member of one of the most radical Baptist congregations in London, Allhallows the Great, she rubbed shoulders with many of the most influential—and controversial—separatist preachers of her day.[2] Like a number of them, she was also a Fifth Monarchist: a millenarian believer in the imminence of the Day of Judgment and the return of King Jesus to rule in person. Such beliefs were in themselves neither exceptional nor extreme—indeed, Oliver Cromwell, governing the country at the time, shared many of them—but they acquired a particular urgency and political iconoclasm in the hands of the group of which Trapnel was a part.

If her background and her religious affiliation rendered her voice "other" to the mainstream, so too did her mode of speaking. Trapnel was a prophet, uttering her stormy tirades against the government of Oliver Cromwell and his allies in a series of visionary trances, the best known of which overtook her in January 1654 while she was attending the examination of Vavasor Powell, a fellow Fifth Monarchist, in the Palace of Whitehall, the former chief royal residence in London and the seat of government then as now.[3] For eleven days, fasting, she lay in a room in a nearby inn, where crowds of curious onlookers gathered, and spoke in verse and prose her words of angry lamentation at Cromwell's betrayal and of ecstatic anticipation of the coming millennium. As a prophet, she quite literally spoke as "the other voice," for she claimed that she spoke not of her own volition but at the insistence of God—indeed, that she was "made a voice, a sound ... a voice within a voice, another's voice, even thy voice through her."[4] Her voice needs to

2. Figures such as John Simpson, Christopher Feake, and William Greenhill were of great importance to Trapnel, and as such appear in her *Report and Plea* (London, 1654).

3. On the history of Whitehall Palace, see Ben Weinreb and Christopher Hibbert, eds., *The London Encyclopædia* (London: Macmillan, 1983), 959–60; and Simon Thurley, "The Lost Palace of Whitehall," *History Today* 48.1 (1998): 47–52.

4. Trapnel, *Cry*, 45.

be understood as "other" not only to the dominant culture but also—and powerfully—to herself.

It was the prophetic words spoken in the inn near Whitehall that formed her first publications. Two versions of these visionary prophecies were quickly published, her words having been transcribed by someone in the room identified only as "the relator."[5] This alerts us to yet another way in which her voice might be said to be "other," for her route into print was not via an act of straightforward authorship, her own words transmitted by her own pen into her own, authorized, text. Instead, she speaks words prompted by the Lord, in a trance of which she can recall nothing once she comes to herself again, and transcribed by a well-meaning but imperfect "relator" who cannot catch everything she says. This relay of voices speaking through a variety of textual collaborations and mediations reminds us that "authorship" has no simple or monolithic form and allows us to hear still other voices alongside and as a part of Trapnel's own.

Trapnel was a woman of the middling sort, a committed member of an oppositional religious movement speaking out insistently for a political agenda that put her at odds with the government of the day, a visionary prophet, and a collaborative author. As such, her profile challenges many of our expectations as to where and how an early modern woman's voice might be heard. Yet to catalogue the many ways in which her voice might be understood as other to the dominant modes of spoken and written discourse of her time is to risk corralling her into a position where that voice sounds always responsive, defensive, secondary, perhaps even impotent—a beleaguered counterpoint to the dominant discursive strain. *Anna Trapnel's Report and Plea*, the text republished here in its entirety for the first time since it appeared in 1654, however, quickly dispels any such categorization. Here, in the final text of hers to be published in that most remarkable year, Trapnel's voice sounds out loud and clear. It is assured, sometimes angry. It is unapologetic, politicized, not only literate, steeped as it is in the language of the Bible, but also rhetorically adept, as it makes its case—against all the odds, perhaps—that she is "a woman like others, that were modest and civil,"[6] undeserving of the opprobrium that is heaped upon her.

It is also a voice that, in the *Report and Plea*, moves between the genres of autobiography, travel narrative, polemic, and personal defense. It not only tells her own remarkable story of her journey into Cornwall, in the far southwest of the country, and her subsequent imprisonment in Bridewell Prison, back in London, but also examines her fears regarding her prophetic calling and her hopes for the restitution of the ways of God in a nation she believed to be losing its way. It is a voice that claims for itself a place in the public life of the nation, such that its

---

5. The two texts were Trapnel, *Cry*, and Anna Trapnel, *Strange and Wonderful Newes from White-Hall* (London, 1654).

6. 122. Page numbers for the *Report and Plea* refer to the present edition.

characteristics as "other" become no less than the rationale for their being rein-scribed as indispensable.

"The world's stage": Anna Trapnel's Historical Context

"The report was, I went from place to place, aspersing the government."[7] This sentence, taken from the closing pages of Trapnel's *Report and Plea*, brings into sharp relief just how much was at stake as a consequence of her prophesying, pub-lishing, and traveling.[8] The events recorded in this text, and indeed the very figure of its author, caused reverberations that went right to the heart of the public life of the day. To "asperse" the government was to speak "seditious words"; and sedition, a treasonous act, was punishable by death.[9] To prophesy in the way that Trapnel did was to give voice to words that the prophet claimed were God's own, and in so doing fearlessly to speak truth, as she saw it, to temporal power. Whether one interprets such an act as reckless or courageous, deluded or inspired, it unques-tionably brought her into situations where she was vulnerable to the weight of government retribution.

Anna Trapnel lived in tumultuous times, when a good deal more than small-scale acts of sedition was in contention. In 1642, twelve years before her journey to Cornwall, the Civil Wars had first broken out, with the armies and supporters of King Charles I lining up against those of Parliament. At issue were not only ques-tions of taxation, the King's "personal rule" (from 1629 to 1640 Charles I ruled alone, without calling Parliament), or the power of the prerogative courts, but also more fundamental and far-reaching questions of monarchical power, its origins and its limits, and thus the nature of tyranny and freedom. The Parliamentary armies finally prevailed in 1647, capturing the King, trying him, and in January 1649 executing him. Shortly afterwards, the monarchy itself was abolished, as was the House of Lords. England was declared a Commonwealth, or Republic, to be governed by a small Council of State, its members drawn from Parliament and the

---

7. 76.

8. See 85n250.

9. *The Weekly Intelligencer* 243 (May 30–June 6, 1654), 280, recorded that Trapnel "is for some sedi-tious words brought up from *Cornwall* by Order of the Council." An act identifying what offences shall be "adjudged high treason" had been passed on January 19, 1654; it included the words: "if any person or persons shall maliciously or advisedly either by writing, printing, openly declaring, preach-ing, teaching or otherwise, publish, That the Lord Protector and the people in Parliament assembled are not the Supreme Authority of this Commonwealth, … Or that the said Authority or Government is Tyrannical, usurped, or unlawful, … Then every such offence shall be taken and adjudged to be High Treason." C. H. Firth and R. S. Rait, eds., "19 January 1654: An Ordinance Declaring that the offences herein mentioned, and no other, shall be adjudged High Treason within the Common-wealth of England, Scotland, and Ireland, and the Dominions thereunto belonging," *Acts and Ordinances of the Interregnum, 1642–1660*, 2:831–35 (London: Stationery Office, 1911), 832.

Army, and led by the increasingly powerful figure of Oliver Cromwell. A Member of Parliament since 1640 and an officer in the Parliamentary armies since 1642, Cromwell rose to become the New Model Army's Lord General (commander-in-chief) in 1650. In 1653, he dissolved the Barebone's (or Nominated) Parliament, the short-lived assembly that had seemed briefly to offer radicals like Trapnel the promise of a social and political order premised on the millenarian beliefs they espoused. At the same time, Cromwell accepted the title of Lord Protector, a move proposed by his fellow rulers but seen by radical groups as dangerously close to the assumption of the crown.[10] It was in the wake of these momentous and (to her) treacherous acts that, in January 1654, Trapnel went to Whitehall—the center of government—to attend the examination of a fellow radical, the Welsh preacher Vavasor Powell, by the Council of State. There she fell into a visionary trance that lasted eleven days and during which she uttered the prophecies published as *The Cry of a Stone* in February 1654. There, in Whitehall, began the train of events that kept Trapnel in the public eye for the best part of a year.

Such an account gives little sense, however, of the complexity, the uncertainty, and the turmoil generated by the unprecedented and fast-moving events of the 1640s and early 1650s. While the main political fault line of the times undoubtedly lay between Royalist and Parliamentarian, the subdivisions among the Parliamentary supporters were many and complex. In the 1640s, for example, there were two main factions in Parliament itself. On one side were the Presbyterians, "conservatives" who favored negotiation with the King, feared the increasing power of Cromwell's New Model Army, and supported the establishment of a Presbyterian and antisectarian religious system. On the other side were the more radical Independents (who ultimately prevailed), aligned with the Army and arguing for religious toleration. London, the capital city and seat of government, was the forum in which the political consequences of the Civil Wars were fought out most intensely, not only among Parliamentarians themselves but also among the many popular political groups that formed and agitated in these years, of whom the Levelers, led by John Lilburne, are only the best known. With the demise of the old system of censorship in 1641, there was a proliferation of cheap printed pamphlets and petitions, by means of which groups such as these made their cases and argued their corners in unprecedented numbers. So it was, as Nigel Smith has suggested, that the events of these years effected a revolution of words still more far-reaching even than the revolution in government and the social order. "In that all but the poorest now had the possibility of authorship," he writes, "we can say that the English Revolution was more thoroughgoing in the extension of

---

10. For a fascinating account of the momentous events of the 1640s and 1650s from the point of view of one of Trapnel's fellow Fifth Monarchists, see Christopher Feake, *A Beam of Light, Shining in the Midst of Much Darkness and Confusion* (London: J. C. for Livewell Chapman, 1659).

the possession and use of words than it was in property redistribution."[11] Popular contributions to political debate, in the form of a plethora of pamphlets and petitions as well as debates and disputes, took place on an unprecedented scale and played a significant part in shaping the events and agendas of these years.

These pamphlets—topical, ephemeral, often quickly produced and comprising only a few pages—debated political issues still recognizable as such today. These include issues of parliamentary representation, property and land ownership, taxation, law reform, the justice or injustice of monarchical rule, and so on. But they also rehearsed matters of great complexity and burning urgency that today we would be more likely to categorize as religious rather than political. At issue were questions of the nature of salvation and the bestowal of God's grace, church governance and congregational autonomy, and interpretations of current events in the light of biblical prophecies. In the seventeenth century, however, arguments about religion were also debates about politics, and vice versa. At stake in them all was the matter of a godly society. What would this comprise? How should it be constituted, so that God's will for his people be best ensured? Who would rule, and how? Whose voices could legitimately be heard, in what form, and in what kinds of situation? How much room should there be for diversity of religious views and practices? Which translation of the Bible should be used? Thomas Edwards, a conservative Presbyterian who deplored this outpouring of discussion and dissent, published a three-volume collection of what he saw as reprehensible and blasphemous contemporary religious opinion. Entitled *Gangraena; or, A Catalogue and Discovery of Many of the Errors, Heresies, Blasphemies, and Pernicious Practices of the Sectaries of this Time* (1646), it gives a vivid, if expostulatory, sense of the ferment and scope of religious ideas at this time.

Not all commentators, however, responded with the fear or revulsion of Edwards. For an indication of the excitement and sense of possibility that such debate could also engender, we do better to listen to the poet, pamphleteer, and Parliamentarian John Milton. In *Areopagitica* (1644), his pamphlet against prepublication censorship, he celebrates the English people as "a Nation not slow and dull, but of a quick, ingenious and piercing spirit, acute to invent, subtle and sinewy to discourse." Such a people, he argues, can be trusted to discern the difference between God's truth and the erroneous opinions that were in circulation. The work of revolution, Milton insists, is as much about the hammering out of ideas as it is about the fashioning of the "instruments of armed Justice," and he argues that his readers should celebrate the fact that "there be pens and heads there, sitting by their studious lamps, musing, searching, revolving new notions and ideas … others as fast reading, trying all things, assenting to the force of

11. Nigel Smith, *Literature and Revolution in England, 1640–1660* (New Haven: Yale University Press, 1994), 6.

reason and convincement."[12] The argument that this was a revolution of words and ideas as well as of military force was as current then as now.

The matters so hotly contested might now seem arcane, but at the time they were urgent, fraught, and contentious, for the 1640s and 1650s were not only years of political upheaval but also marked the culmination of decades of religious disputation and fragmentation. The Reformation in England—the separation from the Roman Catholic Church and the establishment of an English Protestant church—had precipitated an unparalleled level of intense debate about the proper interpretation of the Bible, the ordinances and practices of the church, and the beliefs that underpinned them. With this debate came a splintering of the national body of believers, and the establishment of a number of separate autonomous groups such as the Independents (later the Congregationalists), the Baptists, and the Quakers, committed to worshipping as their consciences and their beliefs dictated. Trapnel belonged to the "Particular Baptists," a group whose origins lay in the previous century but whose numbers proliferated in the 1640s. The epithet "Particular" in their name referred to the belief that salvation was predestined only for the few, rather than potentially available to all, as the "General Baptists" believed.[13] The two groups were united, however, in their rejection of the practice of infant baptism.

Whereas the General Baptists were "Arminian"—that is, they believed that people could act, for good or ill, so as to affect their own progress toward salvation—the Particular Baptists, like the majority of the many radical religious groups of the time, subscribed to Calvinist doctrines of election and predestination. These held that Christ had died to save only particular individuals, the predestined "elect," the chosen few or (in Trapnel's terminology) the "Saints." This emphasis on predestination—the belief that God had decided "before the foundations of the world were laid" who would be saved and who would be damned— brought with it a stress on the inability of a believer to intervene in their own spiritual progress.[14] Salvation could not be earned but was the unmerited gift of a beneficent God; as St. Paul put it, "For by grace are ye saved through faith; and

12. John Milton, "Areopagitica," in Milton, *Prose Writings*, ed. K. M. Burton, 145–85 (London: Dent, 1958), 176, 177.

13. On these groups, and others, see Christopher Hill, *The World Turned Upside Down: Radical Ideas During the English Revolution* (London: Maurice Temple Smith, 1972; this ed. Harmondsworth: Penguin: 1975); J. F. McGregor and Barry Reay, eds., *Radical Religion in the English Revolution* (Oxford: Oxford University Press, 1984); and Andrew Bradstock, *Radical Religion in Cromwell's England: A Concise History from the English Civil War to the End of the Commonwealth* (London: I. B. Tauris, 2011).

14. From Article XVII of the "Articles of Religion" (39 Articles) of the Church of England, first prepared under Edward VI and revised under Elizabeth I, and included in *The Book of Common Prayer* (1571; this ed. London: Eyre and Spottiswoode, n.d.), 691.

that not of yourselves: it is the gift of God."[15] Together these elements produced a religious discourse of both remarkable intensity and extraordinary variety. The spiritual autobiography of a Particular Baptist such as John Bunyan, for example, is an unremitting record of uncertainty, self-doubt, and torment, as he sought to navigate the inevitable indeterminacy of his spiritual destiny. "How can you tell you are Elected? and what if you should not: how then?" he asks himself, and records that "By these things I was driven to my wits end."[16] For Anna Trapnel, in contrast, the doctrine of election and reprobation, and the consequent relinquishment of all sense of individual spiritual agency, seems to have released her from fear of sin and temptation into a frequently ecstatic and blissful state: "I had exceeding raptures of joy very frequent, little or no intermissions, no questions or doubtings in the least measure."[17] Confident in her sense of God's love, and of his providential hand intervening in the world to protect her and to subdue her enemies, she concludes with disarming simplicity in the *Report and Plea* that "it's a lovely life the life of faith."[18] The doctrine of Calvinism and the cultures and affective responses it generated, therefore, were not monolithic. While they were certainly frequently productive of anxious, sometimes anguished, discourse such as Bunyan's, the insistence on human powerlessness in the face of divine omnipotence could also be, as it was for Trapnel, a source of liberation, joy, comfort, and even confidence and courage.

As well as being a Baptist, Trapnel was a Fifth Monarchist: that is, a millenarian who believed (as so many people—John Milton and Oliver Cromwell among them—did at the time) that the revolutionary events currently unfolding in England represented the fulfillment of biblical prophecies, and that the political turmoil presaged the imminence of Christ's Second Coming. Of particular importance for Fifth Monarchists in this respect were the books of Daniel and Revelation, with their prophecies of the demise of the four earthly monarchies and the institution of the fifth monarchy, when King Jesus would return to rule on earth, in person.[19] The Fifth Monarchists are notoriously difficult to locate in relation to specific religious groupings or doctrinal positions, and indeed the historian Bernard Capp writes that "their genesis was political rather than religious." Nonetheless, they were drawn principally from the Independents and the Particular Baptists, and Fifth Monarchist groups coalesced within these congregations, from

15. Ephesians 2:8.

16. John Bunyan, *Grace Abounding, with other Spiritual Autobiographies*, ed. John Stachniewski with Anita Pacheco (Oxford: Oxford University Press, 1998), 20.

17. Anna Trapnel, *A Legacy for Saints; Being Several Experiences of the Dealings of God with Anna Trapnel, In, and After her Conversion* (London: Thomas Brewster, 1654), 10.

18. 52.

19. On the importance of the books of Daniel and Revelation, see Bradstock, *Radical Religion*, xii–xviii, 117–19, 136, 163–64. He also discusses Trapnel: see 125–28, 130–34.

which they differed "only in certain details of eschatology, and in their political attitude. But they saw themselves as a distinct group ... and their meetings had a religious as well as a political function."[20] In Trapnel's case, the congregation of which she was a part, Allhallows the Great, on Thames Street in London, was one of the "very capitals of the Fifth Monarchy," as the historian Austin Woolrych calls it. There, the movement's leading preachers and spokesmen John Simpson and Christopher Feake were weekday lecturers and held a number of rousing meetings where they prayed that "all *Corrupt, Wicked, and ungodly Magistrates* might be removed, and put out of place and power; and that a Righteous generation of Rulers might be set up in their stead."[21] Religion and politics, as these words show, together spoke a single language.

The *Report and Plea* makes clear just what an important source of community and comfort, as well as political expression, the congregation was to Trapnel. She visits Feake and Simpson in jail in Windsor Castle before she embarks on her journey to Cornwall; she thinks of her congregation repeatedly, and with some longing, in the course of her travels, and sends them letters; and when she is imprisoned in Bridewell, members of the congregation not only visited her there but also stayed with her to take care of her, and intervened with the authorities on her account. In July 1654, while she was still in Bridewell, they also published on her behalf *A Legacy for Saints*, a collection of her autobiographical accounts, prophecies, and letters. The congregation was thus much more than a body of like-minded believers. It provided an environment as emotionally intense, as supportive, as irritating, and sometimes as explosive as that more typically associated with the family.[22]

Separatist congregations such as Trapnel's at Allhallows the Great drew as many women to them as men; indeed, Bernard Capp has found that the surviving church lists show that "women easily outnumbered men."[23] These religious groupings proved to be important for women's entry in significant numbers into the world of public debate, writing, and publication. While the ratio of women's writings to men's did not change significantly in this period, their overall quantity did rise substantially. Trapnel's publications constitute just one instance among

20. B. S. Capp, *The Fifth Monarchy Men: A Study in Seventeenth-Century English Millenarianism* (London: Faber and Faber, 1972), 172, 182.

21. Austin Woolrych, *Commonwealth to Protectorate* (Oxford: Clarendon Press, 1982), 18; and Feake, *A Beam of Light*, 41. A lecturer was a preacher; see Trapnel, *Report and Plea*, 69n170; and Paul S. Seaver, *The Puritan Lectureships: The Politics of Religious Dissent, 1560–1662* (Stanford: Stanford University Press, 1970).

22. One of Trapnel's letters to Allhallows from Cornwall shows her clearly irritated by her congregation's failure to reply to her last letter; see introduction, 22. For the later split in the congregation of Allhallows the Great, see Capp, *Fifth Monarchy Men, 276–78*.

23. Capp, *Fifth Monarchy Men*, 82.

many of sectarian women's accession to print in this period. Other women who traveled this route to publication include Mary Cary, Katherine Chidley, Sarah Jones, Margaret Fell, Jane Turner, Barbara Blaugdone, and Anne Wentworth. As the twentieth-century feminist historians and literary critics who were instrumental in returning the work of these writers to public view noted, this period marks a sea-change not only in women's entry into print culture but also in the unprecedented access to it assumed by women of the middling sort.[24] Alongside their male counterparts—and sometimes head-to-head with them—these writers staked their claims in the great conversation that unfolded through the revolutionary years.

It was not as a religious polemicist, political commentator, or biblical exegete, however, that Trapnel first found her way into print, but as a prophet. For sectaries such as Trapnel, "prophecy" was not so much, or not only, the foretelling of events, but rather, in the historian Diane Purkiss's words, "any utterance produced by God through human agency."[25] This frequently involved the interpretation of current events and phenomena in the light of biblical teachings. It is, therefore, a very capacious category, comprising a range of different kinds of divinely originating discourse. The Fifth Monarchist Mary Cary, for example, believed that "all might prophesy, that is (in the lowest sense) be able to speak to edification, exhortation and comfort."[26] Trapnel's prophetic mode, however, was less quotidian in its form. Her prophecies were the result of the "bringing of my Spirit into this extraordinary praying and singing, and visions."[27] Frequently, this involved a period of fasting and the advent of a trance state, often of long duration, during which she extemporized prayer and prophecy, in verse and prose, and of which she had no recollection once the trance ended.

Prophecy, whether uttered by women or men, was a mode of expression to which people during the revolutionary years were more than usually open. The historian Phyllis Mack has suggested that "over four hundred women prophesied at least once during the second half of the seventeenth century."[28] In a providentialist society, where it was understood that the hand of God routinely intervened

24. For one study of early modern print culture, and of women's place in it, see Joad Raymond, *Pamphlets and Pamphleteering in Early Modern Britain* (Cambridge: Cambridge University Press, 2003).

25. Diane Purkiss, "Producing the Voice, Consuming the Body: Women Prophets of the Seventeenth Century," in *Women, Writing, History, 1640–1740*, ed. Isobel Grundy and Susan Wiseman, 139–58 (London: Batsford, 1992), 139.

26. Mary Cary, *A New and More Exact Mappe or Description of New Jerusalems Glory* (London: W. H., 1651), 237. See 1 Corinthians 14:3.

27. 73.

28. Phyllis Mack, "The Prophet and her Audience: Gender and Knowledge in the World Turned Upside Down," in *Reviving the English Revolution: Reflections and Elaborations on the Work of Christopher Hill*, ed. Geoff Eley and William Hunt, 139–52 (London: Verso, 1988), 150n1.

in human affairs, and with the polity in such a state of flux and already attuned to millenarianism, prophecy for a short time found an audience open to its claims to divine inspiration.[29] Not all who encountered such prophets were persuaded by them, of course. As Trapnel found, her opponents were quick to attribute her utterances to the wiles of Satan, to witchcraft, to willful sedition, or to madness. But she, like other prophets, was convinced that such opposition was just part of the great struggle between God and the devil in these last days.

With its characteristic seamless mix of religion and politics, of the biblical and the contemporary, of anger and joy, prophecy is a form of discourse likely to be profoundly unfamiliar to a twenty-first century readership. It is also, however, one that offers an unusually immediate, affective, and telling perspective on this historical juncture. As Trapnel played her part on "the world's stage," as she put it, she did so not only tirelessly and inventively but also by articulating an idiom entirely and compellingly evocative of the extraordinary historical moment in which she lived.[30]

"From her own hand": The Life and Work of Anna Trapnel

Although it is possible to glean some information about her family from parish records, everything of substance that we know about the life of Anna Trapnel, we know from her own writing. Since the events of her life were crucial evidence of her credentials as a prophet, she details them extensively. Her status as a prophet thus ensured in two distinct ways that she did not disappear from the historical record. First, it brought her to public notice and created an appetite for her prophecies, and second, it required the invocation of details about her life to underwrite the claims she made for the godly origins of her utterances.

Anna was the daughter of William Trapnel and his wife, Anne. She was baptized at the church of St. Dunstan and All Saints, Stepney, on September 10, 1620, at ten days old.[31] The Trapnels had lived in this parish for several generations. Her grandfather, William Trapnel, married his first wife, Ellen Quarby, there on June 2, 1588. Their son William, Anna's father, was baptized there on April 13, 1589, and their daughter Betteris on August 29, 1591. Ellen was buried on August 9, 1597, and William, her widower, married Mary Brooke the following month. The register does not record when William, Anna's father, married his wife, Anne, but their son William was baptized there on April 8, 1617. No further records of

29. On providence, see Blair Worden, "Providence and Politics in Cromwellian England," *Past and Present* 109 (1985): 55–99.

30. Trapnel, *Report and Plea*, 122.

31. Saint Dunstan and All Saints, Register of Baptisms, September 1608–January 1637/8, P93/DUN, Item 256. London Metropolitan Archives. I am grateful to Brian Austin, historian of the Trapnel (or Trapnell) family, for first drawing the importance of these records to my attention.

William, Anna's brother, have been found, and Anna herself never refers to him. Her father died very soon after her birth: he was buried on December 5, 1621, when Anna was just a year old. The parish records show an Anne Trapnell, widow, marrying Richard Hanley, a shipwright, on July 16, 1629. Although the evidence is inconclusive, this may be a reference to Anna's mother. If it is, this invites further speculation: since there is no record of Hanley in Trapnel's writings, and since she inherited property from her mother following her death in 1643, perhaps her stepfather Hanley also died in the course of Anna's childhood.

What is certain is that William Trapnel, Anna's father, had also been a shipwright, or shipbuilder, in Poplar in east London, where he probably worked in the East India Company's shipyards in nearby Blackwall, on the river Thames. Shipyards, as Purkiss reminds us, were dangerous places, full of inflammable materials, fires burning, timber being sawn and hewn, heavy weights being moved around with ropes and pulleys.[32] Perhaps working in such an environment caused the early deaths of William Trapnel and Richard Hanley. While we know nothing of Anna's early family experiences, the shipbuilding context certainly made its mark on her religious life and her linguistic resources: it is striking how frequently she reaches for a nautical metaphor to flesh out a spiritual point. In *A Legacy for Saints* (1654), for example, she writes of a metaphorical "Sea in which my spirit first received trouble and dark dissertion," and in the *Report and Plea* she warns that the "council ships" and "Parliament ships" cannot be held together by "clergy nails," but, being "made of wood; and pitch, and rosin, and tar, and oakum … will burn to ashes when the fire comes."[33] Such a detailed enumeration of the materials involved in building and caulking ships suggests a childhood spent in close proximity to the shipyard where her father and stepfather worked. Moreover, her subsequent reference to her heavenly father as the "great Ship-Wright" allows speculation that her earthly father figures provided a paternal model of loving authority on which she could later draw in her prophetic work.

Poplar was a small hamlet in Stepney, a large parish to the east of the City of London, and long associated with reformed, radical, and separatist religion. Huguenots sought refuge there from Catholic persecution in France in the sixteenth and seventeenth centuries. The first General Baptist group in England was formed in Spitalfields in 1612, and the first Particular Baptist church was formed in nearby Wapping in 1633.[34] Poplar had no place of worship of its own until 1654, when a chapel paid for by public subscription was built on land donated

---

32. Diane Purkiss, *The English Civil War: A People's History* (London: Harper Perennial, 2007), 41. On the history of shipyards, see David Loades, "The English Maritime Community, 1500–1650," in *The Social History of English Seamen, 1485–1649*, ed. Cheryl A. Fury, 5–26 (Woodbridge: Boydell, 2012), 6–8.

33. Trapnel, *Legacy*, 17; Trapnel, *Report and Plea*, 133.

34. *VCH, Middlesex*, 11:74–75.

by the East India Company.[35] Trapnel's early religious life, therefore, would have centered on Stepney's parish church, St. Dunstan and All Saints, where she had been baptized. This church had its own claim to radical innovation, in that it was the first to petition to be allowed to appoint its own lecturers. These were preachers, not always ordained, taken on to give additional sermons on Sundays and weekdays. William Greenhill was one of two such lecturers to be appointed by St. Dunstan's in 1641; he later gathered an Independent congregation there and was made vicar of Stepney in 1652.[36] Alongside other influential nonconformist ministers, Greenhill is named by Trapnel in *The Cry of a Stone* as one of her supporters, someone who could vouch for her spiritual—and, in all likelihood, family—credentials.

Trapnel's sketch of her early religious life, given most fully in *A Legacy for Saints*, conforms to the conventions of the Puritan conversion narrative, with its characteristic stages of sin, conviction of guilt, and assurance, and accompanying affective states, such as fear, doubt, and joy.[37] Despite its conventionality, the account also conveys a sense of the ways in which her avowedly godly context shaped her. Her parents set the tone, "living and dying in the profession of the Lord Jesus," and their godliness is probably what resulted in her being "trained up to my book and writing." Literacy would not have been commonplace for someone of her social position but was frequently taught within dissenting congregations to allow firsthand reading of the Bible.[38]

Trapnel's account of her childhood reproduces the common Puritan emphasis on the ubiquity and inevitability of human corruption. Hers, she writes, was a nature "as corrupt as any ... forward to do evil."[39] At the age of fourteen, she began to take an active interest in prayer and in hearing sermons, but she remained convinced that her own sinful nature meant that she was not one of the elect, those chosen by God for eternal salvation: "I then went home full of horror, concluding my self to be that stony ground Christ spake of in the parable of the sower."[40] This period of "terrors and perplexities, and sore plunges" continued for several years until, on January 1, 1643, a Sunday, she heard John Simpson, the controversial but charismatic preacher who had held a lectureship at St. Dunstan's

---

35. A later version of this chapel still exists as the Church of St. Matthias, Poplar. See http://www.mernick.org.uk/thhol/stmatthi.html (accessed December 17, 2015).

36. On Trapnel's London networks of influences and supporters, see Diane Purkiss, "Anna Trapnel's Literary Geography," in *The Intellectual Culture of Puritan Women*, ed. Johanna Harris and Elizabeth Scott-Baumann, 162–75 (Basingstoke: Palgrave Macmillan, 2011).

37. On the *Ordo Salutis* ("order of salvation"), see John von Rohr, *The Covenant of Grace in Puritan Thought* (Atlanta, GA: Scholars Press, 1986).

38. Trapnel, *Cry*, 6.

39. Trapnel, *Legacy*, 1.

40. Trapnel, *Legacy*, 2.

since March 1642, preach on Romans 8:9: "Now if any man have not the spirit of Christ, he is none of his."[41] From this text, Simpson "shewed that the Spirit might be in that soul that was very dark, and much confused in its apprehensions of Christ."[42] Trapnel took this to heart. No longer was her sense of sin, of confusion or doubt, a necessary barrier to election. The effect of this interpretation on Trapnel was immediate and life-changing. As she writes,

> suddenly my soul was filled with joy unspeakable, and full of glory in believing, the spirit witnessing in that word, Christ is thy welbeloved, and thou art his; my soul was now full of joy as it could hold, now I saw all my sins laid upon Jesus Christ, and when he was sacrificed, all my sins were sacrificed with him.[43]

While periods of fear and temptation continued to dog her in the coming months and years, she never lost this sense of personally belonging to, and being saved by, Christ. From then on, the predominant emotion she records with regard to her spiritual life is no longer terror, but joy.[44]

The heightened emotional state precipitated by Simpson's sermon was intensified by subsequent events. Two days later, Trapnel stayed overnight with her uncle and aunt in Stepney. In the morning, her aunt brought her news: "Cosen, the Lord hath taken your mother from you, now labour to be married to Christ, you have nothing to take up your time, but to labour for Christ."[45] The death of her mother is framed above all as a spiritual event: her dying words were "Lord! Double thy spirit upon my child," uttered three times. Her aunt presents her mother's death as freeing her niece from family responsibilities, so as "to be married to Christ," and her friends tell her that when she "mourned for the loss of my tender mother, that Christ would be more tender."[46] Family ties and affections give shape to, and make way for, spiritual experiences and bonds.

---

41. Trapnel, *Legacy*, 6, 8. The year given for this event in *Legacy* is 1642, but Trapnel, like most of her contemporaries, dated the first day of the New Year as March 25. For details of the seventeenth-century calendar, see "Editorial Principles and Practices," 38–39.

42. Trapnel, *Legacy*, 8.

43. Trapnel, *Legacy*, 9. For a discussion of Trapnel's conversion, see David R. Como, *Blown by the Spirit: Puritanism and the Emergence of an Antinomian Underground in Pre-Civil-War England* (Stanford: Stanford University Press, 2004), 435–41; and Hilary Hinds, "The Transvaluation of Body and Soul in the Spiritual Autobiographies of Anna Trapnel," in *Paradigms, Poetics, and Politics of Conversion,* ed. Jan N. Bremmer, Wout J. van Bekkum, and Arie L. Molendijk, 107–21 (Leuven: Peeters, 2006).

44. On Simpson's importance in Trapnel's move to the congregation of Allhallows the Great, see Purkiss, "Anna Trapnel's Literary Geography," 166–67.

45. Trapnel, *Legacy*, 10.

46. Trapnel, *Cry*, 6; Trapnel, *Legacy*, 10, 13.

Her mother's death may have freed Trapnel to pursue her union with Christ, but it also marked the end of a life of domestic stability.[47] She continued to keep house for a while with the means left her by her mother, but then, having donated her mother's legacy to the "public use," she thereafter lived with friends and relations. For a while in the mid-1640s she lodged with Mrs. Spenser, a minister's widow, and her daughter, Mrs. Harlow, in the Minories, near the Tower of London. Then for six years, from 1648 to the end of 1653, she lived with her kinswoman Mrs. Wythe, the wife of a merchant, who lived both in the city, in Fenchurch Street, and in the countryside at Hackney, at the time still a rural village (Samuel Pepys went there to play at shuffleboard and to "eat cream and good cherries") but increasingly favored as a country retreat by wealthy merchants, who were building houses there.[48] This arrangement definitively ended only when, following "threatening speeches" made by those in power following the Whitehall prophecies, Mr. Wythe became nervous and "was afraid to receive me for losing his place."[49] The Minories, Fenchurch Street, and Mark Lane (where she also sometimes stayed) were all in the City of London, within half a mile or so of Thames Street, where the congregation of Allhallows the Great met, which was to become such an important site of identification for Trapnel and her prophetic work. While her familial, political, and spiritual circumstances were all in a state of profound and simultaneous flux, therefore, this period of thoroughgoing uncertainty also generated the changes that allowed her accession to her new identity as a prophet. They contributed to the material "undoing" of Anna Trapnel—a process of dissolution or destabilization that also characterized her spiritual life, where "the pouring forth of thy spirit … makes the body to crumble, and weakens nature."[50] This material "undoing," however, provided the ground for her spiritual remaking. Trapnel's familial and material losses, and the consequent changes to where and how she lived, were as instrumental in her access to her prophetic voice as were her transformative spiritual experiences, which played out in her body as well as her spirit.

The changes set in motion by Simpson's sermon and the death of her mother both fell within the first year of the Civil War, a further source of instability in her life. Trapnel is keen to convey her commitment to the Parliamentary cause

---

47. Trapnel, *Report and Plea*, 123–25.

48. These details of her habitations are drawn from Trapnel, *Cry*, 7, 9, 10, 12, and 13; Trapnel, *Legacy*, 10; and Trapnel, *Report and Plea*, 123–25. On Mrs. Wythe, see *Report and Plea*, n474. Samuel Pepys, *The Diary of Samuel Pepys: A Selection*, ed. Robert Latham (London: Penguin, 1987), 393 (Saturday, June 11, 1664). On Hackney, see Margaret Pelling, "Skirting the City? Disease, Social Change, and Divided Households in the Seventeenth Century," in *Londinopolis: Essays in the Cultural and Social History of Early Modern London*, ed. Paul Griffiths and Mark S. R. Jenner, 154–75 (Manchester: Manchester University Press, 2000), 158, 162.

49. Trapnel, *Report and Plea*, 125.

50. Trapnel, *Cry*, 29.

through these years. Defending herself against the charge of vagabondage, she reminds her readers that she paid her taxes "not grudgingly, but freely and will-ingly" to support the army. She sold her plate and rings, gave away the money left to her by her mother, and worked hard to raise money, all for "the public use." Her own "public-spiritedness," as she calls it, is one of the touchstones of her justifica-tory self-presentation and extends to her civic engagement and contribution, as well as to her prophetic work.[51]

It was not until three years after hearing Simpson's sermon, in 1646, that Trapnel's spiritual life took another decisive turn. In June of that year, she became ill with a fever, during which God promised to revive her, and after which "the Lord made use of me for the refreshing of afflicted and tempted ones."[52] Her sense of a special calling as God's chosen instrument had begun: "Particular souls shall not only have benefit by thee," promises the Lord, "but the universality of saints shall have discoveries of God through thee."[53] These discoveries were to be made via the medium of visionary prophecies.

By this time, Trapnel was beginning to associate with the congregation gathered at Allhallows the Great on Thames Street, where Simpson and Feake were both lecturers, and her subsequent prophetic visions and fasts were in-creasingly interpreted within this radical context.[54] Some of these visions were straightforwardly related to current political events concerning the triumph of the Parliamentary armies against the forces of the King, of Cromwell's forces against the Scots at the Battle of Dunbar, of the English fleet against the Dutch, or of the dissolution of the Barebone's Parliament. Other visions, more opaque, were wrought broadly from the symbolic repertoire of the Bible. She had visions of towers, of oaks, of thrones and winged angels, and of children bathed in light. Most contentiously, she had visions that explicitly brought together politics and Scripture, including her most famous vision of a company of cattle, the foremost of which, with a face "perfectly like unto Oliver Cromwell's," charged at Trapnel "with his horn to my breast."[55] This took place in December 1653, as the Bare-bone's Parliament was being dissolved and Cromwell installed as Protector, events

---

51. Trapnel, *Report and Plea*, 73.

52. Trapnel, *Cry*, 6.

53. Trapnel, *Cry*, 6.

54. Not all in her circle welcomed her fasts and trances: "I was judged by divers friends to be under a temptation, as H. J. [Henry Jessey] and Jo. S. [John Spencer] to be under a temptation for not eating"; Trapnel, *Cry*, 8. Jessey was a well-known weekday lecturer at Allhallows; see Stephen Wright, "Jessey, Henry (1601–1663)," *Oxford Dictionary of National Biography*, ed. Lawrence Goldman (Oxford: Oxford University Press, 2004–) (accessed January 7, 2015) at http://www.oxforddnb.com/; all sub-sequent references to the ODNB are to the online edition. Spencer was a Baptist preacher and a Fifth Monarchist but was loyal to the Protectorate; see Capp, *Fifth Monarchy Men*, 262.

55. Trapnel, *Cry*, 15.

that Trapnel and her fellow Fifth Monarchists experienced as a profound betrayal of the millenarian cause. The vision's outright condemnation of Cromwell set the tone of subsequent prophecies. When she underwent her eleven-day trance in Whitehall in January 1654, which began as she watched the examination by the Council of State of her fellow Fifth Monarchist, the preacher Vavasor Powell, her prophetic visions were either ecstatic anticipations of the coming millennium or furious castigations of Cromwell and his treachery.

This very public prophetic trance—in a Whitehall "ordinary" or eating house, close to the heart of the nation's government—moved Trapnel decisively into the public eye. She became the object of government attention. The journalist Marchamont Nedham, Cromwell's informer, kept an eye on her and sent an account to the Protector of a meeting he had attended at Allhallows: "The congregation is crowded, the humours boiling, and as much scum comes off as ever, but more warily," he wrote. As for Trapnel herself, Nedham noted that there were plans afoot, both to publish her Whitehall prophecies, which are "desperate against your person, family, children, friends and the government," and to send her around the country "to proclaim them *vivâ voce*."[56] He was right on both counts. Trapnel was soon invited by Captain Francis Langdon, one of four Cornish MPs in the recent Barebone's Parliament and a visitor to Trapnel during her Whitehall visions, to visit Cornwall to continue her prophetic work there. Resistant at first, she was reconciled through prayer and following discussion with the recently imprisoned Fifth Monarchist preachers Feake and Simpson, whom she visited in Windsor Castle. She set off by coach on Monday, March 6, and arrived at Langdon's house, Tregassow, near Truro, on Saturday, March 18, where news of her arrival soon spread. Following some prophetic episodes, she was arrested and appeared in court in Truro on April 7, bound over to good behavior and to appear at the next Assizes. Her trial, however, never took place, for it was preempted by an order issued by the Council of State in London for her arrest. Under armed guard, she was shipped from Plymouth to Portsmouth and then escorted to London, where she was imprisoned in Bridewell, the House of Correction where vagrants, whores, and other miscreants were incarcerated. She stayed there from June 2 until the order for her release was made on July 26.[57]

Meanwhile, accounts of her words and experiences had begun to be published, with four appearing in the space of about eight months. The first, published in February before she left for Cornwall, was *The Cry of a Stone*. Subtitled

---

56. "Marchamont Needham to the Protector," *CSPD*, February 7, 1654. On Nedham, see Joad Raymond, "Nedham [Needham], Marchamont (*bap.* 1620, d. 1678)," *ODNB*; and Blair Worden, *Literature and Politics in Cromwellian England: John Milton, Andrew Marvell, Marchamont Nedham* (Oxford: Oxford University Press, 2007).

57. Fuller details regarding her arrest and court appearance are given in footnotes to the text; see 78–93.

"A relation of something spoken in Whitehall," it comprises a brief autobiographical section, and then extensive transcriptions of her Whitehall prophecies, "taken from her own mouth" by a nameless figure referred to only as "the relator."[58] In March, a much abbreviated and somewhat expurgated version of these prophecies was published under the title of *Strange and Wonderful Newes from White-Hall*. Only eight pages (as against *The Cry of a Stone*'s seventy-six), it reproduced in close paraphrase the autobiographical section and some of the most noteworthy prophecies of the earlier book, such as the vision of the cattle, and of Cromwell as Gideon, reminding him that, since he now occupies "the highest place," he must "see justice done in all Places, Courts, or councels, and Committees, that they may not feed upon the Poor."[59] In July, while Trapnel was in Bridewell, the elders of the congregation at Allhallows the Great published on her behalf *A Legacy for Saints*, a composite text combining an extended first-person account of her spiritual progress, an earlier prophecy of 1646, and some letters she had sent from Cornwall to London, giving early accounts of her arrest and trial in Truro.[60] These were recounted more fully in her final 1654 publication, the *Report and Plea*. This text, published some time in or soon after September, is the only one to be written entirely by her own hand and to name her as author on the title page. It is very different in tone from the earlier three. Concerned principally with recent events rather than her early life or the substance of her prophecies, the text has an immediacy, energy, and vitality all of its own.

This text marks, however, almost the last that we know of Trapnel's life and activities. From time to time, newsbooks give fleeting sightings of her. In 1655, *The Publick Intelligencer* records that she had returned to Cornwall to visit the radical Member of Parliament John Carew, then imprisoned in the castle of St. Mawes, on the coast near Truro; she went there again in 1656.[61] A little later, two further collections of her prophecies were printed: *A Voice for the King of Saints and Nations*

---

58. Trapnel, *Cry*, 5. The full title of this was *The Cry of a Stone; or, A Relation of Something Spoken in Whitehall, by Anna Trapnel, being in the Visions of God. Relating To the Governors, Army, Churches, Ministry, Universities: And the Whole Nation. Uttered In Prayers and Spiritual Songs, by an Inspiration Extraordinary, and Full of Wonder. In the eleventh moneth* [sic] *called January. 1653* [1654 by the modern calendar: see "Editorial Principles and Practices," 38–39] (London: s.n., 1654). The title page of the copy in the British Library includes the handwritten date on which it was acquired by the contemporary collector of Civil War pamphlets, George Thomason: 20 February. See David Stoker, "Thomason, George (ca. 1602–1666)," *ODNB*.

59. Trapnel, *Strange and Wonderful Newes from White-Hall*, 8. The text was printed for Robert Sele, and the title page was hand-dated March 11 by Thomason.

60. *A Legacy for Saints; Being Several Experiences of the Dealings of God with Anna Trapnel, In, and After her Conversion* was printed "for T. Brewster, at the three Bibles in *Pauls* Church-yard, near *London*-House, 1654". Thomason hand-dated the title page "July 24."

61. *The Publick Intelligencer* 13 (December 24–December 31, 1655): 193–94; *Mercurius Politicus*, 312 (May 29–June 5, 1656): 6997–98.

(1658) and a one-thousand-page folio, extant now in only one known copy, with no title page, held by the Bodleian Library in Oxford.[62] While these give insight into her later prophetic preoccupations—she was, for example, repeatedly exercised and antagonized by the Quaker movement—they shed no light on her life after the extraordinary events and exceptional textual records of 1654. Any later possible sightings—such as the Anne Trapnel who married Thomas Semicraft at St. Mary's, Woodbridge, in Suffolk on July 2, 1662, for example—remain tantalizing but only speculative.[63] Despite her moment of fame in the 1650s, her end was still more unmarked than her beginning: we know neither when nor where she died. She had predicted in *The Cry of a Stone* that her place on the public stage was to be temporary: "When thy servant has done thy work, she shall be willing to lock up herself in her closet again, and not to be seen of men."[64] Whether this is indeed what happened, we may never know. However, with the demise of the brief experiment in English republican government at the end of the 1650s, Anna Trapnel's moment in the public eye came, as she had foreseen, to a close.

"Well observe the ensuing discourse": Reading Anna Trapnel's Report and Plea

Of all Anna Trapnel's publications, her *Report and Plea* is the one that speaks most directly to twenty-first-century readers. Where her other writings, both the prophecies and the conversion narratives, require of contemporary readers a good deal of contextual historical and religious knowledge, the *Report and Plea* has an intimate voice and an engaging and compelling narrative. All Trapnel's writings are recounted in the first person, but this is the only one in which that first-person voice focuses solely on the recent experiences, thoughts, and feelings of its author-narrator. In this respect, therefore, the text takes on the characteristics of what we might now categorize as a piece of life-writing, in which the detailed account of her visit to Cornwall, her arrest and trial in Truro, her journey under guard back

---

62. The British Library's copy of *A Voice for the King of Saints and Nations* lacks a title page and contains no publication details. The one-thousand-page folio volume without a title page can be found in the catalogue of the Bodleian Library, Oxford, under the title "Poetical addresses or discourses delivered to a gathering of 'Companions' in 1657 and 1658," where it is tentatively dated 1659.

63. James Holstun notes this possibility, strengthened by the fact that Frederick Woodall, a Fifth Monarchist before the Restoration, led a gathered church there from 1652 to 1681; see his *Ehud's Dagger: Class Struggle in the English Revolution* (London: Verso, 2000), 300. Germane to this, though whether it strengthens or weakens Holstun's case is moot, is the fact that there were a significant number of other Trapnells in Suffolk in the mid- and late seventeenth century, including a William Trapnell who married at the same church as Anne Trapnel and Thomas Semicraft, once in 1656 and again in 1658; see parish records for St. Mary's Woodbridge, Suffolk, at www.ancestry.co.uk

64. Trapnel, *Cry*, 45.

to London, and her subsequent imprisonment in Bridewell offers a recognizable and familiar point of access to the text.

The *Report and Plea* yields the reader many of the pleasures associated with autobiographical writing from earlier times, not least by giving vivid insight into the material conditions of life in the mid-seventeenth century. It conveys, for example, a sense of the prevailing modes and conditions of travel. To get from the east of the City of London, where Trapnel lived, to Whitehall in the west, Trapnel went not via the streets but by boat up the Thames, as would have been the norm—an unremarkable detail that nonetheless brings into sharp focus the river as a busy and populous thoroughfare. Subsequently, having left Westminster by coach to travel to Truro in Cornwall, a distance of some 270 miles, she took thirteen days, eleven of them on the road, to reach her destination. The roads were poor, particularly in Devon and Cornwall; indeed, the word "road" indicated only "a right-of-way, a route, rather than any particular surface or structure."[65] Some forty years after Trapnel was there, the intrepid traveler Celia Fiennes made a journey through Cornwall, on horseback. Her diary includes the following description of the road near Looe, along which Trapnel traveled, also by horse, on her journey out of the county:

> The raine the night before had made it [a deep clay road] very dirty and full of water; in many places in the road there are many holes and sloughs where ever there is clay ground, and when by raines they are filled with water its difficult to shun danger; here my horse was quite down in one of these holes full of water.[66]

Unsurprisingly, Trapnel's progress was slow; the coach traveled at little more than walking pace, averaging around twenty-five miles a day. Cornwall, as contemporary commentary reiterates, was remote from the capital. To undertake a journey from the one to the other required a major commitment of time, resources, and fortitude.

As well as offering a view of travel conditions, the *Report and Plea* gives a fascinating glimpse of the conduct of social and public life at the time. It conveys the bustle and jostle of Truro on a day when the court was sitting, as the crowds in the street "mocked and derided" her, pulling at her arms and "making wry faces." The courtroom to which she was taken seems unceremonious and somewhat disorganized, with people interrupting each other and not following due procedure. Moreover, in line with the practice of the time, Trapnel had no

---

65. Paul White, *The South-West Highway Atlas for 1675* (Launceston: Tamar Books, 2005), 7.

66. Christopher Morris, ed., *The Journeys of Celia Fiennes* (London: The Cresset Press, 1947), 255. Trapnel's journeys were themselves not without incident, her coach overturning on the road between Portsmouth and London; see 106.

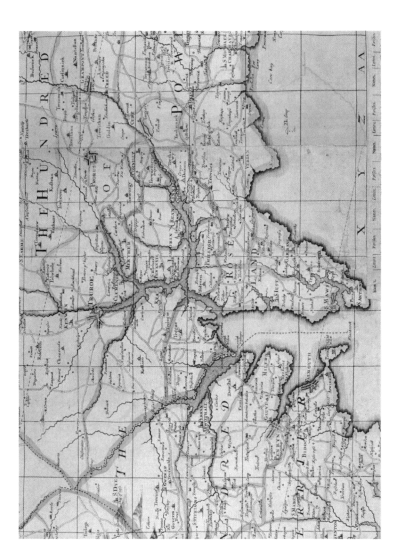

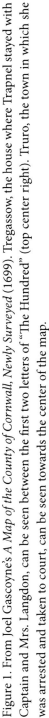

Figure 1. From Joel Gascoyne's *A Map of the County of Cornwall, Newly Surveyed* (1699). Tregassow, the house where Trapnel stayed with Captain and Mrs. Langdon, can be seen between the first two letters of "The Hundred" (top center right). Truro, the town in which she was arrested and taken to court, can be seen towards the center of the map.

legal representation but answered the indictment and addressed the Justices of the Peace on her own behalf.[67] However, if her account is to be believed, this was no disadvantage, as it allowed her to get the better of her inquisitors during the back-and-forth of their questioning. The dramatic quality of this exchange is suggested as much by the form in which she records this section of the text as by its content, set out as it is like a play-text. Later, the account of the conditions she endured while she was held in Bridewell—a House of Correction intended to reform those deemed to be social delinquents—is graphic in its portrayal of the cold and damp, the filth, stench, and rats, the noise, and the hard labor to which many of the inmates were subjected. Adding insult to injury, "Bridewell birds" had to pay for their accommodation. In Trapnel's case, this was five shillings a week, forty shillings in all over the eight weeks she was there, equivalent now to about £298 (US$435).[68]

As fascinating as these glimpses into the early modern courtroom and prison cell are, equally revealing are the passing details about the habits and practices of city life, friendship, and community. Trapnel moves frequently between the houses of her friends in different parts of the city, sometimes staying with them for quite extended periods. Her women friends routinely care for her when she has been in a visionary trance, including passing the night alongside her. They subsidize her accommodation costs; many of them visit her in Bridewell (she asks the Bridewell Court for permission to receive six of them at a time); and one is even permitted to stay with her there.[69] The text also shows just how central letter writing was to social networks and to the maintenance of friendships, as well as to the conduct of business. Letters from Mr. and Mrs. Hill of Truro arrive at the Langdons' house at Tregassow, inviting their visitor and them to visit. Letters arrive from London, ordering Trapnel's arrest and transportation back to London. Trapnel herself sends regular updates of events to her friends in London and elsewhere—and she is not averse to chastising them when they do not reply swiftly enough: "I sent you a Letter," she wrote to her London congregation from Plymouth Fort, where she was held for several weeks on her way back to London, "wherein I desired your Counsel and Exhortation, but I have no Answer: I believe you do not forget me; yet I am grieved you do not write to me now in my bonds."[70] While the *Report and Plea* is a text entirely constructed through reference to the figure of Trapnel, it is also one that lays bare the multiple ways in which that singular figure was upheld by an expansive, enabling, and constitutive network of friendships.

67. Fuller details regarding her indictment are given in footnotes to the text; see 78–85.

68. Calculations of monetary equivalence have been undertaken using the "Measuring Worth" website: www.measuringworth.com/index.php. See, too, 86n254.

69. See 116n420.

70. Trapnel, *Legacy*, 64.

The *Report and Plea*'s framework of social and material detail is matched by its author's commitment to chronological and textual accuracy. She shows a rigorous exactitude with regard to the calendar and the passage of time. Precision clearly mattered to her. She notes in court in Truro that this was a "fast-day, set apart by authority." Cromwell had called a Fast Day as a day of "Mourning, and great Abasement of soul" before God, to take place in London and Westminster on March 24, and two weeks later in the rest of the country. This detail allows us to date Trapnel's court hearing to Friday, April 7. From here, we can trace her itinerary backward, to find that she left Westminster on Monday, March 6, and arrived at Tregassow on Saturday, March 18. We can follow it forward, to find her arrested by order of the Council of State on April 17, to arrive in London on May 23 or 24. When she notes that something happened on a first day or a second day of the week (Sunday or Monday), and when there is other evidence—the documents included in the *Calendar of State Papers: Domestic*, for example—the dates tally, at least in the vast majority of cases. And when she reflects on "the rocks I passed by," she would indeed, at that stage of her journey, have been close to the rocky outcrops of Bodmin Moor. Trapnel's *Report and Plea* is concerned throughout with her reliability and her moral rectitude, its latter pages largely concerned to demonstrate what a loyal and law-abiding citizen she has always been. Her reliability extends not only to her tax-paying but also to her record-keeping. In its calendrical precision, her text silently and unwittingly confirms the accuracy and dependability of her powers of witness.

If the text reveals a solid scaffolding of verifiable reference to the external or social world and its chronologies, it also offers an unusually rich and textured account of Trapnel's inner world, shaped by immaterial forces as powerful as these material ones. As well as recounting her travel itinerary and recording whom she visited, when, and where, the text conveys an extraordinary sense of the interiority of its narrator. This is true throughout the text. In court, for example, Trapnel notes not only what she actually said but also what she did not say—in fact, what she thought better of saying because of how it would negatively impact her case. But it is in the early pages of the text, in which she recounts the process of inward struggle whereby she became reconciled to going to Cornwall, that this is most striking. It is also in these pages that her interiority is perhaps most clearly legible as what we would call "early modern," comprising equally the forces of the divine and the human, the spiritual and the dispositional. As she wrestles with her own reluctance to go to Cornwall, she represents the tussle as a debate or dispute in which the spiritual combatants, God and Satan, battle over her decision and the safety of her eternal soul, but they also address her directly, respectively reassuring or undermining her. However elemental this struggle might be, it is conceived in the most intimate, even prosaic, terms. God speaks to her, saying, "*Don't pray against it* [the journey to Cornwall] *any more: for there thou must go*," while Satan both addresses her directly ("*go not thy journey*, said Satan, *for that extraordinary dispensation of prayer and singing shall not be with thee*") and reveals himself in the punishing inner dialogue of her own fearful thought processes: in her fleeting desire to be permanently hoarse so as to be unable to continue her prophetic work, for example, or to throw herself down the stairs so that she cannot travel.[71] Such accounts, in which the narrator is the object of a struggle between the cosmic forces of good and evil, are familiar from the very many other spiritual autobiographies published in the course of the seventeenth century—records of spiritual torment and temptation, despair and doubt, and, intermittently, hope and joy.[72] Trapnel's text rehearses a spiritual battle familiar from countless other contemporary accounts.

The ground on which this elemental struggle is conducted, however, is carefully chosen, for these external forces mesh with what are clearly Trapnel's own very human fears regarding the journey. For example, Satan plays on her apprehension about being so far away from her familiar and trusted community by asking, "*Being in a strange place, how sad then will it be with thee? And they are but strangers to thee; acquaintance with them hath been but a little while: therefore don't go.*"[73] Such anxieties are glossed as having their origins not only in the satanic but also much closer to home: "Thus Satan and my fearful nature joined together to frustrate what I had spoken from the Lord concerning my going."[74] Trapnel finds in her fears and troubles a spiritual and cosmic dimension, the malevolent intervention of Satan, but she also identifies the importance of her own imperfect human temperament (though whether it is rooted in the mind or in physiology is not specified)—what she calls her "fearful nature." She diagnoses the interplay between the two, Satan and her nature, as generating a specific inflection of temptation all her own: one honed by Satan, that is, to take advantage of her particular vulnerability. Her anguish is bespoke, custom-made for her. While Trapnel's text is driven by a vivid sense of God's active providentialist intervention in, and Satan's cunning assaults on, the life of the frail human subject, these interactions play out both within and beyond that subject. Moreover, they combine with an acute sense of the importance of the disposition of this particular human mind in the generation of, and the response to, the drama of these supernatural attacks and rescues.

If the *Report and Plea* conveys a vivid sense of the world *beyond* the text—the worlds both material and immaterial inhabited by Trapnel—then it does so, of course, *by means of* the text. It is testament to Trapnel's skill as a narrator that

---

71. See 48–49, 51, 56.

72. For an analysis of this religious culture, see John Stachniewski, *The Persecutory Imagination: English Puritanism and the Literature of Religious Despair* (Oxford: Clarendon Press, 1991).

73. 51.

74. 52.

these worlds are conveyed as powerfully as they are. The courtroom scene (and, as already mentioned, it is indeed a "scene," set out in part like a play-text) is one such section; so too is the account of her weeks in Bridewell. Many other sectarian writers are eloquent concerning the shaping power of reading in their lives—Protestantism is, after all, a famously bibliocentric religion—but Trapnel is unusual in her reflections on the power and practice of writing.[75] Her *Report and Plea*, she suggests, has a complicated genesis: "I could not have related so much from the shallow memory I have naturally, but through often relating these things, they become as a written book, spread open before me, and after which I write."[76] By this account, the text owes its written form not so much to her memory of the events—her natural memory is but "shallow"—but to the prior accounts she has already given. Repeated relation of her experiences, in earlier letters and also, presumably, in her verbal accounts of her adventures, preconstituted the narrative of her Cornish journey "as a written book," so that all she then has to do is make a fair copy of it. The creation of the written text thereby loses its singularity and fragments into a series of stages, none of them definitive in itself. Moreover, in the process, writing as an act of composition becomes elusive or fugitive, as the written text is presented as preexisting itself, while the author is dissolved and becomes a mere copyist. In this, she makes herself of a kind with the "relator" of *The Cry of a Stone*, who attended her Whitehall prophecies and transcribed her words as best he could as she spoke. In each case, the writer, pen in hand, is amanuensis rather than author.

This notwithstanding, Trapnel also suggests her own acute awareness of the influence of authorial and editorial decisions in the construction of a text. To be sure, she insists that the aim of her text—she writes in order "that truth may silence falsity"—is best ensured by the fact that the spoken words she records here are not her own but the Lord's: "In all that was said by me, I was nothing, the Lord put all in my mouth, and told me what I should say, and that from the written word, he put it in my memory and mouth."[77] God speaks directly to her (in court, the Lord said to her, "*Say not guilty* ... so I spoke it as from the Lord"), but her words are also shaped by her reading.[78] The "written word"—the Bible, with which she was clearly intimately familiar—is lodged in her memory and becomes another source forming her words. Divine intervention and the texts of the Bible combine to assure the godliness of her words.

75. See, for example, Jane Turner, *Choice Experiences* (1653) or John Bunyan, *Grace Abounding* (1666). I discuss the importance of reading in such texts and contexts in Hinds, "Sectarian Writing," in *A New Companion to English Renaissance Literature and Culture*, 2 vols., ed. Michael Hattaway, 1:464–77 (Oxford: Wiley-Blackwell, 2010).

76. 103.

77. 92.

78. 85.

"Truth" is, however, in the hands of a frail and imperfect human subject. Her memory is shallow, she asserts, and she fails "in an orderly penning down these things," yet this nonetheless remains "a true relation of as much as I remember, and what is expedient to be written."[79] Already truth is becoming less of a freestanding and self-evident concept and more one that is both subject to the imperfections of its author and in need of "expediency" in its transmission. In her vindication of the truth, some active editorial intervention is required: "I have left out some things that I thought were not so material to be written: and what I have written of this, it's to declare as much as is convenient to take off those falsities and contrary reports that are abroad."[80] She is conscious of the power and duty of the author to make active selections from the available material, and to include only those elements that will best set the record straight and quash the "falsities" in circulation. Furthermore, she owns the decision to publish quite straightforwardly as her own: "Now to inform all people's judgments, I have thought it meet to offer this relation to the world's view."[81] The "I" in both these statements is very different from the prophetic "I" channeling God's words so familiar from her accounts of her visionary outpourings. Far from claiming that this is a spontaneous outpouring of unmediated "experience," Trapnel shows herself quite willing to claim her place as an "author," well attuned to the processes of writing for a particular audience and with a particular case to make.

Trapnel's experiences in 1654 had already taught her—if it were a lesson still needing teaching by then, which for a prophet was perhaps unlikely—that language needed always to be handled with care. Words were dangerous currency. They could save their speaker or hearer, as Simpson's words had helped save Trapnel on New Year's Day 1643, but equally they could condemn her, as Trapnel's words as published in *The Cry of a Stone* were in danger of doing. The book, after all, was in contention in the Truro courtroom as much as was its author, and Trapnel had to show considerable dexterity to dodge the magistrates' attempts to get her to condemn herself out of her own mouth. As well as being an editor of her written work, she therefore also shows herself to be an active editor of her spoken words. When the magistrates speak all at once, she writes, "I was going to say, *What are you like women, all speakers, and no hearers?* but I said thus, *What do you speak all at a time? I cannot answer all, when speaking at once.*"[82] In danger of tripping herself up by referring to the reputation of women as always speaking and never listening, she corrects herself. Her readers, however, are trusted not to draw the conclusions the magistrates might have, and her suppressed comment is included. Her readers are thus invited to enjoy her quickness of mind in two ways:

79. 103.

80. 92.

81. 92.

82. 88–89.

first, in her ability to come up with an apposite proverb for the circumstance, and, second, in her decision not to speak it. The dangerous ambiguity of language figures on a local scale, as here, but also on a grander scale in her prophecies, when there is the likelihood that her opponents will interpret her utterances as the work of the devil rather than as the divinely inspired words she claims them to be. As such, her textual strategy of "self-inscripturation"—the writing-in of herself, her text, and her life to the Scriptures, whereby biblical texts are repeatedly invoked, paraphrased, and ventriloquized—becomes a potent, because unanswerable, mode of self-authorization.[83] "*I am a double shield to thee*, said the Lord," writes Trapnel, and truly the word of God becomes, in her writing, a shield with which she can protect herself against the blows of her opponents.[84]

The figure and voice of Trapnel herself unite this generically disparate text. The title announces it as both "report" and "plea," an account of her travels and a retort to those who accuse her of being "mad, and under the administration of evil angels, and a witch, and many other evil terms."[85] These two elements are to be found in two discrete sections of the text, a "Narrative, or Relation," and a subsequent and shorter "*Defiance to all reproachful, scandalous, base, horrid, defaming speeches*" that have been leveled against her. There is a third element to the text, however: a lengthy prefatory epistle, addressed "To the Reader." "Pray, Christian Reader, well observe the ensuing discourse," she writes there.[86] This is, in many ways, the crucial plea constituted by this text in its entirety. Without a receptive, attentive, and sympathetic audience, the text will not succeed in its fundamental work of persuading readers of the rectitude of her own account and interpretation of events, as opposed to those of her adversaries. And as the narrative itself demonstrated in Trapnel's arrest and spell in Bridewell, to fail in this act of persuasion had material as well as rhetorical consequences. This serves as a reminder that the text does not just *reveal* aspects of early modern life but is an active and accomplished intervention into them. As Trapnel herself was only too acutely aware, words were as potent a means of intervention as other, more obviously material, ones, and the *Report and Plea* was as complex, dexterous, and compelling an interposition as this shipwright's daughter from Poplar, East London, ever made.

83. Hilary Hinds, "Anna Trapnel, *Anna Trapnel's Report and Plea*," in *A Companion to Early Modern Women's Writing*, ed. Anita Pacheco, 177–88 (Oxford: Blackwell, 2002), 185.

84. 66.

85. 45.

86. 45.

"Reports and Rumors": The Afterlife of
Anna Trapnel's Report and Plea

Like her other writings, *Anna Trapnel's Report and Plea* was not republished after its first appearance in print until recent scholarship rekindled a sense of the fascination and importance of her life and work. Public interest was intense enough for six texts authored by her to be published in six years but also ephemeral enough for these subsequently to drop out of view for more than three hundred years.

While her texts had no intervening afterlife in terms of republication, their author nonetheless never quite disappeared from the historical record. Trapnel fell silent after the Restoration of the monarchy in 1660, publishing nothing after 1659, but her reputation lived on in her contemporaries' reflections on the extraordinary events of the mid-century. The political philosopher Thomas Hobbes alluded to her in his history of the period: "There appeared in Cornwall a prophetess, much famed for her dreams and visions, and hearkened to by many, whereof some were eminent officers. But she and some of her accomplices being imprisoned, we heard no more of her"; strikingly, her short-lived public prominence and subsequent disappearance are already key coordinates in her biography.[87] She also earned a place in the historian James Heath's 1676 chronicle of the Civil Wars, in which he calls her a "Quaking Prophetess" and a forerunner of the early Quaker leader James Nayler, who in 1656 was branded for blasphemy. More overtly condemnatory than Hobbes, Heath notes that she "reported her Visions and Raptures, and was attended by several of the Grandees of the male-contented [*sic*] party."[88] The tone of disapprobation continued in subsequent accounts. In 1678 two figures prominent in the Church of England, Thomas Comber, the future Dean of Durham, and Thomas Tenison, the future Archbishop of Canterbury, published books that recall her by name. Tenison mentions her only in passing, as an instance of someone who "committeth Idolatry with his own imagination," but Comber devotes several paragraphs to her, in which he judges that she "exceeds both the Quakers and most of the other Pretenders, in excessive fastings." He does, however, allow himself a note of grudging admiration when he records her "lucky hits upon several things that came to pass afterwards."[89] Nor was it only

---

87. Thomas Hobbes, *Behemoth; or, The Long Parliament*, ed. Ferdinand Tönnies (first published 1679; this edition London: Simpkin, Marshall and Co., 1889), 187.

88. James Heath, *A Chronicle of the Late Intestine Wars in the Three Kingdoms of England, Scotland, and Ireland*, 2nd edition (London: J. C. for Thomas Basset, 1676), 359–60. Heath's chronicle was one of Hobbes's sources; see Tomaž Mastnak, "Introduction: The Ways of *Behemoth*," in *Hobbes's Behemoth: Religion and Democracy*, ed. Tomaž Mastnak, 1–37 (Exeter: Imprint Academic, 2009), 33.

89. Thomas Tenison, *Of Idolatry a Discourse* (London: F. Tyton, 1678), 309; and Thomas Comber, *Christianity No Enthusiasm; or, The Several Kinds of Inspirations and Revelations Pretended to by the Quakers* (London: T. D. for Henry Brome, 1678), 96.

skeptical seventeenth-century historians of the revolutionary years who recalled Trapnel's work: Natasha Simonova makes a persuasive case for Trapnel's publications continuing to be read and recommended into the late 1680s by readers who shared her radical spiritual agenda.[90] Sometimes parenthetically and reluctantly, sometimes sympathetically, Trapnel's contemporaries and immediate successors granted her a place in their histories of the century's turbulent middle years.

In the eighteenth century, too, despite the growing distance from the events in which she had participated, Trapnel remained intermittently in view. Her work appeared from time to time in booksellers' catalogues of disparate "curious and scarce pamphlets," and accounts of her activities also surfaced during the resurgence of interest in prophecy prompted by the French Revolution, in works that included short accounts of her visions against Cromwell. *Prophetical Extracts. No. IV. Relative to the Revolution in France, and the Decline of the Papal Power in the World* (1794?), for example, included a half-page extract of Trapnel's vision of the horns from *The Cry of a Stone*.[91] The following year, *The World's Doom* included a brief account of Trapnel's prophesying, fasting, and imprisonment, concluding "She predicted, that kingly power was to cease throughout the earth, when the Lord should again open the eyes of the blind."[92] The uncertainties of one republican and revolutionary context prompted interest in the prophetic interventions in an earlier one. Later, in the nineteenth century, Trapnel was afforded a notable change of generic context as she made a cameo appearance in the poet and novelist Horace Smith's historical romance, *Brambletye House; or, Cavaliers and Roundheads* (1835). Here she appears as "Hannah Trapnell the Quaker prophetess," sitting in prison with "a Bible in her hand, and her eyes fixed on heaven in a state of ecstatic abstraction," in the company of James Nayler and other "furious Anabaptists, [and] addle-headed Fifth-Monarchy-men."[93] As one of an assembly of wrong-headed if colorful fanatics, she serves to conjure the extremity of a now-distant and romantic past.

While these sporadic appearances across the two centuries subsequent to her life and work make it possible to trace a faint and intermittent afterlife to her reputation, they do little to explain either the fascination or the threat she

90. Natasha Simonova, "New Evidence for the Reading of Sectarian Women's Prophecies," *Notes and Queries* 60.1 (2013): 66–70.

91. Thomas Davies, *A Catalogue of a Large Collection of Curious and Scarce Pamphlets* (London: s.n., 1771; Henry Chapman, *A Catalogue of Near Twenty Thousand Volumes of Curious Books* (London: s.n., 1785); and Johann Amos Comenius, *Prophetical Extracts. No. IV. Relative to the Revolution in France, and the Decline of the Papal Power in the World* (London: G. Terry, 1794?), 40–41.

92. Anon., *The World's Doom; or, The Cabinet of Fate Unlocked,* (London: B. Crosby, 1795), 1:21. The same account is in Anon., *Literary and Critical Remarks* (London: B. Crosby, 1794), 1:457, and in Richard Brothers, *Wonderful Prophecies* (London: M. Ritchie for B. Crosby, 1795), 33.

93. Horace Smith, *Brambletye House; or, Cavaliers and Roundheads*, revised edition (London: H. Colburn, 1835), 1:128.

represented in her own time. It was the twentieth century that provided the historical and political medium in which a serious if slow growth of interest in her work could take place. Two articles, some fifty years apart, provided key reference points for this rehabilitation. The first, Champlin Burrage's "Anna Trapnel's Prophecies," describes comprehensively the Bodleian folio with the missing title page, and identifies it as the work of Trapnel.[94] The second, Keith Thomas's "Women and the Civil War Sects," broke new ground both by delineating the extensive and complex radical religious context for her writing and by focusing the discussion through the lens of gender.[95] This combination, together with the articles' refusal of the dismissive or patronizing tone toward her work frequently found in her brief appearances in histories of the revolutionary period, set the terms of the discussion that then expanded exponentially with the advent of feminist literary and historical criticism from the 1980s onward.[96]

The impetus behind feminist historians' and critics' interest in Trapnel was, in the first instance, the recovery of lost or marginalized writing by women writers of earlier centuries. This enterprise was undertaken not only in a spirit of retrieval and celebration but also with an acute interest in the critical debates raised by the work's disappearance and reappearance. This included questions about, for example, canon formation, about the relationship between gender and genre, about authorship and literary authority, and about the complex interrelation of early modern politics and notions of "public" and "private." So, for example, Christina Berg and Philippa Berry, in their 1981 article, included Trapnel in their examination of the gendered politics of women's prophecy, and her work also figured in Elaine Hobby's comprehensive study of seventeenth-century women's writing as an instance of the genre of political prophecy, newly significant in the political circumstances of the mid-century.[97] The 1980s also saw the beginning of the publication of anthologies of early modern women's writing that included

---

94. Champlin Burrage, "Anna Trapnel's Prophecies," *English Historical Review* 26 (1911): 526–35. The Bodleian folio is discussed above, 19.

95. Keith Thomas, "Women and the Civil War Sects," *Past and Present* 13.1 (1958): 42–62.

96. Examples of this dismissive tone include Edward Geoffrey O'Donoghue, *Bridewell Hospital, Palace, Prison, Schools* (s.l.: John Lane, 1923), 99, who writes of her as "seized with hysteria, accompanied by delusions and the torrential volubility of disordered emotions," and Austin Woolrych, *Britain in Revolution, 1625–1660* (Oxford: Oxford University Press, 2002), 581, 550, who suggests that she "threw a spectacular trance" that "had something of the pull of a raree-show."

97. Christine Berg and Philippa Berry, "'Spiritual Whoredom': An Essay on Female Prophets in the Seventeenth Century," in *1642: Literature and Power in the Seventeenth Century,* ed. Francis Barker et al., 37–54 (Colchester: University of Essex, 1981); and Elaine Hobby, *Virtue of Necessity: English Women's Writing, 1649–88* (London: Virago, 1988).

extracts from Trapnel's work, allowing new readerships to engage firsthand with her texts.[98]

The increasing availability of her writing, together with diverse and searching critical analysis of her work, has contributed not only to the transformation of the teaching of early modern literature in universities over the past twenty-five years but also to the steady increase in critical discussion of Trapnel and her publications. Indeed, this work exists in such quantity now that it is no longer possible to do full justice to all who have contributed to it. In what follows, therefore, rather than seeking to produce a comprehensive overview of the many excellent studies of her work, I indicate the broad areas of critical debate to which analyses of Trapnel's writings have been most significant. Gender, genre, and questions of political and literary authority have continued to be of central concern to these discussions, but of equal significance have been considerations of subjectivity and agency, of the prophetic body and soul, and of print culture.

Studies of Trapnel's work have continued to engage and examine the particularity of the political and social circumstances of its production: revolutionary, sectarian, and unlicensed. Phyllis Mack's *Visionary Women* remains an indispensable reference point for its nuanced location of Trapnel's work in the broader context of women's prophetic activity, while James Holstun's *Ehud's Dagger* offers a lively and astute account of the political theater of her Whitehall prophecies.[99] His interest is in the ways in which Trapnel's work is legible in terms of its articulation of and allegiance to a particular social rank. Other critics position it politically as radical and revolutionary (David Loewenstein, Maria Magro), as oppositional

---

98. Examples of anthologies that feature Trapnel's writing include Elspeth Graham, Hilary Hinds, Elaine Hobby, and Helen Wilcox, eds., *Her Own Life: Autobiographical Writings by Seventeenth-Century Englishwomen* (London: Routledge, 1989); Charlotte F. Otten, ed., *English Women's Voices, 1540–1700* (Gainesville: University Press of Florida, 1992); Kate Aughterson, ed., *The English Renaissance: An Anthology of Sources and Documents* (London: Routledge, 1998); Stephanie Hodgson-Wright, ed., *Women's Writing of the Early Modern Period, 1588–1688: An Anthology* (Edinburgh: Edinburgh University Press, 2002); Helen Ostovich and Elizabeth Sauer, eds., *Reading Early Modern Women: An Anthology of Texts in Manuscript and Print, 1550–1700* (London: Routledge, 2004); and Hilda L. Smith, Mihoko Suzuki, and Susan Wiseman, eds., *Women's Political Writings, 1610–1725* (London: Pickering and Chatto, 2007). While welcoming such anthologies, Nigel Smith has argued that much critical work remains to be done to ensure that writing such as Trapnel's continues to challenge the tenets of canon-formation: where, he asks, is a critical engagement that "bring[s] out complex puns, reversals and plays, ... [and] is sensitive to the ups and downs of phrasing"? Smith, "The Rod and the Canon," *Women's Writing* 14.2 (2007): 232–45 (235). For a formalist study of Trapnel's work, however, see Lucy Munro, *Archaic Style in English Literature, 1590–1674* (Cambridge: Cambridge University Press, 2013), 124–36.

99. Phyllis Mack, *Visionary Women: Ecstatic Prophecy in Seventeenth-Century England* (Berkeley: University of California Press, 1992); and Holstun, *Ehud's Dagger*, 257–304. For a recent historical account of the importance of gender for an understanding of this period, see Ann Hughes, *Gender and the English Revolution* (London: Routledge, 2011).

(Susannah Mintz), as antimonarchist (Catie Gill), or as a part of the early formation of what later became glossed as political liberalism (Katharine Gillespie).[100] Such studies demonstrate that the public and the private, the political and the domestic, however conceptualized, are terms that continue to warrant critical pressure being exerted on them, as their scope and limits differ so profoundly from their twenty-first-century formulations.

Unsurprisingly, given the distinctiveness and historical specificity of the genre, many studies of Trapnel's work have focused on the politics and rhetoric of prophecy—a genre that exists in the *Report and Plea* only as a matter of report, rather than in transcription as in *The Cry of a Stone*. Others, however, have been interested in the constitution of the speaking and authorial subject across the range of her writing, with considerable attention paid to the *Report and Plea*. They consider the implications of an oeuvre in which the prophet speaks not in her own voice but as a conduit for the word of God—"a voice within a voice, another's voice, even thy voice through her."[101] Where and how, critics ask, is the "I" of the first-person account to be located and characterized in this decentered and disaggregated series of first-person voices?

Such questions have helped focus and extend the continuing critical problematization of the assumptions underlying the Enlightenment notion of a unified and accessible individual or subject-position. Trapnel's writings require readers to engage with texts that constitute their first-person narrators in a range of diverse ways. In some instances, the text is produced somewhere between the fasting body, the entranced mind, and the vacated consciousness of the prophet. In others, it emanates from the divine voice that fills and overcomes her. Elsewhere, it results from the avowedly imperfect powers of transcription of the "relator" or amanuensis and is therefore as dependent on the medium of the spoken as of the written word, on public performance more than private composition. Consequently, readers may well conclude, with Sue Wiseman, that Trapnel's texts "present us with no unified and gendered subject-position," nor a singular originary author-figure.[102] Far from comprising a series of first-person texts cohering

---

100. David Loewenstein, *Representing Revolution in Milton and his Contemporaries: Religion, Politics, and Polemics in Radical Puritanism* (Cambridge: Cambridge University Press, 2001); Maria Magro, "Spiritual Autobiography and Radical Sectarian Women's Discourse: Anna Trapnel and the Bad Girls of the English Revolution," *Journal of Medieval and Early Modern Studies* 34.2 (2004): 405–37; Susannah B. Mintz, "The Specular Self of *Anna Trapnel's Report and Plea*," *Pacific Coast Philology* 35.1 (2000): 1–16; Catie Gill, "'All the Monarchies of this World Are Going Down the Hill': The Anti-Monarchism of Anna Trapnel's *The Cry of a Stone* (1654)," *Prose Studies* 29.1 (2007): 19–35; and Katharine Gillespie, *Domesticity and Dissent in the Seventeenth Century: English Women's Writing and the Public Sphere* (Cambridge: Cambridge University Press, 2004).

101. Trapnel, *Cry*, 45.

102. Sue Wiseman, "Unsilent Instruments and the Devil's Cushions: Authority in Seventeenth-Century Women's Prophetic Discourse," in *New Feminist Discourses: Critical Essays on Theories and Texts*, ed.

around the legible identity and voice of its author-narrator, Trapnel's work instead articulates a multiply constituted and only partially available "self." This has led to discussions, on the one hand, of her collaboratively constituted subjectivity *and* texts, and, on the other, of the first person as an exercise in community-making rather than self-exposition.[103] This is as true of her nonprophetic texts, such as the *Report and Plea*, as it is of the prophecies. Here, Trapnel speaks as God directs her, and recounts a first-person narrative whose events, in particular her visionary experiences, are vouchsafed her by her network of supporting friends. Both the prophetic and the social voices of Trapnel's texts are multiply constituted, underwritten by the community on which their author depends. As Wray concludes, "behind the apparent singularity of 'I am Anna Trapnel' ... lies an intricate edifice of figuration and reproduction, conversation and construction, and moulding and solicitation."[104] In the light of such a multiplicity of contributing voices, readers may discern, hidden in the singular declaratory "I am Anna Trapnel," the first-person plural "We are Anna Trapnel."

Inseparable from Trapnel's verbal utterances is the body from which these inspired and/or politically invested words emerge, whether it be the entranced prophetic body, speaking from beyond herself in Whitehall or Cornwall, or the active and agentic social body, walking home after her eleven-day visionary trance "in health and strength," traveling from London to Cornwall, or carefully piecing together its narrative of events.[105] Purkiss's 1992 article made a powerful case for the importance of the prophetic body as an eloquent if silent component of the composite prophetic utterance, its "disavowed flesh" simultaneously serving as "a mere cover for the masculine voice" and as an authorizing sign of divine

Isobel Armstrong, 176–96 (London: Routledge, 1992). On Trapnel's fasting body as an element within her construction of political authority, see Teresa Feroli, *Political Speaking Justified: Women Prophets and the English Revolution* (Newark: University of Delaware Press, 2006).

103. Ramona Wray, "'What Say You To [This] Book? ... Is It Yours?' Oral and Collaborative Narrative Trajectories in the Mediated Writings of Anna Trapnel," *Women's Writing* 16.3 (2009): 408–24; Achsah Guibbory, "England's 'Biblical' Prophets, 1642–60," in *Writing and Religions in England, 1558–1689: Studies in Community-Making and Cultural Memory*, ed. Roger D. Sell and Anthony Johnson, 305–26 (Farnham: Ashgate, 2009); Tom Hayes, "Diggers, Ranters, and Women Prophets: The Discourse of Madness and the Cartesian *Cogito* in Seventeenth-Century England," *Clio: A Journal of Literature, History, and the Philosophy of History* 26.1 (1996): 29–50; Marcus Nevitt, "'Blessed, Self-denying, Lambe-like'? The Fifth Monarchist Women," *Critical Survey* 11.1 (1999): 83–97; Hilary Hinds, *God's Englishwomen: Seventeenth-century Radical Sectarian Writing and Feminist Criticism* (Manchester: Manchester University Press, 1996); Hinds, "*Anna Trapnel's Report and Plea*"; and Naomi Baker, "'Break Down the Walls of Flesh': Anna Trapnel, John James, and Fifth Monarchist Self-Representation," in *Women, Gender, and Radical Religion in Early Modern Europe*, ed. Sylvia Brown, 117–38 (Leiden, Boston: Brill, 2007).

104. Wray, "'What Say You,'" 420.

105. Hilary Hinds, "Sectarian Spaces: The Politics of Place and Gender in Seventeenth-Century Prophetic Writing," *Literature and History* 13.2 (2004): 1–25.

intervention through its capacity to withstand, even thrive on, extended periods of fasting.[106] Since then, other work has broadened the focus to consider the non-prophetic manifestations of Trapnel's body as also part of the matrix authorizing and underwriting the prophecies.[107] In a close examination of the text's "specular dynamics," for example, Mintz reads the *Report and Plea* as pivoting on Trapnel's body both as the object of the gaze of others and as the viewing subject, returning the gaze. In this, the most resolutely social of Trapnel's texts, Mintz argues that the gaze, in both directions of travel, is directly constitutive of Trapnel as prophetic subject: "If it is objectifying to be the recipient of someone else's gaze, Trapnel implies than one can also be actualized by being looked at."[108] By this account, understandings of "subject" and "object" as distinct categories begin to be reframed.

The body figures in Trapnel's work not only as authorization of its prophetic utterances but also as an index of the relationship of the believer to her God, in the course of her progress toward salvation. In a formulation that demonstrates succinctly how erroneous it would be to think of the body and the soul, the physical and the spiritual, as being in polarized relation to each other, Trapnel's texts demonstrate repeatedly the ways in which the two dimensions, in seamless continuity, comprise the believing subject.[109] *A Legacy for Saints*, for example, makes clear that to live in the assurance of salvation is to live fully in the body, not in its denial, as Trapnel describes her spiritual ecstasy in strikingly material terms. Christ, to whom she hopes she is "married," brought "love tokens to my soul, … my meat was sweet meats from heaven, my drink wine upon the lees, wines well refined."[110] Longfellow and Clarke have both pursued the rhetorical consequences of Trapnel's recourse here and elsewhere to the trope of marriage and to the erotics of the biblical Song of Songs as a metaphor—and a conventional one—for the relationship between Christ and his church, while Warren considers the common ground in such metaphors of embodiment between women's spirituality as articulated in the early modern period and in the medieval period.[111]

106. Purkiss, "Producing the Voice, Consuming the Body," 158.

107. See Hinds, "Sectarian Spaces"; Mintz, "Specular Self"; Marcus Nevitt, *Women and the Pamphlet Culture of Revolutionary England, 1640–1660* (Aldershot: Ashgate, 2006); Tamsin Spargo, "The Father's Seductions: Improper Relations of Desire in Seventeenth-Century Nonconformist Communities," *Tulsa Studies in Women's Literature* 17.2 (1998): 255–68; and Sue Wiseman, "Margaret Cavendish among the Prophets: Performance and Gender in and after the English Civil War," *Women's Writing* 6.1 (1999): 95–111.

108. Mintz, "Specular Self," 9, 8–9.

109. For a critique of the polarization of body and soul in an early modern context, see Mary Floyd-Wilson et al., "Shakespeare and Embodiment: An E-Conversation," *Literature Compass* 2 (2005): 1–13.

110. Trapnel, *Legacy*, 28–29, 10, 14.

111. Elizabeth Clarke, *Politics, Religion, and the Song of Songs in Seventeenth-Century England* (Basingstoke: Palgrave Macmillan, 2011); Erica Longfellow, *Women and Religious Writing in Early Modern England* (Cambridge: Cambridge University Press, 2004); Nancy Bradley Warren,

Finally, Trapnel's publications, as well as offering critical engagement with extratextual matters of embodiment, subjectivity, and political agency, have also been read as instances of a rapidly changing print culture, if one crosscut by continuing traditions of manuscript transmission and orality. Margaret Ezell, for example, considers Trapnel's among other "performance texts, which both record oral performance and in their formats mirror it, remind[ing] us of the complicated interchanges between oral performance, handwritten documents, and printed pages," while Marcus Nevitt considers Trapnel's work as a signal and indicative instance of the ways in which pamphlet culture negotiates a gendered position of agency for its women authors, in part, again, by means of its invocation of extratextual phenomena. Whereas these studies read Trapnel's work in part for the light it sheds on the development of print culture, Rebecca Bullard's quietly virtuoso article on the *Report and Plea* instead starts from the material traces of the pamphlet's journey into print. These prompt her hypothesis of a series of finely judged decisions made in the course of the text's publication, designed to secure the best position of narrative authority from which the pamphlet might speak. In so doing, Bullard makes a powerful case for Trapnel criticism to pay as much attention to the body *of* the text as it has to the prophetic body *in* the text.[112]

As this discussion has demonstrated, Anna Trapnel's afterlife has, in recent years, been conducted for the most part in the pages of scholarly publications. It is gratifying, therefore, given her own aspirations to speak to as diverse and plentiful an audience as possible, to end this account with reference to a very different kind of engagement with her life and work. Inspired by Trapnel's outspoken prophetic utterances and celebrating her resistance to the oppressive Cromwellian regime in London, a community opera entitled "On London Fields" was staged in Hackney, London, in November 2004. Written by Matthew King and Alasdair Middleton and directed by Martin Lloyd-Evans and Jonathan Gill, the production involved 250 performers from the local community working alongside professional musicians, including the renowned chamber orchestra of the Academy of St Martin in the Fields, with the mezzo soprano Sally Burgess taking the part of Trapnel. The novelist Margaret Drabble praised the production as "one of the most exciting community events I've ever seen—a great show, great teamwork, bold and

---

The Embodied Word: Female Spiritualities, Contested Orthodoxies, and English Religious Cultures, 1350–1700 (Notre Dame, IN: University of Notre Dame Press, 2010). See, too, Hilary Hinds, "Soul-Ravishing and Sin-Subduing: Anna Trapnel and the Gendered Politics of Free Grace," *Renaissance and Reformation* 25.4 (2001): 117–37; Hinds, "The Transvaluation of Body and Soul"; and Matthew Prineas, "The Discourse of Love and the Rhetoric of Apocalypse in Anna Trapnel's Folio Songs," *Comitatus* 28 (1997): 90–110.

112. Margaret J. M. Ezell, "Performance Texts: Arise Evans, Grace Carrie, and the Interplay of Oral and Handwritten Traditions during the Print Revolution," *ELH* 76 (2009): 49–73 (69); Nevitt, *Pamphlet Culture*, 1–20; and Rebecca Bullard, "Textual Disruption in *Anna Trapnel's Report and Plea* (1654)," *The Seventeenth Century* 23.1 (2008): 34–53.

exciting material, and a really keen audience."[113] The scale and grassroots character of this production, together with such effusive critical responses as Drabble's, chime perfectly with many of the sentiments and aspirations articulated by Trapnel in this volume.

Trapnel's work may still be best known in academic circles, but "On London Fields" serves as a salutary and heartening reminder that the words and actions of a seventeenth-century prophet from Poplar in east London can continue to enthuse contemporary audiences seeking historical precedents for popular activism and creative ways of speaking truth to power. The figure of Anna Trapnel served them well in both regards.

Editorial Principles and Practices

The text for this edition is based on the copy of *Anna Trapnel's Report and Plea* in the Library of the Religious Society of Friends, London (Friends' Library), shelf-mark Box 579/4. The *English Short Title Catalogue* identifies other copies of *Anna Trapnel's Report and Plea* at (in the UK) the British Library and Edinburgh University Library, and (in the USA) at Harvard University Library, Haverford College Library, and the Henry Huntington Library.[114] Rebecca Bullard has published a detailed analysis (bibliographic, textual, and interpretative) of the most significant difference between, on the one hand, the Friends' Library, Edinburgh, British Library, and Harvard copies of the text and, on the other, the Haverford and Huntington copies: namely, that the former all have an additional gathering of four pages that is absent from the latter (the "d" gathering, which recounts part of the court hearing). She concludes that these pages were most likely a late addition to the pamphlet as it was prepared for the press.[115]

I have not been able to undertake a systematic comparison of the basetext with all the other extant copies. I have not been able to consult the Huntington Library edition at all, and, since the original of the Haverford College Library edition is now missing, it can be consulted only as a poor quality photocopy of the missing original; I have checked this as far as the poor copy quality allows. I have made a more comprehensive comparison, however, between the basetext and the copies in the British Library and Edinburgh University Library. I have also made a detailed comparison of the basetext and the Harvard University Library copy via

---

113. http://www.hmdt.org.uk/hmdt_happybirthday_1.html (accessed July 3, 2015). The program and script are available on the Hackney Music Development Trust website (http://www.hmdt.org.uk/hmdt_downloads_1.html).

114. For a list of libraries holding copies of the text, see the *English Short Title Catalogue*: http://estc.bl.uk/.

115. Bullard, "Textual Disruption."

its facsimile on *Early English Books Online*.[116] These detailed comparisons show some significant variations between the basetext and the other three copies, as follows: in the basetext, the signature on page 1 ("Here begins the Narrative or Relation") is B, whereas in the other copies this page is marked A2, and there is no B gathering. Otherwise, the signatures in the copies I have examined are the same. The basetext also includes three typographical errors: on page 13, "unwilling" appears as "nnwilling"; on page 18, "authority" appears as "anthority"; and on page 39, the catchword "and" appears as "aud." These errors have all been corrected in the British Library, Edinburgh University Library, and Harvard University copies. Additionally, the Haverford copy includes a further typographical correction: on page 46 of the basetext, and of the British Library, Edinburgh, and Harvard copies, "And" appears as "Aud," but in the Haverford copy this has been corrected to "And."

As is the case with all the volumes in the Other Voice in Early Modern Europe series, I have modernized spelling in this edition. American spellings have been used. The exceptions to this are that "my self" and "any thing" have been retained as two words, as the modern contracted forms "myself" and "anything" risk losing nuances of meaning important to the text. I have silently expanded contracted words (so that "w^ch" becomes "which," for example), and expanded "&" to "and," and "&c." to "etc." I have modernized obsolete word forms, so that "then" (in, for example, "far more then old Eli") is emended to "than." Where variant forms of a word appear in the basetext ("handmaid" and "hand-maid," "mayst" and "mayest"), I have regularized in line with the *Oxford English Dictionary* (*OED*). Names have been modernized only when reference books consistently agree on a different spelling: so "Mrs. Grose" is rendered "Mrs. Grosse." These instances are footnoted. Capitalization follows guidelines in the fifteenth edition of the *Chicago Manual of Style*, so that (for example) "Clergy" becomes "clergy." The exception to this is where the noun in question refers to God, Christ, or the Bible (hence "Savior," "Creator," and "Scripture"), to legal titles, instruments, or buildings (such as "Justice," "Protector," "Bill of Indictment," "Assizes," "Sessions-house," or "Court"), or where titles are used refer to specific people (such as "Governor" or "Matron"). In such instances, where capitals were used in the basetext they have been retained. Where the basetext uses capitals inconsistently (as with the "order" issued for Trapnel's arrest), lower case has been used. Additionally, a capital is retained when Trapnel refers to her "Spirit" (the soul, or immaterial, divinely originating, and eternal element of her being), to distinguish it from her "spirits" (the immaterial, animating element of her being, as distinct from the corporeal). Where I quote in footnotes from other seventeenth-century texts, spelling has not been modernized. Cardinal numbers have been silently changed to ordinal where

---

116. *Early English Books Online* (*EEBO*) is a database of works published in English between 1475 and 1700. All of the 125,000 titles available there are in facsimile; some are also available in searchable text.

necessary to avoid confusion, so "1 verse of the 8 of the Romans" is rendered "1st verse of the 8th of the Romans." The long "s" of the basetext has been regularized to its modern form.

While I have modernized spelling, I have retained the punctuation (with very few exceptions) as it appears in the basetext. I have retained, for example, the colons that are so frequently used where the modern norm would be a period.[117] The retention of the original punctuation preserves the texture, cadences, and pace of the original prose. The only systematic change to the punctuation is the introduction of possessive apostrophes, as their absence too often risked confusion of the sense. No additional paragraph breaks have been introduced, nor has the page layout been changed.

Where italics in the basetext were used for proper nouns, these have been changed to roman. However, the most significant use of italics in the basetext is to indicate biblical quotations or direct or reported speech, though they are not used consistently. Where italics are used for quotations and to indicate speech, they have been retained, rather than being replaced by quotation marks. The rationale for this is that the transition between direct speech, reported speech, and authorial commentary is not always clearly marked, and the introduction of quotation marks would have required arbitrary and unnecessary editorial decisions to be made about the boundary between speech and commentary. The retention of italics in these instances allows these more fluid transitions to be preserved without any loss of clarity to the prose.

Dates are given as they appear in the basetext but footnoted when they need clarification. This is necessary because there were differing calculations as to when New Year fell. According to the Julian (Roman) calendar, the year began on January 1. This dating practice survived into the Christian era, with the Church calculating its calendar in accordance with the solar framework of the Julian calendar and retaining January 1 as the New Year. From the twelfth century, however, the feast of the Annunciation (March 25) became the starting point of the year for most official and legal purposes in England, and this remained the case until the calendar was reformed in 1751. For a time, therefore, these different calculations about when the year began continued side by side: "After 1582 Englishmen had to reckon with the fact that some continental countries (and Scotland, in 1600) had agreed to begin the year on 1 January; and English writers of the next century and a half sometimes give a double year-date for days from 1 January to 24 March."[118] Trapnel's texts take the New Year to begin on March 25. So, for example, when we would today cite two successive dates as March 24, 1652, and March 25, 1652,

117. For a discussion of early modern punctuation principles and practices, see Percy Simpson, *Shakespearean Punctuation* (Oxford: Clarendon Press, 1911).

118. "Appendix III: The Calendar," in Sir Paul Harvey, *The Oxford Companion to English Literature*, 4th ed., revised by Dorothy Eagle, 932–34 (Oxford: Clarendon Press, 1967), 932.

Trapnel would write March 24, 1651, and March 25, 1652. Any dates that might, as a consequence, cause confusion for twenty-first-century readers are therefore footnoted.

Trapnel, like other religious radicals, does not use the names of the months or of the days of the week, since these were of pagan rather than Christian origin; instead, she numbers them. I therefore footnote the name of the month to which she is referring when she writes, for example, of the "second month." For the reason given above, January and February end the calendar year rather than beginning a new one, and hence appear in Trapnel's writing as the eleventh and twelfth months; March is the "first month." Where Trapnel refers to the days of the week as "first day," "second day," and so on, the days to which she is referring are footnoted. Sunday is the week's "first day." Like other religious radicals, too, Trapnel's writing relies heavily on direct quotation or paraphrase of the Bible. For the most part, she uses the King James Bible, and so I have used this version when I cite the Bible in the footnotes. Occasionally her words are closer to the Geneva Bible; when this is the case, it is footnoted.

The basetext ends with a page of Errata, which is retained here. In addition, for ease of reference, these corrections have also been incorporated into the text, and in each case a footnote has been added to indicate the original wording.

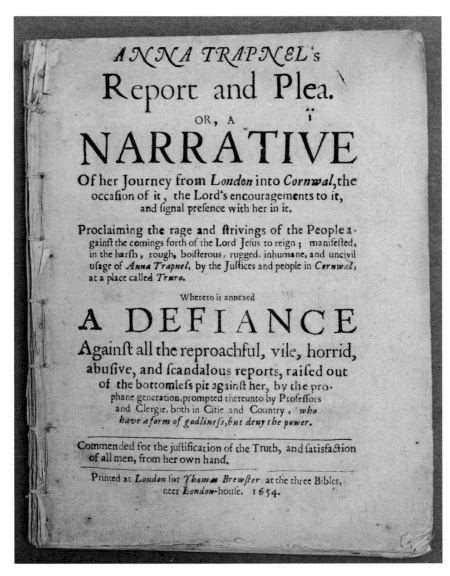

ANNA TRAPNEL's

Report and Plea.

OR, A

NARRATIVE

Of her Journey from *London* into *Cornwal,* the
occasion of it, the Lord's encouragements to it,
and signal presence with her in it.

Proclaiming the rage and strivings of the People a-
gainst the comings forth of the Lord Jesus to reign ; manifested,
in the harsh , rough, boisterous, rugged, inhumane, and uncivil
usage of *Anna Trapnel,* by the Justices and people in *Cornwal,*
at a place called *Truro.*

Whereto is annexed

A DEFIANCE

Against all the reproachful, vile, horrid,
abusive, and scandalous reports, raised out
of the bottomless pit against her, by the pro-
phane generation,prompted thereunto by Professors
and Clergie, both in Citie and Country , *who
have a form of godliness,but deny the power.*

Commended for the justification of the Truth, and satisfaction
of all men, from her own hand.

Printed at *London* for *Thomas Brewster,* at the three Bibles,
neer *London*-house. 1 6 5 4.

Figure 2. The title page of *Anna Trapnel's Report and Plea* (1654).

ANNA TRAPNEL'S

Report and Plea.[1]

Or, A

NARRATIVE

Of her Journey from London into Cornwall, the
occasion of it, the Lord's encouragements to it,
and signal presence with her in it.
Proclaiming the rage and strivings of the People
against the comings forth of the Lord Jesus to reign; manifested,
in the harsh, rough, boisterous, rugged, inhumane, and uncivil
usage of Anna Trapnel, by the Justices and people in Cornwall,
at a place called Truro.

Whereto is annexed
A DEFIANCE
Against all the reproachful, vile, horrid,
abusive, and scandalous reports, raised out
of the bottomless pit against her, by the
profane generation, prompted thereunto by Professors[2]
and Clergy, both in City and Country, *who
have a form of godliness, but deny the power.*[3]

*Commended for the justification of the truth, and satisfaction
of all men, from her own hand.*
Printed at London for Thomas Brewster,[4] *at the Three Bibles.*[5]
near London House.[6] *1654.*

---

1. Both of these terms have specific legal meanings in addition to their more general connotations: a report is "a written account of a case heard in a court (esp. as prepared for publication)," and a plea is "a formal statement, written or oral, made by or on behalf of a prisoner or defendant." Oxford English Dictionary, 2nd edition, *Oxford University Press*, 1989. Online edition, http://www.oed.com/ (accessed January 7, 2015). All subsequent references to the *OED* are to the online edition.

2. Those who have all the outward signs of faith but live ungodly lives; always used derogatorily by Trapnel and other religious radicals.

3. A paraphrase of 2 Timothy 3:5. The chapter identifies the "last days" as perilous times during which people lose their way and become "despisers of those that are good." From these people, "having a form of godliness, but denying the power thereof," the godly should turn away. The reference demonstrates Trapnel's prophetic role and her millenarian concern with the sweeping away of the old corrupt order in preparation for the imminent personal rule of King Jesus.

4. A London bookseller who, with Giles Calvert and Henry Hills, had been official printer to the Council of State until the end of 1653: see Henry R. Plomer, *A Dictionary of the Booksellers and Printers who were at Work in England, Scotland, and Ireland from 1641 to 1667* (s.l.: Bibliographical Society, 1968), 32.

5. The name of the bookseller's business, identifiable by a sign showing three Bibles rather than by a written name. Many booksellers had their premises in St. Paul's churchyard.

6. The town house of the Bishops of London, also in St. Paul's churchyard: see Henry Benjamin Wheatley and Peter Cunningham, *London Past and Present: Its History, Associations, and Traditions* (London: John Murray 1891), 2:430–31. During the Commonwealth and Protectorate, episcopacy was abolished and so the building was used for other purposes: the Fifth Monarchists, for example, held meetings at London House on Sundays. On such uses of London House, see Anon., *Reasons Humbly Offered in Justification of the Action, of Letting a Room in London-House unto Certain Peaceable Christians, called Anabaptists* (London?: s.n., 1642); William Erbery, *The Bishop of London* (London: s.n., 1653), 1–8; and Humphrey Hathorn, *The Old Leaven Purged Out* (London: s.n., 1658); see, too, B. S. Capp, *The Fifth Monarchy Men: A Study in Seventeenth-Century English Millenarianism* (London: Faber and Faber, 1972), 59–60, 277.

To the READER.

The Lord, and my Father (Courteous Reader) having put me upon this work and employment, I pray don't call it idleness, lest you would be likened to those *who call good evil, and evil good; and put darkness for light, and light for darkness;* against whom there is a woe pronounced from the Lord (Isaiah 5:20[7]): and is it not dreadful to come under the woe of the Lord? Sure it is much better to come under men's threats, scourges, and contempt; and when for well-doing too, what *shall harm you if you be followers of that which is good* (1 Peter 3:3)? Whatsoever is done to the upright in heart,[8] it's no harm: *If ye suffer for righteousness sake, happy are ye; and be not afraid of their terror, nor be troubled.*[9] I bless the Lord, my sufferings are for righteousness' sake, and I go not about to vindicate my self, but Truth; which indeed stands in no need of mine or anyone's vindication; but I would show love and respect to it, in opposition to those, who with spades and shovels dig up mire and rubbish[10] to throw upon it. Power and spear is drawn against the Lord and his anointed, for the holy unction that the holy one hath given his,[11] they suffer, and who can be sad? Whatsoever is laid upon them by men or devils, when thereby they are not losers, but great gainers from the Lord, though losers from men: and therefore men may give losers leave to speak to them, which have offered them so much injury. But the Lord knows, I would not reach out tongue, hand nor pen, to right my self, or to seek restoration[12] of my loss,[13] I waive that, such a thing is below my spirit. I bless the Lord, and truly I do not herein boast, neither would I glory in any thing, save in my infirmities; not in my sins, but in reproaches, and

7. In the few cases when biblical references appeared in the basetext as marginal notes, they are given, as here, in parentheses.

8. A common biblical trope for godliness; see for example Psalms 7:10, 15:2, 32:11, 97:11, and 119:7.

9. 1 Peter 3:14. See, too, Matthew 5:10: "Blessed are they which are persecuted for righteousness' sake: for theirs is the kingdom of heaven."

10. See Isaiah 57:20: "But the wicked are like the troubled sea, when it cannot rest, whose waters cast up mire and dirt."

11. See 1 John 2:20: "But ye have an unction from the Holy One, and ye know all things." Unction is both an anointing and the oil or ointment used for anointing.

12. Spelled "restauration" in basetext. Neither specialized sense of the word thus spelled (i.e., "the reinstatement of man in the divine favour or in a state of innocence," or "the restoration of a person to a former status or position") seems intended here, though the former sense, associating the subject with divine favor and innocence, would not have been unwelcome (*OED*).

13. Presumably, the loss of her reputation occasioned by the accusations made against her in Cornwall; for an account of these, see in particular her "Defiance" in this text, 122–35.

vilifyings, which the Apostle saith, He will glory in: (2 Corinthians 11:30) *I will,* saith he, *glory of the things which concern mine infirmities.* He could glory in the Lord's fatherly strokes, as looking unto all things to work for the good of his soul, seeing his Father's love in all that was done unto him, giving him a thousand-fold for his outward damage. And though I am a poor inferior, unworthy to be compared with any of the holy men or women reported of in the Scripture; yet I can say with Paul, Through grace I am what I am;[14] and I live, yet not I, but Christ lives in me; and the life that I live, is by the faith of the Son of God, who died, and gave himself for a weak handmaid,[15] as well as for a strong Paul.[16] And my desire is to imitate that approved Hannah in 1 Samuel 1, who was in bitterness of soul, and prayed unto the Lord, and wept sore for a Samuel, wherein God might be glorified and advanced in and by that typical prophet,[17] who held forth Christ that great prophet, that lives for ever, who maketh fruitful, and removes barrenness.[18] And if handmaids[19] in these days pray and weep for their Lord, begging his coming to rule in them, and in the nation, and to teach all sorts of people his statutes, that so the statutes of Omri[20] might be utterly ruinated, such praying cannot be borne by the inhabitants of this nation; there is such an old evil spirit of misconstruing, and judging holy actions to carry in them evil consequences. Eli the Priest of the Lord, is imitated in his worst part.[21] England's rulers and clergy do judge the Lord's

14. 1 Corinthians 15:10.

15. A female servant.

16. Galatians 2:20: "I am crucified with Christ: nevertheless I live; yet not I, but Christ liveth in me: and the life which I now live in the flesh I live by the faith of the Son of God, who loved me, and gave himself for me."

17. A prophet who was a "type," that is, a person from the Old Testament who prefigured someone (frequently Christ himself) from the New Testament; hence Samuel here "held forth" (prefigured) Christ.

18. Hannah prayed for a son: "O Lord of hosts, if thou wilt indeed look on the affliction of thine handmaid, and remember me, and not forget thine handmaid, but wilt give unto thine handmaid a man child, then I will give him unto the Lord all the days of his life" (1 Samuel 1:11). She subsequently gave birth to Samuel, dedicated him to God, and he later became a prophet. Trapnel's comparison brings together God's granting of the wishes of a supplicant (and therefore desiring) handmaid with the prophesying of the coming of Christ.

19. Here, servants of the Lord, such as female prophets like Trapnel, rather than female servants.

20. A military commander who became king of Israel, but who ultimately "wrought evil in the eyes of the Lord, and did worse than all that were before him" (1 Kings 16:25). The "statutes of Omri" (Micah 6:16) were oppressive measures introduced by him. Trapnel is here metaphorically referring to Cromwell, who had led the New Model Army to victory over the armies of Charles I in the 1640s, and had very recently, at the end of 1653, been made Lord Protector. For Trapnel's response to this, see introduction, 5.

21. See 1 Samuel 1:12–14. Eli mistakes Hannah's silent praying as a sign of her drunkenness, just as, Trapnel suggests, in her own time the signs of true godliness are misunderstood as signs of spiritual error or immodesty.

handmaid to be mad, and under the administration of evil angels, and a witch, and many other evil terms they raise up to make me odious, and abhorred in the hearts of good and bad, that do not know me.

Pray, Christian Reader, well observe the ensuing discourse, whereby you may understand the voice of malice and envy uttered and acted by the clergy and rulers against me, who hath showed much love and friendship to them for many years, and yet is no enemy to her enemies; but prayeth for them. I am sure they have sinned far more than old Eli, who said of Hannah, She was drunk. This grieved her, and made her reply and say, *Don't count thy handmaid for a daughter of Belial, for out of the abundance of my complaint and grief have I spoken hitherto. Then Eli said, Go in peace, and the God of Israel grant thy petition that thou hast asked of him.*[22] Here is a recantation quickly manifested; and it's probable, he was exceedingly troubled, for afflicting the afflicted. What rash judgers imitate him in this part? Though he was the chief priest in his days, yet he thought it no disparagement to talk with a poor handmaid, being a sober holy woman. Therefore I instance this example, Reader, that thou mayst take notice how far short the great rabbis come of Scripture rule in these days of the Gospel, wherein they should abound, not in pride, haughtiness and lofty carriages; but in humility, and in acknowledging the wrong and evil judgment that they have brought forth, and passed upon the innocent. And as to what they have said, and passed sentence, may not Judas[23] rise up in the Judgment-day of the Lord, and condemn these men, who acknowledged his evil? And likewise Simon Magus,[24] who confessed his sin, and desired prayer; and many heathens did so, recorded in Scripture, and in many histories besides, which the learned are not ignorant of? And shall heathens, and a vile Judas, a spirit-abusing Simon Magus, condemn those that are accounted Christians, great in wisdom and knowledge, and eloquent speeches, and full of gilded words, brave orators, great headpieces,[25] so called; but is it not more commendable to be in heart, than in head? *My son, give me thy heart.*[26] And the Lord saith, when Israel did so word it with him, *Oh that there were such an*

---

22. 1 Samuel 1:16–17.

23. One of Christ's twelve disciples, whose betrayal of him to the Romans resulted in the crucifixion. Matthew 27:3–5 suggests that Judas repented his betrayal and hanged himself.

24. A sorcerer who converted to Christianity, but, by offering money to the apostles Peter and John in return for the miraculous powers he saw them to have, exposed his corrupt and self-serving desire merely to enhance his own magical powers. When Peter and John condemned him, Simon asked them to pray for forgiveness for him; see Acts 8:9–24. Trapnel here invokes two archetypal traitors who repented their sins but who nonetheless should not expect forgiveness at Judgment Day.

25. Men of intellect (*OED*).

26. Proverbs 23:26.

heart![27] Here is brave[28] language, fair promises; but, *Oh that there were such an heart!* Deuteronomy 5:28.[29] An heart comparable with such words, God loves, which brings sayings out into doings; he delights in golden actions, not in gilded words;[30] he esteems reality, not falsehood. Who can forbear taking up a lamentation concerning poor England, whose prophets prophesy falsely, and the priests bear rule by their means, and the people love to have it so; but what will they do in the end thereof? for sure the end will be sad, when the Lord shall come out as a swift witness against the seers of England, for strengthening Baal's priests,[31] and upholding the Pope's dominion, and dressing the Scarlet Whore[32] in new clothes, so as to blind and deceive cities and countries, telling them, that it's the true genuine fruit of the womb of the church, and spouse of Christ,[33] when it will indeed be discovered to be from the harlot's brood, and so a bastard, which is sentenced by the Lord according to Scripture, surely to die, and the day of the Lord's vengeance will slay it; for the Lord hath pronounced destruction to Babylon's brats,[34] as well as to Babylon: why then should contention be for the Whore's brats?

Reader, I beseech this of thee, whosoever thou beest; under forms, or without forms; obedient to ordinances for the Lord's sake, or yet in the dark concerning them:[35] I beseech all sorts of people, high and low, to weigh in the balance

---

27. Deuteronomy 5:29.

28. Fine.

29. See n27. The quotation is misattributed here: it is actually to Deuteronomy 5:29.

30. An allusion to an opposition much cited by sectaries between "doers of the word" and "hearers only, deceiving your own selves" (James 1:22).

31. The priests of false gods.

32. Religious radicals (and other Protestants) frequently identified the Whore of Babylon, "drunken with the blood of the saints, and with the blood of the martyrs of Jesus" (Revelation 17: 6), with the Roman Catholic Church. See Christopher Hill, *Antichrist in Seventeenth-Century England* (London: Oxford University Press, 1971); and Peter Lake, with Michael Questier, *The Antichrist's Lewd Hat: Protestants, Papists, and Players in Post-Reformation England* (New Haven and London: Yale University Press, 2002).

33. The church was frequently figured as the Bride of Christ: see Matthew 25; Luke 5; Ephesians 5:25; and Revelation 21. For analysis of the importance of this trope, see Elizabeth Clarke, *Politics, Religion, and the Song of Songs in Seventeenth-Century England* (Basingstoke: Palgrave Macmillan, 2011); Erica Longfellow, *Women and Religious Writing in Early Modern England* (Cambridge: Cambridge University Press, 2004); and Pamela S. Hammons, *Poetic Resistance: English Women Writers and the Early Modern Lyric* (Aldershot: Ashgate, 2002).

34. See Psalm 137:8–9: "O daughter of Babylon, who art to be destroyed; happy shall he be, that rewardeth thee as thou hast served us. Happy shall he be, that taketh and dasheth thy little ones against the stones." Babylon was the mystical city of the apocalypse, applied polemically to Rome or papal power (*OED*). The Roman Catholic Church was construed by early modern Protestants as the descendant, or offspring, of "Babylon."

35. Trapnel is emphasizing that her text is not addressed only to saints, God's elect, but to all, in an appeal to all of God's friends, "known and unknown," to reject the rumors circulating about her. "Forms"

of the sanctuary[36] the true relation which followeth; for I shall relate the truth without addition: though I cannot (it may be) remember all the passages in order, yet as many as the Lord brings to my mind, I shall relate, for the satisfaction of the Lord's friends known and unknown in all parts where the rumor hath run.

A declaration from my own hand shall follow, not being put on by any, save by the great Instructor, who counselleth with his eye, who beareth me out[37] before men and devils. The Lord is on my side, I will not fear men, what they can do; the Lord is my help and refuge.[38] Farewell.

Your servant that loves
Christ in sincerity,
A. T.

---

referred to outward ceremonies or formalities (*OED*). The term "ordinances" was used by Baptists instead of "sacraments" for baptism and the Lord's supper; they saw these as religious or ceremonial observances or practices, of great symbolic importance but not necessary for salvation.

36. "to weigh (or examine) with the weights (or scales) of the sanctuary: to test by the standard of divine revelation" (*OED*).

37. To bear out is to confirm or corroborate.

38. Psalm 46:1: "God is our refuge and strength, a very present help in trouble."

Here begins the
NARRATIVE *or* RELATION.

First, I shall give an account of my invitation from friends,[39] which said, *Pray go down with us to Cornwall;*[40] *there you may do good to poor souls, with the variety of experiences God hath given you.* But I said, *There's a far journey indeed! Do you think I would leave all my friends, to go so far from them? They would take it very ill, surely.* They said to me, *We have invited you; we pray you spread it before the Lord, and hearken to his mind in it; and we will pray and wait for the Lord's answer.* I said, I would pray against going to Cornwall: if I should find any inclination or motion to go, I would not hearken to it, my mind was so strongly bent against that journey. But two days after, in the night, I was praying to the Lord in my bed secretly;[41] and I desired I might abide near my London friends, that so I might enjoy society with them that I was in church-order with,[42] who were so dear to me, and were written in my heart. But the Lord that night persuaded my heart to pray to him for his presence in the journey to Cornwall, saying, *Don't pray against*

39. Captain Langdon and Colonel Bennet, both Members of Parliament (MPs) for Cornwall in the recently dissolved Barebone's Parliament. This Parliament, also known as the Parliament of Saints or the Nominated Parliament, had been welcomed by Fifth Monarchists because among its members were a number of Fifth Monarchist sympathizers (Capp, *Fifth Monarchy Men*, 68, identifies twelve), including Langdon and Bennet. With the dissolution of the Parliament in December 1653, the Fifth Monarchists "went into permanent and unwavering opposition" to the Protectorate of Cromwell that followed it. Capp, *Fifth Monarchy Men*, 75. On Langdon and Bennet, see introduction, 17, 21–22; nn130 and 132; and Anna Trapnel, *The Cry of a Stone; or, A Relation of Something Spoken in Whitehall, by Anna Trapnel, being in the Visions of God* (1st edition: London: Thomas Brewster, 1654. This edition: edited by Hilary Hinds. Tempe, Arizona: Arizona Center for Medieval and Renaissance Studies, 2000), 4.

40. County in the far southwest of England, some 270 miles from London. Regions at such a distance from the capital often had the reputation of being hard to govern and rebellious: for example in 1549, the Prayer Book Rebellion or Western Rising, a popular revolt in Cornwall and Devon against the introduction of the Protestant Book of Common Prayer, was violently suppressed. In the Civil War of the 1640s, Cornwall had been loyal to the King until forced to surrender to Parliamentarian forces in 1646. On Cornwall in this period, see Mary Coate, *Cornwall in the Great Civil War and Interregnum, 1642–1660* (1st ed.: Oxford: Oxford University Press, 1933; this ed.: Truro: D. Bradford Barton Ltd., 1963); Ronald Hutton, "The Experience of the Civil War in the West," *Somerset Archaeology and Natural History: The Proceedings of the Somerset Archaeological and Natural History Society* (1995): 1–6; M. J. Stoyle, "'Pagans or Paragons?': Images of the Cornish in the English Civil War," *English Historical Review* 111.441 (1996): 299–323; and Diane Purkiss, *The English Civil War: A People's History* (London: Harper Perennial, 2007), 357–72.

41. Matthew 6:6 commends praying "in secret."

42. Her fellow-worshippers in the congregation of Allhallows the Great, Thames Street.

it any more: for there thou must go. And much persuasion was given in to my heart, by the secret whisperings of the Spirit. And the Scripture-sayings I had that night, were these: The first was Joshua 1:9. *The Lord thy God is with thee whithersoever thou goest.* And again, I had that saying, *Where canst thou flee from my presence, or where canst thou go from my Spirit?* Psalms 139:7. I then said, *Truth, Lord, whither can I go from thy Spirit, or flee from thy presence? Then don't fear to go to Cornwall, though it be a long journey,* said the Lord, *for I will go with thee:* then I said, *Lord, let me have thy Spirit and presence in places near London; why should I go so far, and among strangers?* The answer was, *Fear not, be not discouraged:*[43] *thy God, who is thy Father, goeth with thee:* then I mourned before the Lord, and said, *I pray Father let me not go:* then the Lord said, *Thou reasonest as Moses did when he was to go to Pharaoh: he caviled against the mind of God,*[44] *and so dost thou:* then that saying was given into my heart, *The Lord hath purposed thy going there, and his purpose and counsel shall stand, and he will do his pleasure; it pleaseth him, thy going there:* and then I had that Scripture in Isaiah 41:10. *Fear thou not, for I am with thee: be not dismayed, for I am thy God: I will strengthen thee, yea, I will help thee, yea, I will uphold thee with the right hand of my righteousness;*[45] *therefore,* said the Lord, *be willing to go:* and then my reasoning gainsaying spirit fell flat before the Lord, and I prayed, *Thy will, O Lord, be done;*[46] *thy word coming with such power and great authority on my heart, I can no longer contradict it;* then I had this saying, *Out of the mouth of two or three witnesses things are confirmed.*[47] *I have,* said the Lord, *given thee many confirming Scriptures for thy establishment concerning thy journey: therefore be strong in thy Father's strength; rely upon him that will not forsake thee, nor leave thee; but will be thy guide unto death.*[48] Then I told my sister,[49] *I thought I must go to Cornwall;*

---

43. Deuteronomy 1:21.

44. See Exodus 6. God commands Moses to go to Pharaoh to ask that the Israelites be allowed to leave Egypt; Moses objects, on the grounds that "the children of Israel have not hearkened unto me; how then shall Pharaoh hear me, who am of uncircumcised lips?" (Exodus 6:12).

45. Isaiah 41:10.

46. Trapnel is here citing the Lord's Prayer: "thy kingdom come; thy will be done; on earth as it is in heaven."

47. Deuteronomy established the principle that no one should be condemned on the word of a single witness, but that "at the mouth of two witnesses, or at the mouth of three witnesses, shall the matter be established" (Deuteronomy 19:15). The principle is also cited a number of times in the New Testament; see Matthew 18:16; 2 Corinthians 13:1; 1 Timothy 5:19; and Hebrews 10:28. Since there is accusation being made against Trapnel here, the text serves as an early indication of the importance that witnessing comes to have in her later court hearing in Cornwall. On the history of this precept in English law, see L. M. Hill, "The Two-Witness Rule in English Treason Trials: Some Comments on the Emergence of Procedural Law," *American Journal of Legal History* 12.2 (1968): 95–111.

48. Psalm 48:14.

49. Fellow believer.

the which she liked not; but contradicted. And the day after this night's debating and arguing, I told some of the church I walk with,[50] *That I was persuaded to go to Cornwall*: they were much against it, and said to me, *You will not we hope do so, we are against your leaving us to go so far; and will you leave us in such a time as this?*[51] Many of my sisters were troubled at my first speaking of going; but when I had related the Scriptures I had for my going, then they were silent for that time; and I told them, *That if I had not a further call from God to the journey, I would not go; it being such an extraordinary journey, I would not go without an extraordinary call further from the Lord, sealing me up*[52] *thereunto*. And going down to Hillingdon[53] near Uxbridge, by the way, as I rode, I still was filled with apprehensions of my journey into Cornwall, the joy I should have by the way, and what benefit others would have through a poor creature. And when I came to my friend's house[54] at Hillingdon, I lay all next day silent, but exceedingly filled with the presence of the Lord, who showed me a vision of my Cornwall journey: I beheld high rocky hills, and variety of places and towns, and how I should be as I rode in the coach, much melody I should have;[55] this I saw, and heard this saying, *That as sure as Paul in Acts 16:9 had a vision appeared in the night: There stood a man of Macedonia and prayed Paul, saying, Come over into Macedonia and help us;*[56] and the Lord said, *as truly do I thy Lord call thee to Cornwall by this vision*: then I answered, and said, *Paul was to preach there, what is that word to me?* Then reply was, *But as sure as his was a vision from the Lord to go to Macedonia, so as sure had I a call and true vision to go to Cornwall*: then singing triumph was given me concerning the journey thither, how filled I should be by the way: which was so. And then after I had thus sang and prayed, I rode to see

50. A reference to her congregation at Allhallows the Great. "Walk" here means to be associated with, to work or worship with.

51. The congregation at Allhallows the Great was under duress at this time, as their minister, John Simpson, and weekday lecturer (or preacher), Christopher Feake, were in prison in Windsor Castle, having been arrested for preaching against Cromwell and the Protectorate: see Capp, *Fifth Monarchy Men*, 101. On the position of "lecturer," see n170.

52. Pledging me irrevocably.

53. Town in the county of Middlesex, about sixteen miles west of London.

54. In *Cry*, Trapnel notes that she went to Hillingdon in April 1653, where she visited "one Mr. William Atcroft's house" and experienced a number of visions over a period of seven days. The minister of Hillingdon from 1650–1660, Philip Taverner, witnessed these visions; see Trapnel, *Cry*, 12, and n87. Trapnel's friend Ursula Adman also lived in Hillingdon in the 1660s: see n414.

55. As the account on 58–64 shows, Trapnel's vision of what will characterize her forthcoming journey is accurate.

56. In Acts 16:9, Trapnel is citing a verse in which the next stage of Paul's missionary journey, which could have continued in a number of different directions, is determined by a vision.

the Lord's two ambassadors which were imprisoned in Windsor Castle[57] for the testimony of Jesus, Mr. Simpson,[58] and Mr. Feake,[59] who were filled with the Spirit abundantly: and when I a while beheld their courage for King Jesus, I departed, with other friends, back to my friend's house at Hillingdon, and the next day rode to a friend's house six miles off, where I abode two nights. And as I was walking in the fields, I was suddenly very hoarse, and I could not well speak, but softly: and I was greatly tempted as I walked in the fields, that I should be hoarse while I lived, like as a woman of the congregation was, with whom I walk; so should I be not able to speak but hoarsely.[60] *And therefore go not thy journey,* said Satan, *for that extraordinary dispensation of prayer and singing shall not be with thee; then they will not regard thee whom thou goest with, for they look at that, and not at thee; and that departing from thee, thou wilt not be regarded by them; and being in a strange place, how sad then will it be with thee? And they are but strangers to thee; acquaintance with them hath been but a little while: therefore don't go.*

57. About ten miles southwest of Hillingdon, Windsor Castle (a royal residence) had been taken over early in the Civil War by Parliamentarian forces. Royalist prisoners, including Charles I, were held prisoner there. In 1649, after the execution of the King, Windsor Castle was "kept for the public use of the Commonwealth." *VCH, Berkshire,* 3:18.

58. One of the leading Fifth Monarchists. In 1642 John Simpson had become lecturer at St. Botolph's, Aldgate, and in 1652 its rector; in 1647 he was made lecturer and pastor of the Baptist congregation at Allhallows the Great, Thames Street, which had been founded by the Welsh Independent minister Walter Cradock. Simpson prophesied against Cromwell following the dissolution of the radical Barebone's Parliament of 1653. As a result, he (along with Christopher Feake) was imprisoned in Windsor Castle from January to July 1654; see Trapnel's letter to them in Anna Trapnel, *A Legacy for Saints; Being Several Experiences of the Dealings of God with Anna Trapnel, In, and After her Conversion* (London: Thomas Brewster, 1654), 57–60. Trapnel records in *Legacy,* 9, how in January 1643, while listening to Simpson preach, she first experienced fully the presence of the grace of God. She describes the transformation effected by her conversion in vivid detail: "Suddenly my soul was filled with joy unspeakable, and full of glory in believing, the spirit witnessing in that word, Christ is thy wel-beloved." See Bernard Capp, "Simpson, John (1614/15–1662)," *Oxford Dictionary of National Biography,* ed. Lawrence Goldman (Oxford: Oxford University Press, 2004–) (accessed January 7, 2015) at http://www.oxforddnb.com/. All subsequent references to the *ODNB* are to the online edition; and *BDBR,* 3:176–77.

59. Christopher Feake was minister of Christ Church, Newgate, and lecturer at St. Anne's, Blackfriars, and at Allhallows the Great, Thames Street. He was one of the best-known leaders of the Fifth Monarchist movement from 1651 to 1660, during which period he was frequently imprisoned. Like Simpson, he had preached against the dissolution of the Barebone's Parliament in January 1654. He and Simpson were imprisoned in Windsor Castle on January 28. Owing to his continued insistence on the illegality of the government, Feake remained in prison on and off until 1658. Feake had visited Trapnel during her eleven-day prophetic trance in Whitehall: see Trapnel, *Cry,* 5. See, too, *BDBR,* 2:270–71; and Brian Ball, "Feake, Christopher (1611/12–1682/3)," *ODNB.*

60. Hoarseness would have terminated Trapnel's prophetic activities, which were dependent on her voice. In the temptation that follows, Satan seeks to exploit her ambivalence about her journey by tempting her to wish for an end to her powers of prophecy: her friends, he says, are interested only in her prophetic voice, not in her.

Thus Satan and my fearful nature[61] joined together to frustrate what I had spoken from the Lord concerning my going, being sealed up[62] for the journey; and always after sealing unto any work of the Lord, Satan tempts me; but such is the goodness of the Lord to me, who lets not out Satan till he hath first established[63] me; and then before I have the mercy, the sentence of death is put upon what is in order to the bringing it forth to view:[64] so that the Lord thereby strengthens me the more, and makes me live by faith, which is the life of the just:[65] it's a lovely life the life of faith. But further, as for Satan's temptations, they lasted but for half a day, and a little part of the night, and they were removed; for in the night in my sleep the Lord refreshed me with many Scriptures, as being my refuge,[66] stay,[67] and defense,[68] and strong tower,[69] guide,[70] and succorer.[71] And at break of day I awoke out of sleep, refreshed as one with new wine; and indeed I had that night such well-refined wine, as Scripture makes mention of.[72] And hearing the birds

61. Satan tempts Trapnel by targeting her weak point, her "fearful nature" (she fears that her hoarseness might prohibit her ability to prophesy). Trapnel notes that this becomes a pattern: on any occasion that she has committed herself "unto any work of the Lord," Satan tempts her.

62. See n52.

63. Confirmed, settled, given steadiness to (*OED*).

64. The sense here is that before something new can come into being, that which was previously in place has to receive "the sentence of death."

65. For Protestants, justification (whereby God frees the believer from guilt) and salvation were by God's grace and through faith alone, not dependent on any desert of the believer; "will" and "works," one's own life, and intentions or deeds were irrelevant. See Ephesians 2:8–9: "For by grace are ye saved through faith; and that not of yourselves: it is the gift of God: Not of works, lest any man should boast." The "just" are those made righteous before God, by his grace, their faith a sign of their elect (or saved) status. See John von Rohr, *The Covenant of Grace in Puritan Thought* (Atlanta, GA: Scholars Press, 1986); and Dewey D. Wallace, Jr., *Puritans and Predestination: Grace in English Protestant Theology, 1525–1695* (Chapel Hill: University of North Carolina Press, 1982). On Trapnel's "free grace" theology, see Hilary Hinds, "Soul-Ravishing and Sin-Subduing: Anna Trapnel and the Gendered Politics of Free Grace," *Renaissance and Reformation* 25.4 (2001): 117–37.

66. See Psalm 46:1; Isaiah 25:4; and Jeremiah 16:19.

67. See 2 Samuel 22:19 and Psalm 18:18.

68. See Psalm 62:2, 6.

69. See Psalm 61:3 and Proverbs 18:10.

70. See Psalm 48:14.

71. God is not described in the Bible as a "succorer." The word appears there once only, where a woman, Phebe, is commended as "a servant of the church" and "a succourer of many" (Romans 16:1–2). However, see 2 Corinthians 6:2: "We then, as workers together with him, beseech you also that ye receive not the grace of God in vain. (For he saith, I have heard thee in a time accepted, and in the day of salvation have I succoured thee: behold, now is the accepted time; behold, now is the day of salvation.)"

72. See Isaiah 25:6: "And in this mountain shall the Lord of hosts make unto all people a feast of fat things, a feast of wines on the lees, of fat things full of marrow, of wines on the lees well refined." "Lees"

chirrup in the morning early, about my chamber window; I had this saying[73] given into my heart, *Thou hearest those birds in their notes and motion, which pleaseth thy ear: And doth the great Creator take care of birds, still maintaining them with a supply of food suitable for them, that so they may live, and be lively in their service to man?*[74] *And doth God take care of fowls, that not a sparrow shall fall to the ground without the Father's providence or ordering it to be so?*[75] *Then what care and provision doth he make for rational created pieces,*[76] *which the whole Trinity was in the make*[77] *thereof: as for other pieces,* he said, *Let it be, and it was so;*[78] *but as to man's make, the whole Trinity gave their judgment. And,* said the Lord to me, *hath God honored thee with this first honor, in making thee a rational piece, and also giving thee a share and interest in the death and resurrection of his Son, and hath made thee partaker of the divine nature,*[79] *of that heavenly-born state, of that second creation in Christ, spoken of in* Ephesians 2:19?[80] *Art thou thus provided for, to be made a possessor of two creation-works, a first and a second? and also hast thou the Spirit of adoption whereby thou canst cry, Abba, Father?*[81]

---

is a heavy sediment of dead yeast cells, grape pulp, and pips; keeping wine "on the lees" (with its sediment) for a while is thought to improve its flavor.

73. The passage that follows is an extended allusion to Christ's Sermon on the Mount, from Matthew 6:25–34, though the phrasing is Trapnel's own.

74. See Matthew 6:26: "Behold the fowls of the air: for they sow not, neither do they reap, nor gather into barns; yet your heavenly Father feedeth them. Are ye not much better than they?"

75. See Matthew 10:29: "Are not two sparrows sold for a farthing? and one of them shall not fall on the ground without your Father."

76. "Piece" could mean person, individual (*OED*). Trapnel's meaning is that human beings, alone among God's creatures, are made in his image, which is threefold. The Son (Logos, the Word of God), is an intermediary between God and his creation, and is identified with reason.

77. Creation, constitution.

78. The phrasing "Let … and it was so" recurs in the creation story in Genesis 1.

79. 2 Peter 1:4: "Whereby are given unto us exceeding great and precious promises: that by these ye might be partakers of the divine nature, having escaped the corruption that is in the world through lust."

80. Ephesians 2:19: "Now therefore ye are no more strangers and foreigners, but fellow citizens with the saints, and of the household of God." More relevant here to the notion of a "second creation in Christ" are Ephesians 4:20–24: "But ye have not so learned Christ; If so be that ye have heard him, and have been taught by him, as the truth is in Jesus: That ye put off concerning the former conversation the old man, which is corrupt according to the deceitful lusts; And be renewed in the spirit of your mind; And that ye put on the new man, which after God is created in righteousness and true holiness"; and 1 Corinthians 15:47–49: "The first man is of the earth, earthy; the second man is the Lord from heaven. As is the earthy, such are they also that are earthy: and as is the heavenly, such are they also that are heavenly. And as we have borne the image of the earthy, we shall also bear the image of the heavenly." See, too, John 3:3: "Jesus answered and said unto him, Verily, verily, I say unto thee, Except a man be born again, he cannot see the kingdom of God."

81. See Romans 8:15: "For ye have not received the spirit of bondage again to fear; but ye have received the Spirit of adoption, whereby we cry, Abba, Father." In Jewish and early Christian prayers, "Abba"

Then having done thus much for thee, will he withhold any thing that's good for thee? He will not.

And I felt my hoarseness removed from me presently, and all my temptations which I told you the day before did so seize upon my Spirits: and the Lord renewed my faith concerning my journey, and made me to rejoice over Satan. And I arose, and rode that day to meet with some of the Lord's servants, where a day of thanksgiving[82] was kept, for many special favors received from the Lord, and for his upholding comforting presence in sufferings; and there I stayed till night: in which day I beheld much of divine presence and glory coming towards the Saints,[83] and great ruin unto the enemies, which were presented to me like a tottering house, that stands shaking and ready to fall. And I had that saying, *So doth and shall totter all the towers and Babels*[84] *builded and reared up in contempt to King Jesus, who will confound all such builders and their work,* as the Apostle saith, *They that build hay, or wood, or gold, or silver, or any thing of their own materials, it shall be burnt,* 1 Corinthians 3.[85] *This foundation will admit of nothing of man's corruptible stuff to be joined with it; for it is complete, and will complete his servants that build upon him.* Then when this thanksgiving-day was ended, I rode to my friend's house at Hillingdon, where I was filled with joy and singing most part of that night; and the next day I rode to another friend's, where I stayed; the next day, being the first day of the week,[86] that day I went to hear a minister[87] which preached a mile off, in

---

was a name by which God was addressed (as here). "The Spirit of adoption" continues the theme of being reborn in Christ, and thus of the elect.

82. A day of religious services and prayer, held in recognition of divine favors.

83. The "sanctified" holy elect, destined for eternal life; used by Fifth Monarchists to refer to the godly ones chosen to prepare the way for the return of King Jesus to establish his kingdom on earth.

84. See Genesis 11. The tower of Babel was a sign of the Babylonians' overweening ambition and arrogance, as punishment for which God "confounded" human language, so that thereafter people spoke different languages and no longer understood each other. This story was much cited in the mid-seventeenth century, with the tower of Babel frequently used to signify confusion and disagreement: "Babel served both as a representation of the war of words in the press and as a figure for ideological difference." Sharon Achinstein, "The Politics of Babel in the English Revolution," in *Pamphlet Wars: Prose in the English Revolution*, ed. James Holstun, 14–44 (London: Frank Cass, 1992), 18. See, too, Umberto Eco, *The Search for the Perfect Language*, trans. J. Feutress (Oxford: Blackwell, 1995).

85. 1 Corinthians 3:11–15.

86. Sunday. See introduction, 39.

87. The minister of Hillingdon, Philip Taverner, had heard Trapnel speak on an earlier visit: see Trapnel, *Cry*, 12. Edmund Calamy described Taverner as "a grave, peaceable divine, of unblameable life, but who chose to live retired." Calamy, *The Nonconformist's Memorial: Being an Account of the Ministers, Who Were Ejected Silenced after the Restoration, particularly by the Act of Uniformity*, ed. Samuel Palmer, 2 vols. (London: W. Harris, 1775), 2:283. Taverner was a contributor to the public dispute with Quakers held at West Drayton in January 1658: see A. G. Matthews, *Calamy Revised: Being a Revision of Edmund Calamy's Account of the Ministers and Others Ejected and Silenced, 1660–2* (Oxford: Clarendon Press, 1934), 476.

whose ministry the Spirit much warmed my heart, and refreshed my spirits;[88] and though I was ill in my outward man all that day, yet the matter I heard was so reviving, being spiritual, that at night thinking of it, and walking in a curious[89] garden, where I saw the pleasant trees, and plants, and walks, and fish-ponds, and hearing the birds' pleasant notes, all this begat such an harmonious apprehension of God in my heart, that I began to sing forth his praises, and continued while it was so late in the evening, that my friends that walked with me thought it convenient to lead me into the house; which they can best give an account of; for I minded not the time, nor those that were with me, neither can I tell whether I felt the ground I walked upon; my Spirits[90] was so much in divine rapture, and my spirits so heat with Spirit-fire, which produced singing-melody while[91] midnight, the which singing speech was directed to the whole family,[92] and those belonging to it at that time; which family consisted of many persons, grave, and judicious, and learned, understanding persons, before whom I thought my self unfit to speak, when I was in an ordinary capacity;[93] but being filled extraordinarily, I wanted not words com-

88. Vital power, energy, or vigor: Trapnel's heart is warmed by the Holy Spirit, resulting in the refreshing of her own "spirits." In early modern physiology, the spirits were the fluids supposed to permeate the blood and chief organs of the body. They took the form, variously, of animal spirits (responsible for sensation and movement), the natural spirits (responsible for growth and nutrition), and the vital spirits (which supported and sustained life).

89. Skillfully or artfully designed, intricate. This, together with the garden's "walks" and fishponds, suggests that Trapnel is staying in a substantial house, of which there were a number in Hillingdon: "from the 17th century onwards a number of houses on Hillingdon Heath were owned by persons of importance: most of these estates deserve notice rather by virtue of their owners or the character of the houses and adjoining pleasure gardens, than for their size." *VCH, Middlesex*, 4:74. Trapnel frequently experiences communion with God in gardens, not only here, but also at Tregassow, Captain Langdon's house, and at Mr. and Mrs. Hill's house in Truro (see 65–67, 82, and 93). A number of gardens feature in the Bible as places of divine significance, from the Garden of Eden, to the *hortus conclusus* ("A garden inclosed is my sister, my spouse; a spring shut up, a fountain sealed" [Song of Solomon 4:12]) and the Garden of Gethsemane, the latter in particular a place of prayer and privileged communication with God. For a discussion of the importance of gardens in Trapnel's writing, see Longfellow, *Women and Religious Writing*, 168–70. See, too, Hester Lees-Jeffries, "Literary Gardens, from More to Marvell," in *A New Companion to English Renaissance Literature and Culture*, 2 vols., ed. Michael Hattaway, 1:379–95 (Oxford: Blackwell, 2010); and Jennifer Monroe, *Gender and the Garden in Early Modern English Literature* (Aldershot: Ashgate, 2008).

90. Her immaterial being and immortal soul rather than her vital spirits (see n88), though the two senses were related, as the subsequent phrase ("my spirits so heat with Spirit-fire") makes clear: her passionate spiritual rapture results in the heating of her bodily spirits.

91. Until.

92. All members of the household, including servants.

93. Her normal human senses and capabilities, as distinct from her "extraordinary" capacities, which prevail when she experiences prophetic visions or trances. At such times, her awareness of the presence of others and her need for sleep, food, or drink are suspended, and her powers of human speech

posed and orderly, and learning for the learned. Herein I don't boast, but in the rich free love of God,[94] who gives to whom he pleaseth. Then after that singing, I was put to bed, being weak in body and head, between two friends, where I lay and prayed till the morning; and coming into my ordinary capacity, I rose and had strength of body: though I could not eat the day before, nor after this night thus speaking so much; yet I was not dry, neither could I take any creature-refreshing,[95] though I had much offered me. This I mention, to advance Christ, and not for any by-end.[96] Then my friends sent me in their coach to London, where I prepared for my Cornwall-journey all that week.

Coming to my habitation[97] the second day of the week, that week I had much of the Lord's presence in marvelous joy, and yet many temptations between whiles; the tempter tempted me against my journey: and when I went up a pair[98] of stairs, I was tempted that I should fall from the top to the bottom of the stairs and break my limbs, so that I should in such a way be hindered my journey; and I was often tempted that week before I went, that some evil should befall me to hinder me from going to Cornwall; or some would hear of my going, that would stop it. And then Satan said, *What will become of all thy faith, and the singing report[99] concerning it?* And sometimes I was thus hurried, yet I staggered not in my faith concerning the truth of what I had mentioned about my journey, that it should surely be as I had believed; and I waited for the accomplishment of it. And

---

give way to powers of divinely inspired prophecy, often manifesting in outpourings of extemporary verse (as in Trapnel, *Cry*). While she is usually in a physically weakened state at such times, when she returns to her "ordinary" capacity, she usually notes (as here) that her physical strength immediately returns to her.

94. Rather than God's love being earned or deserved by the sinful human being, it was instead seen as bestowed freely by him; see nn65 and 186.

95. Food or drink.

96. Secret and selfish purpose.

97. Trapnel records a number of different "habitations." A report of her Whitehall prophecies dated January 12–19 (while the prophecy was still continuing) describes her as "a Maid that lives at *Hackney*, near the City of London." *Severall Proceedings of State Affaires in England, Scotland, and Ireland*, 225 (January 12–19, 1653 [1654 by the modern calendar: see "Editorial Principles and Practices," 38–39]): 3562. Trapnel's account of these prophecies ends with her walking "in health and strength" from Whitehall to Hackney (where she lived with a kinsman, Mr. Wythe) and then to Mark Lane, where she had been staying with a Widow Smith in late 1653: see Trapnel, *Cry*, 10, 79. She had previously lodged in the Minories and in Fenchurch Street, both streets just to the west of Tower Hill. Hackney, to the northeast of the City of London, was in the seventeenth century a rural parish in the county of Middlesex; see introduction, 15.

98. Flight.

99. "Reports" of her Whitehall prophecies, some of which were delivered in song, were published as *The Cry of a Stone* (in February 1654) and *Strange and Wonderful Newes from White-Hall* (in March 1654).

the sixth day of that week I took my leave of my Tower friends,[100] sitting up till the morning with them, all the night praying and praising with them with joy, more than an ordinary capacity[101] could hold. And in the morning I went to bed, and lay some hours, and then rose, and abode there that day and night: and the next day, being the first day[102] of this following week, I bid my Tower friends farewell; and so departed from them, taking my leave also of other friends by the way as I went to Allhallows,[103] where I met with the congregation that I am in fellowship with, which use to[104] break bread[105] there. And I that day saw great shinings, and tasted much of my Savior that day, who presenting his loveliness in the ministry, and his sweetness in the supper of breaking bread, which filled my heart with joy unspeakable and glorious in believing. And then after the ordinances[106] were ended, I took my leave of many friends there, who gave me their exhortations with counsel and prayer for my well-doing; and I departed from them, begging their prayers for me when absent in the body: and half a score of my sisters kept that night in prayer with me at my friends' house from whence I was to take my journey the next day. And having thus spent the night in sweet communion with God, I was prepared for my journey: I wanted not sleep nor food-preparation, having had the cordial revivement liquors from my Lord Jesus,[107] which strengthened me for my traveling to Cornwall. And I said to my friends, *I pray be much in spiritual communion together, and don't forget to mention before the Lord your unworthy sister at a distance.* Thus desiring their remembrance of me, they departed from me; and I and my friends for the journey, went by water from Southwark[108] to Whitehall

100. Trapnel knew a number of people in the vicinity of the Tower of London: see n97.

101. See n93.

102. Sunday.

103. Trapnel was a member of the congregation of Allhallows the Great, a thirteenth-century church on the south side of Upper Thames Street, near what is now Allhallows Lane. John Simpson, one of the leaders of the Fifth Monarchists, was a lecturer (preacher) here; see n170; introduction, 9, 16–18; and Trapnel, *Legacy*, 8–10. The Fifth Monarchist movement had first taken shape in December 1651 at a meeting at Allhallows, and, together with Christopher Feake's church of St. Anne's in Blackfriars, it continued to be a center for the movement. For details of the beliefs of this millenarian group, see introduction, 8–10. The church was destroyed in the Great Fire of 1666.

104. In order to.

105. Take Holy Communion.

106. Religious observances or ceremonies: here, Holy Communion. The other principal ordinance for Baptists was baptism.

107. Communion wine. "Cordial," in relation to medicines, food, or drinks, meant "stimulating, 'comforting', or invigorating the heart; restorative, reviving." "Revivement" refers to something that has a reviving or restorative effect (*OED*).

108. A London borough on the south bank of the Thames; connected to the City, on the north side, by London Bridge, the capital's only bridge.

Stairs,[109] where we landed, and went to the inn where we took coach;[110] and many friends came to bid us farewell, and among them came one who said to some after I was gone, that *if he had known me, and had known I was going into his country, he would have procured the Council's order*[111] *to have stopped my journey, for the love he bore to his country; which sure he thought I would corrupt, and make like my self:* which he thought to have hindered; but the Lord prevented his desire: for my Father would have me go there, and Satan nor men could not hinder me.

So we rode on our journey toward the West:[112] and in the first day's journey, my thoughts were taken up with the work of the praying Saints, which met that day at Allhallows, it being the second day,[113] which they use to keep for the restoration of the kingdom of Israel,[114] praying and speaking for that concernment,[115] which is so glorious; and my thoughts were very seriously intent upon generation-work,[116]

---

109. These gave access to the river at Whitehall; the River Thames was an important and busy city thoroughfare, and, as there was only one bridge, most river crossings were made by boat. Whitehall was the principal royal residence, in Westminster, on the north side of the river, to the west of the City of London. It continued as the seat of government during the Interregnum. The inn in which Trapnel had uttered her January prophecy, which had brought her considerable public attention, was in Whitehall.

110. There were a number of coaching inns in Whitehall. When Trapnel returns to London from Cornwall, she crosses to Whitehall from Fox Hall (or Vauxhall) by water and stays the night at the George, a coaching inn on King Street: see nn351 and 352. There were no public coaches to Cornwall at this time, so she is likely to have traveled in a coach belonging to one of the other travelers, presumably Captain Langdon, to whose house she is traveling.

111. The Council of State had been the executive body of government since the execution of the King in 1649. It had recently been reformed under the Instrument of Government, following the dissolution of the Barebone's Parliament and the installation of Cromwell as Lord Protector in December 1653. It was empowered to issue orders stopping such journeys, and indeed it was on an order from the Council that Trapnel was later arrested in Truro and detained in Bridewell.

112. Trapnel's journey west to Cornwall was approximately 270 miles. The route from London to Cornwall was an important one: the cartographer John Ogilby, who published his map in 1675, called it "in general a very good road as any in the kingdom, and as good entertainment." Quoted in Paul White, *The South-West Highway Atlas for 1675* (Launceston: Tamar Books, 2005), 24. Trapnel traveled by coach, at a rate of between twenty and thirty miles a day. Internal textual evidence (see n241) suggests that they left London on Monday, March 6.

113. Monday.

114. In Acts 1:6, just before Jesus ascends to heaven, the apostles ask him, "Lord, wilt thou at this time restore again the kingdom to Israel?" In effect, therefore, Allhallows dedicated every Monday to praying and preparing for the return of the kingdom of God to earth. As millenarian Fifth Monarchists, Trapnel and many of her congregation were expecting the imminent return of King Jesus to earth to rule.

115. Concern or matter.

116. The Fifth Monarchist John Tillinghast had, in *Generation-Work* (London: M. Simmons for Livewell Chapman, 1653), 7, 23, defined generation-work as *"that worke, or those workes which the way or manner of Gods dispensations in the age a Saint lives in, calls him unto"*; it is *"of all others the greatest*

praying with them at Allhallows in the Spirit, though I was absent from them in body: and meeting with a dear friend by the way, who told me he intended to go to Allhallows meeting that day; I said, *I pray remember what was earnestly desired of you, that you would assist the church in the wilderness, and be helpful in the second day's meeting, keeping close to the work of the present day: and I desired his prayer for me in my absence;* more words passed between us as he rode by the coach-side a little way: then he bid farewell, and departed; and my joy was increased at the sight of that precious servant of Christ, whose words left a fragrancy upon my spirits some part of the day; and the enjoyment of prayer in the Spirit with them at Allhallows, took up the other part of the day; only speaking a little sometimes to my friends, with whom I went. At night we came to our inn, where I had much refreshings in a little meditation of God's goodness to me that day: and after prayer I went to my bed, and was refreshed with sights of the Lord in my sleep; and rose in the morning, taking another day's journey: and in much discourse we spent that second day's journey. And I rode the next day with the same persons as I did the day before, and my Spirit then was all that day in a praying and singing frame, and so it remained till night; and then we came to Salisbury,[117] where we parted with the judge that rode in the coach with us; for there the judges met in their circuit:[118] and there I was mightily filled with apprehensions of Christ's circuit he was taking in the earth, and of that blessed time that the Saints should judge the earth, when in that time the earth should not pass their false judgments on the Saints: and most part of that night I was thus: and they that were with me, saw and

---

worke, *and neglect herein the greatest sin." He enumerated "the worke of the present generation" thus: "The conversion of the Jews. Propagation of the Gospell, in order to a greater harvest of Gentiles. Joynting [sic] Saints (Christs mystical body) into one. Pulling downe of all high and lofty things and persons that oppose Christ. The establishment of Justice and Righteousnesse in the world. Striving with God in a more especiall manner for a greater degree of his spirit, more light and grace then Saints in former generations have had; together with the exaltation of Christ as King both in his Churches and also over the world"* (70–71; all italics original). Tillinghast (1604–1655) was a Fifth Monarchist and Independent minister, "the most learned of the Fifth Monarchists and the only one capable of publishing a systematic analysis of the prophetic texts that were basic to the movement": *BDBR*, 3:242. The Fifth Monarchist writer John Rogers also wrote of the need for the Barebone's Parliament to undertake "Generation-worke … which is, to *model* and *conforme* the *Civil affaires* for *Christs coming*." John Rogers, *Sagrir; or, Doomes-Day Drawing Nigh* (London: R. I., 1653), 136. See Richard L. Greaves, "Tillinghast, John (bap. 1604, d. 1655)," *ODNB*.

117. A cathedral city in Wiltshire, about ninety miles west of London, where Trapnel's party spent the night of Wednesday, March 8.

118. Assize judges were based in London but traveled from place to place (on their "circuits") throughout the country to hold court hearings. Wiltshire Assizes were held in Salisbury; these were part of the Western Circuit, which also included Devon and Cornwall: see J. S. Cockburn, *A History of English Assizes, 1558–1714* (London: Cambridge University Press, 1972), 46–47. Cockburn, 3, notes a seventeenth-century commentator describing the "lordly judges" riding their circuit "to frighten people with their bloody robes, state and pomp."

felt on my outward man,[119] which was like a dead clod, I was so cold a great while. And the fourth day's journey I sang and prayed almost the whole day: and so I did the fifth day's journey, singing much of the creation-excellencies, as trees, grass, and several plants, and corn that grew as I went by. And though I rode through towns,[120] I minded not any speakings of creatures; for indeed I was not capable of[121] outward sayings or doings, nor of the rattling of the coach those two days. And the last day of that week we came to Exeter;[122] which day I was very cheerful in the Lord, though not so very much as the days before: there we inned at an old disciple's house, a widow, one Mrs. Winter's, a house that many years had entertained and lodged Saints,[123] which in their traveling still took up their quarters there: and I lay there three nights: and the day after, being the first day of another week, I went to hear the Word preached at the castle in Exeter, where I kept this first day with the church that met there; and there I saw my London friends, that a

---

119. The body (as distinct from the soul).

120. After leaving Salisbury, Trapnel's party travels for three more days before arriving in Exeter. Ogilby's map suggests that the most likely towns she would have passed through would have been Shaftesbury, Sherborne, Crewkerne, Axminster, and Honiton; see White, *South-West Highway,* 24.

121. Not able to comprehend.

122. The county town (administrative center) of Devonshire, about ninety miles from Salisbury, and six days' travel from London. Trapnel's party arrived there on Saturday, March 11. Exeter had strong associations with Puritanism and, by this time, with the Parliamentarian cause. There had been a strong Baptist presence in the city since the Parliamentary armies took control in 1646; at first they met in the open air or in private houses, but later, some time between 1649 and 1654, the dining room of the old Deanery Hall was "fitted up as a Baptist meeting house, while the rest of the building was made into dwellings for working-class people whose homes had been destroyed during the siege of the city [in 1643]." Allan Brockett, *Nonconformity in Exeter, 1650–1875* (Manchester: Manchester University Press, 1962), 14. This work had been commissioned by the Fifth Monarchist MP John Carew (1622–1660). He had sat for Devon in the Barebone's Parliament of 1653, as had Trapnel's friends Francis Langdon and Robert Bennet. It may have been these Baptist and Fifth Monarchist connections that led Trapnel to spend several days in the city. Such conjecture might be supported by the fact that the following year, when Carew was imprisoned at St. Mawes, in Cornwall (February 1655 to October 1656), Trapnel visited him: *The Publick Intelligencer* 13 (December 24–31, 1655), 193–4. Thurloe 7:542 includes a letter from John Fox (see nn291 and 324) in which he claimed that Trapnel's visits to Carew had turned the head of the daughter of the governor of St. Mawes castle, Susan Keckwitch, who now "is oft-tymes in her singing trances, and soe continues 12 or 14 hours, if not longer." See J. T. Peacey, "Carew, John (1622–1660)," *ODNB.*

123. Sectaries frequently stayed with religious sympathizers when they traveled. Quakers (the movement with the most extensive records) had very well-developed networks of fellow-believers who lodged their traveling ministers: see Rosemary Moore, *The Light in Their Consciences: The Early Quakers in Britain, 1646–1666* (University Park: Pennsylvania State University Press, 2000), 25–30; Kate Peters, *Print Culture and the Early Quakers* (Cambridge: Cambridge University Press, 2005), chapters 1–3; and Richard T. Vann, *The Social Development of English Quakerism, 1655–1755* (Cambridge, MA: Harvard University Press, 1969), 10–12, 97–101. Mrs. Winter remains untraced.

while had dwelt in the castle:[124] and I continued till late in the evening with them, relating the goodness of the Lord to me by the way of my journey, and acquainting them with the welfare of London friends; and how joyfully the prisoners at Windsor Castle[125] took their sufferings, it being upon so noble an account. And these friends wondered much at my taking so long a journey, and said, *Sure some extraordinary thing was to be made manifest in my going so far; and therefore they would hearken after it, and observe the Lord's work in it:* for they thought there was something more than ordinary to be brought forth, in that I was carried so far a journey, and having so little acquaintance with them I went with:[126] which made them admire what the Lord would do with me; and so did many: and my self also thought and was persuaded, that the Lord would show some special favors to me, and so he did; I largely thereof enjoyed before my return back again: and I took leave of those friends that night, and came to my lodging at Mrs. Winter's. The next day the Lord greatly ravished my soul with his smiling looks on me, and he filled me that day with prayer, and singing, and discovering the tottering, shaking condition of clergy-function.[127] And likewise praying for many particular friends at London; and specially for them at Allhallows meeting,[128] and for those friends at the castle forementioned, speaking to every one of their conditions; and likewise begging sinners to come to Christ. And I spake to variety of conditions that day, wherein many souls were refreshed. And I lay all that night in a rapture of great joy, and had sights of my further journey, how God would carry me safe, and with much pleasantness to my journey's end; the which we went towards in the morning, it being the third day of the week;[129] in which day we parted with Colonel Bennet,[130] and his daughter,

---

124. Rougemont Castle in Exeter; the gatehouse was used as a jail during the Civil War. Stephen K. Roberts, "Juries and the Middling Sort: Recruitment and Performance at Devon Quarter Sessions," in *Twelve Good Men and True: The Criminal Trial Jury in England, 1200–1800*, ed. J. S. Cockburn and Thomas A. Green, 182–213 (Princeton: Princeton University Press, 1988), 184. I have found no record of a church meeting there, nor traced the "London friends" who had dwelt there.

125. Feake and Simpson, whom Trapnel had visited in prison in Windsor Castle before embarking on her journey to Cornwall; see nn58 and 59.

126. Trapnel had not known Captain Langdon and Colonel Bennet before they visited her in the course of her Whitehall prophecies in January.

127. Trapnel, like most sectaries, had no time for clergy who remained within the Church of England and were thus, as she saw it, hand in glove with the oppressive government, in part because of their livings being funded by tithes; as she puts it later in this text, 80, "one depends upon another, rulers upon clergy, and clergy upon rulers."

128. Monday was the day the Allhallows congregation met for prayer: see n113.

129. Trapnel's party left Exeter on Tuesday, March 14.

130. Colonel Robert Bennet was a committed Baptist, millenarian, and supporter of the regicide. He had served as an officer in the Parliamentarian army in the 1640s, published a pamphlet justifying the regicide in 1649, and become an MP in 1651. He played an active part in selecting the members of the Barebone's Parliament of 1653 (which included himself), and sat on its Council of State; he was "bitterly

and servants; and his wife[131] bore me company, with Captain Langdon,[132] and his wife,[133] and their servants; this was our company that went from Exeter together, and lodged by the way that night: which day's journey was very sweet to us; and we had much of the Lord's preservation with us. Then the next day, which was the fourth day, we came to Colonel Bennet's house,[134] where we lodged that night; and

disappointed" by the Parliament's dissolution in December 1653. Bennet visited Trapnel in Whitehall during her visionary trance in January 1654, and she stayed in the Bennets' house near Launceston, during this journey to Cornwall and during another in 1656. He was reelected to Parliament later in 1654, was defeated in 1656, but reelected in 1659; he retired to Cornwall at the Restoration in 1660. John Morrill describes Bennet as "a man who was pragmatic in his politics but utterly convinced in his separatist and chiliastic religious faith: efficient, pragmatic, determined, honest, egalitarian, godly, visionary—he epitomizes the puritan dimension of the English revolution." Morrill, "Bennett, Robert (1605–1683)," *ODNB*.

131. Bennet's second wife, Anne, who was seven months pregnant at the time of the journey. She gave birth to their sixth child (of nine), Mary, on May 27, and buried her two years later, on July 19, 1656: see *VCV*, 633. Bennet's first wife, Mary, had died following a miscarriage precipitated by being "frighted by a Troope of the Cavaleers" in 1643/4; Mary Coate, "An Original Diary of Colonel Robert Bennet of Hexworthy (1642–43)," *Devon and Cornwall Notes and Queries* 18 (1934): 258. See, too, Morrill, "Bennett, Robert (1605–1683)," *ODNB*.

132. Like Bennet, Francis Langdon (*ca.* 1606–1658) had represented Cornwall in the recently dissolved Barebone's Parliament. He was the sixth son of Walter Langdon of Keverell, in the parish of St. Martins by Looe. This estate had been sequestrated from his brother Walter, who was a Royalist exile; in 1650, Francis petitioned to receive the annuity to which he was entitled (paid by the estate) of £20, on the grounds that he had "with all faithfulness served during all the troubles, and is now employed by Parliament in several commissions in Cornwall." *CCC*, 3:2244. Langdon had served on a number of committees in Cornwall in the 1640s, becoming a Justice of the Peace (JP) in 1649. He became a Baptist in 1652, and was one of the Fifth Monarchist members of the Barebone's Parliament of 1653. Like Bennet, he visited Trapnel in Whitehall in January 1654 while she was in her visionary trance; it was after this that he invited her to Cornwall. *BDBR*, 2:170–71; *CCC*, 5:3298–99; Capp, *Fifth Monarchy Men*; Austin Woolrych, *Commonwealth to Protectorate* (Oxford: Clarendon Press, 1982); and *VCV*, 275. On the history of the Langdon family in the seventeenth century, see A. T. Langdon, "A Cornish Royalist Family in the Seventeenth Century," *Devon and Cornwall Notes and Queries* 25–26 (1953): 89–93, 116–20.

133. Anne Langdon (née Jago) of St. Erme, near Truro. Her brother, John Jago, had been an important figure in the administration of governmental affairs in Cornwall, having been a Commissioner on the Cornish Sequestration Committee, which dealt with the confiscation of the estates and property of Cornish Royalists, and their subsequent fines and penalties. Jago had died in 1652, and had been replaced on the Sequestration Committee by Major Peter Ceely (see n276). Following Francis Langdon's death in 1658, his will left to "my loving wife Anne Langdon & her heires forever my ffee farme Rente of twentie pounds a yere." Great Britain. Public Record Office. PRO Prob/11/281. In 1659 Anne married Robert Doyley, a Baptist preacher from Dorset. See *CCC*, 1:444–45, 515, 614; 3:2001–6; *BDBR*, 2:171; and Coate, *Cornwall*, 229, 261–65.

134. Hexworthy, in the parish of Lawhitton, near Launceston, in Cornwall. It is close to the border with Devon, about forty miles west of Exeter. The house survives, with parts of the seventeenth-century building incorporated: "Hexworthy," English Heritage, List Entry Number 1219191; http://

my heart was very cheerfully carried on in reading over every day's mercy, when I came to my lodging. And the next day after dinner,[135] we took our leave there, and parted with Colonel Bennet's wife at her house, who showed me much love, and told me, *She would send for me to her house again, after a little time expired.* Colonel Bennet, by the way as we journeyed, being taken much with my experiences, said, *They were not to be hid, but they were to be manifested for the benefit of others;* and said, *He would have me ride to some of his friends' houses: for that dispensation of the Lord on me, was not to be concealed.* And indeed he manifested much kindness to me as we journeyed in company together, and charged his daughter to be very tenderly careful of me; for that I was not in a capacity to mind my outward man. This his kindness lasted to Exeter.

But now to come again to my journeying from his house in Cornwall, which I told you we departed from after dinner, and came to Captain Langdon's sister,[136] where we lodged, and were lovingly entertained the fifth day; and there I had much love from God, and from strangers, and a very refreshing lodging, and the creatures[137] were very sweet to my taste there. As for the six days before we came to Exeter, I eat very little: but we went from thence, the sixth day: after breakfast, we took our leave of those relations of Captain Langdon's. And the sixth day at night, we came to Mrs. Langdon's brother's house,[138] where we received a courteous entertainment, and a refreshing lodge; and my heart there was taken up much with the apprehension of the vanity of outward enjoyments, and great attendances, and brave houses: and my thoughts were much upon the rocks I passed by in my journey, and the dangerous rocky places I rode over.[139] And whereas I

---

www.english-heritage.org.uk/ The Bennets were visited in 1656 by the Quakers Sarah Bennett and Mary Prince. They found Colonel Bennet to be "full of wisdom," but his wife to have "A hie spirite in her." They remark too that "hana trapnell was not at his house." Swarthmore Manuscripts, vol. 3 (MS VOL 354/116).

135. The main meal, eaten in the middle of the day.

136. Francis Langdon's youngest sister, Alice, had married Thomas Bligh, son and heir of William Bligh of Botathan in South Petherlin, in February 1631; see Langdon, "A Cornish Royalist Family," 120, and *VCV*, 39. Thomas inherited the estate on his father's death in 1627, so would have been living there with his wife in 1654. Botathan was about ten miles west of Lawhitton, so an easy journey to make in an afternoon.

137. "After 1 Timothy 4:4 ('every creature of God is good'). ... A material comfort; something which promotes well-being, esp. food" (*OED*).

138. Untraced. See n133 on Anne Langdon's brother John, who had died in 1652.

139. Trapnel's route to Truro went around the northern side of Bodmin Moor (named as "Foy Down" and "The Temple Moores" on Joel Gascoyne's 1699 map of Cornwall), the landscape of which is wild and rocky, its contours dominating the surrounding area. In the 1580s, John Norden had commented on the county's rocks as "high, huge, ragged, and craggie ... the Inlande mountayns are so crowned with mightie rockes, as he that passeth throwgh the Countrye beholdinge some of theis Rockes afar off, may suppose them to be great Cyties planted on the hills, wherin *prima facie* ther appeareth

used to be very fearful, when I rode on smooth ground, now I feared not, but was very cheerfully carried on, beholding my Rock, Christ, through those emblems of rocks: and I sat as in a chair upon the high steep hills, without any wearisomeness at all; and the thoughts of the Lord's kindness to me in these things, drunk up my thoughts that night: and the next day we came safe to our journey's end, at Tregassow,[140] at Captain Langdon's habitation, and there we ended our journey the last day of the week, which had been accomplishing thirteen days.[141] And the Lord much appeared to all of us the whole journey; praised be his Name, whose Name was to us indeed a strong tower. The Lord was our munition[142] of rocks, and large provision every way to souls and bodies. And thus I have given an account as briefly as I could of my journey-progress, and blessed fare by the way, and of the extraordinary and ordinary breakings forth of the light[143] of his countenance and communications, all along those thirteen days now expired.

---

the resemblance of towres, howses, chimnies, and such like." John Norden, *Speculi Britanniæ Pars: A Topographical and Historical Description of Cornwall* (London: William Pearson, 1728), 3. On Gascoyne's map, see W. L. D. Ravenhill and O. J. Padel, "Introduction," in Joel Gascoyne, *A Map of the County of Cornwall, 1699* (Exeter: Devon and Cornwall Record Society, 1991).

140. About four miles to the north of Truro, Tregassow Manor is in the parish of St. Erme; see map, 21 above. In the seventeenth century the house belonged to the Coke family, until it was sold by Thomas Coke to Hugh Boscawen, Lord Falmouth, in 1673. It is therefore likely that Langdon rented the house from Coke, as the Cokes were short of money for much of the century. No records have been traced suggesting that the house had been sequestrated. Langdon's brother-in-law John Jago, who died in 1652, had lived close by in the same parish. Langdon was living there by 1652, when he drew up his will, which names him as "of Tregassoe in the Countie of Cornwall." Great Britain. Public Record Office. PRO Prob/11/281. The house survives, but was comprehensively rebuilt in the 1690s, though parts of the sixteenth-century building, including the kitchen fireplace, remain.

141. The journey lasted from Monday, March 6, to Saturday, March 18.

142. Military equipment, such as weaponry or ammunition.

143. Communion with God whether in a visionary ("extraordinary") state or not.

Here follows a Relation, in the next place, of several passages and actings by creatures, in a way of love and hatred, some frowning, few smiling; many rejecting, few receiving: manifested from the first day, to the last day of my abode there in Cornwall, in the West. Also, of my imprisonment in Bridewell, and my enlargement therefrom.

I shall now begin the relation of my first coming to Captain Langdon's house, where there came many of Captain Langdon's acquaintance, to see them at their first coming home; and most of them gave me but a sour greeting, they having been informed before concerning my Spirit, as it was reported to me afterwards; but they frowningly and dissemblingly saluted me, though their hearts were against me, as many of them made it to appear largely afterwards; and some became loving friends among them, that loved me not when I first came; but I seeing these unlovely carriages[144] from the most part of them that came there that evening and afternoon, it made me very thoughtful what it would produce. I sat down in the room a while, where I heard many discourses from them to one another, and with Captain Langdon; and I not relishing the discourse, had a mind to walk in the garden by my self, and so I did a while, wherein the Lord gave me much of his loving-welcome, and kind salutations, saying, *Though thou seest many frown on thee, it shall not make thee sad; for thy Savior will smile on thy soul in all conditions*: and that saying made my heart revive presently; and then the Lord gave me that Scripture-saying, *This he requires of thee, To deal justly, love mercy, and walk humbly with thy God*, Micah 6:8. Then I said, *Lord, what am I to do here?* The Lord said, *I require this, that thou holdest out a just, upright walk with God*[145] *before all people; and in these parts thou shalt manifest the free justification*[146] *received of the Father by the Spirit through Christ to poor souls; telling them thy*

144. Conduct or behavior.

145. Show godly behavior.

146. The stage in the *Ordo Salutis* ("order of salvation") when the Christian was freed from guilt, and to be achieved by faith alone; human will itself had no power to initiate conversion or faith, which was an unmerited gift from God. "The essence of this Protestant piety was a vision of the divine-human relationship as based on the gratuitous mercy of God in the absence of human deserving, with humankind the object of a supernatural renovation worked only by the divine favor." Wallace, *Puritans and Predestination*, viii. Trapnel, Simpson, Vavasor Powell, and others who stressed the primacy of "free grace" argued that justification occurred not in the course of the human subject's life, but at the moment of predestination: "The elect are justified by grace before knowing anything of that grace; to God they are justified from eternity." Wallace, *Puritans and Predestination*, 119–20. Faith, in this view, was subsequent to, and a sign of, justification. See, too, von Rohr, *Covenant of Grace*, 92–93.

experiences there: and thou shalt declare the mercy of thy God, and thy love to it, by shewing thy experiences thereof, which thou hast had in divers manners discovered to thee. Here are some tempted souls, said the Lord, that must be comforted through thy temptations; the mercy thou foundst therein, tell them: love mercy in every kind of it. This saying I had also from the last words of the verse, *Walk humbly with thy God:*[147] *these things he requires of the just, doing and walking, mercy, loving, and a humble deportment in all thou dost.* Then I said, *Lord, make me humble:* said the Lord, *I will make thee humble through sufferings;*[148] *the Lord thy God begun it in thee, when he manifested thy salvation to thee, to be freely given thee, making thee see thy self, the worst of sinners; and he humbled thee more in Satan's prison,*[149] *and he hath brought thee here to humble thee more; for he will teach thee much of his secrets.*

Then my heart was melted as I was thus under divine speakings in the garden, and I said, *Lord, if thou wilt make me a partaker of more of that lovely clothing of humility; then, Lord, I will not matter*[150] *what I suffer here in this world below:* then the Lord said, *Thou must suffer many ways:* then I said, *Lord, balance me with thy word:* the Lord said, *What word wouldst thou have?* I said, *What thou pleasest:* then the Lord said, *Thou shalt have the same word as I gave to my servant Abraham; I told him when he went he knew not whither, that I would be his shield and exceeding great reward,* Genesis 15:1. *And as I was,* said the Lord, *to the father of the faithful, so I will be to the children, they having the same faith, as faithful Abraham had, I will give such the same promises:* then I said, *Lord, I fall short of his faith:* said the Lord, *I look not on the quantity so much as at the quality; I looking at the truth of it, it bearing the same stamp with that of Abraham's, which was the stamp of divine power and Spirit: therefore take the same promise: thou art come into a strange country, among many that don't affect*[151] *thee, and thou art like to suffer by them; but fear not, I thy God have not only given thee faith, as a shield; but I am thy shield and exceeding great reward; I am a double shield to thee,* said the Lord, *so I was to Abraham,*[152] *a shield within a shield: therefore fear not any*

---

147. Micah 6:8: "He hath shewed thee, O man, what is good; and what doth the Lord require of thee, but to do justly, and to love mercy, and to walk humbly with thy God?"

148. In "To the Reader," 43, Trapnel has already made clear that suffering is a sign of righteousness. She also rejoices at the prospect of suffering "for the testimony of Jesus," 67.

149. A year earlier, from February to April 1653, Trapnel had experienced a period of protracted temptation by Satan, comprising bodily torment, temptation to suicide, and temptation to join the Familists, another radical sectarian group; see Trapnel, *Cry*, 10–12.

150. Care about.

151. Like or have affection for.

152. In Genesis 15:1, which Trapnel has just cited, the Lord says to Abram, "I am thy shield, and thy exceeding great reward." While there is no mention in the Bible of a double shield, Psalm 91:4 refers to the truth of the Lord as "thy shield and buckler."

enemy; but look unto thy shield and buckler, and defense, for so Jehovah is to thee.
And the Lord brought to me those Scriptures that he gave me when he made me
willing to go the journey, as that saying, He would go with me, and that his Spirit
and presence should accompany me, and that he would uphold me with the right
hand of his righteousness:[153] which Scriptures were much enlarged on my Spirits,
as I thus walked alone in the garden: and I had such sweetness from the Lord
through the Scriptures, that it made my heart much affected with my journey,
and my Spirit leapt within me, and rejoiced that I was come into a country where
I should suffer for the testimony of Jesus; and I had at that time such cordials[154]
from the Lord, that I could have walked many hours in that garden; but Captain
Langdon's man[155] came, and desired me to walk into the room where his master's
acquaintance were; *For it may be they would not take it well,* he said, *if I did not
come and sit in the room with them.* I was very unwilling; for my communion in
the garden was so delightful to me; yet through much entreaty by him, I went. I
told him, *I could the better bear their sour countenances, and girding*[156] *expressions,
now I had drunk of divine cordials than I could before, when I first saw them, at my
coming into the house.*

So I went into the room among them, that did not care for my company,
and I heard many expressions concerning visions. I perceived what and who
they aimed at; I sat silent among them; there was Major Bawden[157] and his wife,
they were strangers then to me; but they spake very friend-like to me; and it was
not in tongue, but in heart, as afterward appeared: and there was Mr. Vinson[158]

---

153. Isaiah 41:10: "Fear thou not; for I am with thee: be not dismayed; for I am thy God: I will strength-
en thee; yea, I will help thee; yea, I will uphold thee with the right hand of my righteousness."

154. See n107.

155. Servant.

156. Jeering.

157. Major John Bawden, like Langdon and Bennet, had sat as MP for Cornwall in the Barebone's
Parliament of 1653; he also seems to have been a friend and neighbor of Langdon and of John Jago,
Anne Langdon's brother, who had lived in the same parish. Following Jago's death in 1652, Bawden
defended Jago's suit in a long-running dispute with Nicholas Borlace, also of the parish of St. Erme,
about sequestration. Coate, *Cornwall*, 264–65; *CCC*, 1:2004–5; 3:2001–6; Woolrych, *Commonwealth
to Protectorate*; and Capp, *Fifth Monarchy Men*. Bawden was, like Francis Langdon, a Fifth Monarchist
sympathizer; he and Langdon later acted as sureties for Trapnel for her appearance before the Assizes;
see 86. There was a John Bawden, son of John Bawden, at Trelassick in the adjacent parish of Ladock
in the 1690s, about five miles north of Tregassow; this gives a likely location for the Bawden family in
the 1650s, and would have made a short visit to Major Bawden's house feasible (Trapnel says she was
"but once at his house," 76). Cornwall Record Office. Mortgage for £400, Trelassick, Ladock, May 16,
1696. TLP/343.

158. Perhaps Walter Vincent (1631–1680), a barrister, and his wife Jane (née Norsworthy), of Truro.
Walter was elected MP for Truro in 1656, 1658, and 1660. The Vincents and the Norsworthys were
prominent Truro families: see June Palmer, *Truro in the Seventeenth Century: A Pattern of Place*

and his wife, my very loving friends they declared themselves to be: Mrs. Vinson came to me then, and said, *Pray come to my house; for I entertain you upon a Scripture-account, which adviseth to be kind to strangers; and what gain they had in old time, that in entertaining strangers, they entertained angels unawares.* Thus she instanced the Scripture,[159] which made her to speak to me, a poor, undeserving creature to be thus taken notice of; and indeed, I felt humility in my heart springing up much, when she thus spoke: I looked on my self unworthy of such a word, or loving expression to me; but my Father caused that friend, though a stranger, to show me kindness.

Again, further, this evening being spent, I went to my lodging, where the Lord smiled on me, and made it a lovely night, and I was no whit weary after so long a journey; but had refreshing rest; and in the morning Mrs. Langdon came to see me; but I had no mind to rise out of my bed: and that day the Lord filled me with much joy and singing; and I was in the Spirit with my friends at London, who broke bread that day;[160] and I was filled with apprehensions of Christ, the eternal Sabbath, and the glorious Rest, and the first-day-Resurrection, how glorious all this was, meeting in Christ the Savior and Deliverer from all bondage and enthrallment: and my heart was much with my friends in that ordinance of breaking bread; I partook of that sweet supper with them in the Spirit. And thus I spent that first day that I came to Tregassow, which was the first day of the first week that I took up my abiding there; much of Christ's death and resurrection was lively presented to me, and I sang forth his praises. And the second day my heart was heat also with the flame of love, which many waters cannot quench, as the spouse saith in the Canticles,[161] so I felt it; for all that day I had the Spirit's flame, as I had the day before, and I kept praying with, and for my friends at Allhallows, it being their meeting day;[162] those particulars they first thought upon in their beginning that meeting, which were the uniting of Saints in that bond of love, as those were in formerly, in the primitive times,[163] and that they might be of one heart and one mind; and that knowledge might cover the earth, as water the sea:[164] and that Jew and Gentile-fullness might be brought in, and the Kingdom restored

---

and People (Truro: June Palmer, 1989), 24, 40, 74; and http://www.historyofparliamentonline.org/volume/1660-1690/member/vincent-walter-i-1631-80.

159. Allusion to Hebrews 13:2: "Be not forgetful to entertain strangers: for thereby some have entertained angels unawares."

160. Took Holy Communion, as it was a Sunday.

161. Song of Solomon 8:6–7.

162. See n113.

163. Many sects were intent on returning their modes of worship to those "of primitive times," i.e., the New Testament times of the apostles, and still a time of direct divine revelation, prophecy, and miracles.

164. Isaiah 11:9 and Habakkuk 2:14.

to this old Israel,[165] which was the first married wife, as it's recorded in Scripture.[166] And that judges and rulers might be as at the beginning, as Moses, and Joshua, and as Samuel, and Gideon,[167] and other faithful ones, as is made mention of in Scripture. And I besought the Lord for these things, and for the reign of Christ, in, and by which, these things should be brought forth: and for this, every one, professing[168] the Lord, ought to pray. And thus I spent the second day: and it was very sweet to me, and fitted me for what I was to suffer in those parts. And after that second day, my heart was carried on very cheerfully in the apprehensions of the Lord's presence still with me, and I had a great deal of tenderness from my friends I went down with, who were as a tender father and mother to me at all times; and in suffering, their tenderness and care of me exceeded, it abounded as my sufferings abounded: and many that were at the first strange[169] in their carriages to me, after I had been there a while, they were very loving to me; and I had great kindness from the whole family, where I abode, till the wills of men fetched me away with their soldiers.

Further, I shall give people to know, that after I had been a week and a few days there, I was desired to go to Truro to hear the lecture[170] that was kept

---

165. Acts 1:6–7.

166. In Isaiah 54, God addresses Israel as his wife: "For thy Maker is thine husband; The Lord of hosts is his name; and thy Redeemer the Holy One of Israel: The God of the whole earth shall he be called. For the Lord hath called thee as a woman forsaken, and grieved in spirit, and a wife of youth, when thou wast refused, saith thy God" (Isaiah 54:5–6). In subsequent verses, God explains the restoration of Israel, and promises this church that while they might have felt forsaken, they had not been—a comforting thought for Fifth Monarchists in 1654, at a moment when they felt betrayed by the actions of Cromwell and that preparation for the Fifth Monarchy was under threat.

167. Moses was lawgiver and prophet; Joshua was Moses' successor as leader of the Israelites; Samuel was the last of the Hebrew judges and first of the major prophets; and Gideon was a judge and military leader. Trapnel is yearning for the kind of just and godly rule enacted by these archetypal Old Testament figures. Cromwell had until recently been celebrated as a new Gideon by Fifth Monarchists, but since his assumption of the Protectorship, such laudatory identifications had been disavowed; Trapnel recalled thinking that "Oliver Cromwell, then Lord-General, was as that Gideon, going before Israel, blowing the trumpet of courage and valour." By January 1654, however, she proclaimed him to have "backslidden," so that "this was not Gideon of old." Trapnel, *Cry*, 9, 54.

168. Declaring faith in, but whose words were empty; see n2.

169. Hostile, distant or cold.

170. A weekday sermon. The Truro lecture took place "every third day": that is, every Tuesday. A lecturer was "One of a class of preachers in the Church of England, usually chosen by the parish and supported by voluntary contributions, whose duty consists mainly in delivering afternoon or evening lectures" (*OED*). The aim was that lecturers should compensate for the scarcity of preaching ministers. William Arthur Shaw, *A History of the English Church during the Civil Wars and under the Commonwealth, 1640–1660* (New York: B. Franklin Reprints (1900), 2:182. As Trapnel's text exemplifies, lecturers were not restricted to the Church of England, but played an important role in Puritan and separatist congregations. See Paul S. Seaver, *The Puritan Lectureships: The Politics of Religious*

there every third day; so I did: and that morning before we went, there came a letter, which after we had prayed, was read; wherein a gentleman at Truro[171] invited Captain Langdon, and his wife, and my self to his house; the which invitation, we looked upon as answer of prayer, it coming so suitable to those requests put up to the Lord that morning. And we went to Truro, and heard the sermon; and that day, there preached one Mr. Allen,[172] a young man, who spake of many things from the 1st verse of the 8th of the Romans.[173] And when the sermon was ended, we went home with Mrs. Hill[174] to dinner, her husband having invited us by writing, the which I mentioned. And after dinner, there came many to see me, some out of good will, and love to what they had heard was of God in me, and others came to gaze, and others to catch at my words, so as to reproach me; but the Lord taught me how to speak before them all: as in the presence of the great God I spake, who is my Father, who always showed me kindness, and did then before those several sorts of people. I seeing many come into the room, and Mr. Powel[175]

Dissent, 1560–1662 (Stanford: Stanford University Press, 1970); Christopher Hill, God's Englishman: Oliver Cromwell and the English Revolution (London: Weidenfeld and Nicolson, 1970), 46–48; and introduction, 13.

171. Mr. Hill; see n174.

172. Stevie Davies suggests that this was Thomas Allen, a "militant" from Truro. Davies, "Trapnel, Anna (fl. 1642–1660)," ODNB. I have been unable to verify this reference. It is more likely that it was Joseph Allen, later (February 1655) Vicar of Mylor, eight miles south of Truro, and then Vicar of St. Gluvias with St. Budock, the parish church of Penryn, four miles west of Mylor. Matthews, Calamy Revised, 6. Allen was "esteemed a very good man, but very poor. He had a wife and several children, and had his subsistence from charitable friends; principally from the Hon. Hugh Boscawen, Esq." Calamy, Nonconformist's Memorial, 1:287. See, too, n276.

173. Romans 8:1: "There is therefore now no condemnation to them which are in Christ Jesus, who walk not after the flesh, but after the Spirit."

174. There were a number of prominent Hill families in the area, including the Hills of Truro and Constantine: see VCV, 229–30. Palmer, Truro in the Seventeenth Century, 59, 74, notes a merchant by the name of William Hill in Truro in 1650; Joan, daughter of John Norsworthy (the Norsworthys were another influential local family), married James Hill, who was mayor of Truro in 1658. See, too, Veronica Chesher, The Boscawen Street Area, Truro (Truro Civic Society and Buildings Research Group with the University of Exeter Extra Mural Department, 1980), 6.

175. Thomas Powel was Assistant to the Cornish Commission in 1654, and preacher at St. Clements, a parish adjacent to Truro; he became Rector of Truro with St. Clements in 1657. John Tingcombe, Rector of Truro St. Mary's 1649–1652, wrote that Powel was "a man of parts and (I hope) real piety." Matthews, Calamy Revised, 397. Trapnel is using "teacher" as a synonym for preacher or lecturer: see nn170 and 176.

a teacher[176] in those parts, came in with his wife,[177] and another woman, so that being there, I thought to be silent; but some desiring to have me speak, I said, *I was loath to speak before that critical-pated man, who would take my words and put his own sense upon them, and so ensnare me*; and it proved according as I said: but when I had sat a while, and saw so great a room full of people, who desired I should give an account for their edification and satisfactions, what God had done for my soul: there having gone such a rumor abroad concerning me, some saying one thing, and some another, it was therefore thought convenient to speak something among that great company of people that was come to my friend's house; and the Lord bringing that word also, which is recorded by the apostle, 1 Peter 3:15. which is, *to be ready to give an account at all times, when required, of the hope that is in me.* And I being desired to speak, I thought it my duty, though at the first I refused; and when I began to speak, I said to Captain Langdon, who was then discoursing with that Mr. Powel I mentioned, I said, *I remember a word from Mr. Bridges of Yarmouth,*[178] *which was, that we must still either be doing or receiving good: And,* said I, *here is neither of these among us;* and I repeated a word I told them Mr. Greenhill[179] once said to one whom he desired, with many of that congregation then present, who desired experiences to be imparted to them, using that word of David's, who said, *Come you that fear God, and I will tell you*

---

176. Preacher or lecturer. In 1643 the Westminster Assembly had debated the difference between a preacher and a teacher: "The debate on this was carried on for a week … with extraordinary pertinacity and warmth." Some Independents there described the difference thus: "Where two ministers can be had in one congregation, the one is allowed according to his gifts to applie himself most to teaching and the other to exhortation according to Scripture." Shaw, *History of the English Church*, 1:159.

177. In 1655 Thomas Powel was "son in law to Mrs. Simpson, Mr. Sidrake Simpson's widow." Powel's wife was Isabella; see Matthews, *Calamy Revised*, 397; Tai Liu, "Simpson, Sidrach (*ca.* 1600–1655)," *ODNB*; and n218.

178. William Bridge, an Independent minister, lived in Rotterdam and worshipped in Hugh Peter's congregation there, with William Greenhill (see n179), in the 1630s. He returned to England in 1641, and the following year became pastor of an Independent church in Yarmouth, East Anglia, though he was also a prominent lecturer in London, preaching widely, publishing a large number of pamphlets, and advising Cromwell on the composition of the Barebone's Parliament. Richard L. Greaves, "Bridge, William (1600/01–1671)," *ODNB*. John Simpson had visited Bridge during his tour of thirty gathered congregations in East Anglia in 1653. B. S. Capp, "Simpson, John (1614/15–1662)," *ODNB*. See, too, *BDBR*, 1:99–100.

179. William Greenhill, like William Bridge, had lived and worshipped in Rotterdam in the 1630s. A leading Independent minister and spokesman, he had been vicar of Trapnel's family's parish of Stepney since 1652, having been lecturer there since 1641. He had a large number of publications to his name (some jointly authored with William Bridge and John Simpson) and was very influential among Parliamentarians and clergy alike. Richard L. Greaves, "Greenhill, William (1597/8–1671)," *ODNB*; and *BDBR*, 2:25–26. In *Cry*, 6, as she seeks to establish her credentials, Trapnel cites Greenhill as someone to whom she is well known.

what God hath done for my soul:[180] and then I took up Paul's speech he used before Agrippa,[181] having been falsely accused by many, he declares the manner of his life from his youth, Acts 26.[182] And so to others he said, How he had walked in all good conscience before the Lord unto that day he then spoke it, Acts 23.[183] I used these words of the apostle, and said, *This was his practice, when false rumors had gone concerning him; and being that people had reported many things which were very contrary concerning me, I thought it requisite to acquaint them there present with the Lord's dealings concerning me from my childhood.*

And I told them, the first conviction[184] I had at nine years old, and how I remained under a formal work;[185] and then how I was brought into a despairing

180. Psalm 66:16.

181. After his missionary journeys, Paul returned to Jerusalem where he was arrested on "a trumped-up charge; the story describes his various appearances before courts and governors in the course of which he defends himself over against both the Jews and the Romans, protesting his innocence and in effect having it confirmed by the Roman authorities." I. Howard Marshall, *The Acts of the Apostles: An Introduction and Commentary* (Leicester: InterVarsity Press, 1980), 26. Marcus Julius Agrippa II ruled Chalcis, a province northeast of Judea; he was powerful in Jewish religious life as the Romans gave him the right to appoint the high priest, and custodianship of the temple treasure and the high priest's vestments. Judea itself was ruled by the new Roman Procurator, Porcius Festus. Agrippa and his sister Bernice were asked by Festus to assist in the trial of the apostle Paul in Caesaria on charges of sedition and heresy. Paul speaks before Agrippa in what is his final missionary act. Agrippa, well-versed in Jewish law, finds that Paul has no case to answer, but that he nonetheless could not be set free because he had appealed to Caesar, and to fail to honor such an appeal would be to disregard the authority and status of the emperor. See Acts 24, 25, and 26. While the point of her identification with Paul here is her narration of her life story, his subsequent rebuttal of false charges of sedition and heresy also resonates.

182. Paul's defense in Acts 26 is largely autobiographical, comprising an account of his early life and conversion to Christianity.

183. Acts 23 records the opening stages of the proceedings against Paul.

184. State of awareness of her own sinfulness. In *Legacy*, 1, Trapnel recalls, "When a child, the Lord awed my Spirit, and for the least trespass, my heart was smitten." The stages of her spiritual development are broadly conventional, and similar narratives can be found in many contemporary accounts; compare the early pages of George Fox's *Journal*, ed. John L. Nickalls (Cambridge: Cambridge University Press, 1982), for example, or those of John Bunyan, Richard Norwood, John Crook, Lawrence Clarkson, and Agnes Beaumont, collected together in John Bunyan, *Grace Abounding, with Other Spiritual Autobiographies*, ed. John Stachniewski with Anita Pacheco (Oxford: Oxford University Press, 1998). See, too, Stachniewski's analysis of the ways in which this Calvinist apprehension of spiritual development shaped the emerging literary form of the spiritual autobiography: John Stachniewski, *The Persecutory Imagination: English Puritanism and the Literature of Religious Despair* (Oxford: Clarendon Press, 1991).

185. Concerned only with the outward form of religious observance, rather than the spiritual truth and power. "I began to be very eager and forward to hear and pray, though in a very formall manner." Trapnel, *Legacy*, 1.

condition, and was so a while: and then I told them the Work of free grace[186] on me, and the Testimony of the Spirit, bearing witness to my Spirit, that I was in union with the Father, Son and Spirit: and I told them of my desertions and temptations, and of Satan's many cunning wiles, and of freedom many times therefrom: and I related my fit of sickness which was cured in believing, that I had eight years ago:[187] and I related the time and manner of my coming into church-order:[188] and likewise I told them the first bringing of my Spirit into this extraordinary praying and singing, and visions, was six weeks before Dunbar-fight in Scotland,[189] which was a beginning three years before, but did not so much appear to the view of others: and I told them how I prayed against this public-spiritedness;[190] and how the Lord silenced me, from those words in 1 Corinthians 1:27, 28.[191] *But God hath chosen the foolish things of the world, to confound the wise; and God hath chosen the weak things of the world, to confound the things that are mighty; and base things*

186. The phrase "free grace" signifies the belief that God's saving grace was bestowed "freely," without regard to merit or desert. This emphasis on the lack of agency of Christian believers in their own soteriological destiny (whether or not they are of the "elect," destined for salvation) was particularly important for Calvinist Christians such as Trapnel. See nn65, 94, and 146.

187. For an account of this sickness and recovery, see Trapnel, *Cry*, 6: "I being visited with a fever, given over by all for dead, the Lord then gave me faith to believe." See an extended account of her sickness in Trapnel, *Legacy*, 25–42.

188. "A regulation or code of regulations decreed by ecclesiastical or scriptural authority" (*OED*).

189. The Battle of Dunbar, in which Cromwell's Parliamentary army beat the Scots, took place on September 3, 1650, and was regarded as Cromwell's most decisive victory. Trapnel, in *Cry*, 9, wrote that, six weeks before the battle, "I had visions given me concerning that first overthrow of the Scots, where I saw myself in the fields, and beheld our army, and their general, … I saw the Scots fall down before them, and a marvellous voice of praise I heard in our army."

190. A willingness to ignore one's own wishes or predilections in order to undertake work for the good of others. In *Cry*, 40, Trapnel had prayed, "Let thy servants now be of a public spirit," but also acknowledges her own ambivalence about a life of public service, 45: "Thy servant knew that she was beloved of thee, and that she lay in thy bosom from a child, and there she might have lived without the condemnings or reproaches of men, or of this generation; but since Father thou wilt have it so, thy will be done. If the body suffer never so much, if it be for thyself, thy saints, thy kingdom, it is better for her than to be in her own habitation, and in pleasant gardens; and when thy servant has done thy work, she shall be willing to lock up herself in her closet again, and not to be seen of men." In the *Report and Plea*, 122, she also records how reluctant she was to answer this call: "I am forced out of my close retired spirit, by rulers and clergy, who have brought me upon the world's stage of reports, and rumors, making me the world's wonder, and gazing stock." James Holstun takes the notion of "public-spiritedness" as a focus for his discussion of Trapnel: see Holstun, *Ehud's Dagger: Class Struggle in the English Revolution* (London: Verso, 2000), 257–304.

191. Much quoted by religious and social radicals, this is a powerful biblical endorsement of the turning upside-down of the established order—social as well as religious and spiritual—for which groups such as the Fifth Monarchists and the Diggers, the Baptists, and the Quakers were working. See, too, for example, the Baptist Anne Wentworth's use of it to justify her own actions in her *A Vindication of Anne Wentworth* (London: s.n., 1677), 3, 14.

of the world, and things which are despised, hath God chosen; yea, and things that are not, to bring to nought things that are. I could be contented to be made use of under these terms, as a fool, and base, and despised, and as a thing that is not. The Lord knows, I then stooped to his will to do with me as he pleased, when he set home this Scripture to my soul. And this I told them, and a great deal more largely than I will relate, for brevity's sake. I gave a relation of my horrible pit[192] I was in a year ago, and Satan's tyranny over me in that time, and the great freedom the Lord afforded me after that storm, and the pourings out of the Spirit that hath been on my heart ever since. I declared visions I had seven years ago, concerning four sorts of horns[193] presented to me, which related to four several changes of powers one more fierce and sharper still than the other, and the little horn's worst of all, more in its pushings than the former. I spake of so many things, and so largely, that it took up the afternoon for the most part; so that before I spake much of my going to Whitehall, and praying and singing there, I broke forth into singing, my heart being so thoroughly heated with discoursing of God's goodness so many hours. And I sang and prayed a great part of that night; and when I gave over, my friends carried me in a chair into my chamber, and put me into bed, where I lay the remaining part of the night: and the next day sang and prayed many hours: and many souls were much taken in that speaking, concerning the preciousness of Christ to them that believe, 1 Peter 2:7,[194] from this Scripture, and many others, relating to Saints, and to sinners not changed and brought in to Christ which day

192. The basetext reads "horrible fit," corrected by the Errata thus: "for horrible fit, read horrible pit." See n149 on Satan's temptations the previous year.

193. Trapnel's vision of four horns occurred in August 1647, when Cromwell's New Model Army occupied the capital. It is related in full in Trapnel, *Cry*, 8: "I saw four horns, which were four powers, the first was that of the bishops, that I saw was broken in two and thrown aside; the second horn more white, had joined to it an head, endeavouring to get up a mount, and suddenly it was pushed down, and broken to pieces; the third horn had many splinters joined to it, like to the scales upon the back of a fish, and this was presented to be a power or a representative consisting of many men, having fair pretences of love to all under all forms; this I saw broken and scattered, that not as much as any bit of it was left. As to the fourth horn, that was short, but full of variety of colours, sparkling red and white; it was said to me, 'This is different from the three other, because great swelling words and great offers of kindness should go forth to all people from it, like unto that of Absalom, speaking good words to the people in the gate to draw them from honest David.'" Trapnel, like many of her contemporaries, was drawing on the vision of beasts and horns recounted in Daniel 7; here she identifies the first three horns with the bishops, the King, and Parliament; Holstun, 288, suggests that she (retrospectively) identifies the fourth with Cromwell, though it remains ambiguous. Other Fifth Monarchists, such as Mary Cary and William Aspinwall, published books identifying the little horn of Daniel's prophecy with Charles I, but after the dissolution of the Barebone's Parliament, both Trapnel (in another vision of horns that she related to Daniel 7) and Feake were quick to interpret the little horn of Daniel's prophecy as Cromwell. See Capp, *Fifth Monarchy Men*, 101; and Holstun, *Ehud's Dagger*, 278, 286–88.

194. 1 Peter 2:7: "Unto you therefore which believe he is precious: but unto them which be disobedient, the stone which the builders disallowed, the same is made the head of the corner."

was so glorious to me, that Satan stirred up many against me afterwards, because many were convinced, that were prejudiced before by their teachers;[195] and some carnal ones were awed, convincing Scriptures came with such authority; as that, *Behold, ye despisers, wonder, and perish:*[196] and that word in Isaiah 28:22. *Be ye not mockers, lest your bands be made strong.* Many other Scriptures were spoken upon largely that day to sinners: and some said afterwards, *Which of all our ministers can hold out thus many hours without a cordial?*[197]

Now when their ministers thought they should lose their fleece,[198] they began to stir, like that maid's masters spoken of in Acts 16:19. *When her masters saw what was done, they caught Paul and Silas, and drew them into the market-place unto the rulers:* this was for the gift of healing, and casting out that unclean spirit.[199] All people observe how they loved sooth-saying[200] in those times; and I would they did not in these days of more light. But I pray mind the relation, that after that day wherein I was thus carried forth to speak for Christ's interest, the clergy, with all their might, rung their jangling bells[201] against me, and called to the rulers to take me up: that I heard was the speech of Mr. Welstead:[202] and others said, *The people would be drawn away, if the rulers did not take some course with*

195. The syntax here is ambiguous, but the sense is that the text from 1 Peter 2:7, and others, which referred both to saints and to sinners, convinced many who had previously been skeptical; this made the day one of glory to Trapnel, but moved Satan to stir up opposition against her.

196. Acts 13:41.

197. Trapnel's capacity for prolonged periods of visionary praying and singing while fasting was already well-established. Trapnel, *Cry*, 4, notes that during her eleven-day prophecy, she lay in bed, "the first five days neither eating nor drinking anything more or less, and the rest of the time once in twenty-four hours, [she] sometimes ate a very little toast in small beer, sometimes only chewed it, and took down the moisture only, sometimes drank of the small beer, and sometimes only washed her mouth therewith, and cast it out … speaking every day, sometimes two, three, four and five hours together." For "cordial," see n107.

198. Flock, congregations.

199. See Acts 16:16–24. Paul and Silas are taken to the magistrates by the masters of a "soothsaying" maid, angry because, in casting out the spirit of divination in her, they were depriving these men of a source of financial gain. The masters accuse Paul and Silas of causing trouble in the city and have them imprisoned.

200. Foretelling the future.

201. Used metaphorically, as sounding out a warning against Trapnel.

202. Leonard Welstead ("Welsted" in basetext) was the curate of St. Ives, Cornwall, in 1650, and of Madron, near Penzance in Cornwall, from 1657 to 1660. He was also assistant to the Cornish Commission in 1654 (Matthews, *Calamy Revised*, 520), which might explain why he was in Truro at this point. Trapnel, in *Legacy*, 55, calls him "a great Presbyterian Priest." Welstead may have been the "young, silly priest" involved in the arrest of the Quaker leader George Fox in St. Ives in 1656. Fox, *Journal*, 238.

me. They were extremely afraid of losing Diana's repute.[203] And after these two days spent at Truro, I returned to my place of abode at Tregassow; but the clergy gave information in many places of the country, what an imposter, and a dangerous deceiver was come into Cornwall, that the people wondered what strange kind of creature was come into their country: and thus they spit forth venom against me; but it did me no hurt, because my Father made it work for good; my joy was not lessened, but increased. And after a little while I was invited again to Truro, and I went to visit Mrs. Hill, her husband being gone to London, she prayed me to tarry and bear her company. And after that I had sat down a while, word was brought me, that there were two warrants out for to take me, either at Captain Langdon's, or at Major Bawden's: as for Major Bawden's, I was but once at his house; for I kept at my friend's house I went down with, though the report was, I went from place to place, aspersing the government; I did not the one nor the other: I was but twice at Truro. I have told all the places I went to, while I remained at Tregassow. *This report of theirs is as false as the rest.*

But I will come to tell you how they acted against me: after I heard warrants were out for me, I looked when they would come in to the house where I was, to take me. And many people came to see me. And one Holse,[204] a minister, with whom I had some converse, and he said, *I had fully satisfied him in his requests. And for his part,* he said, *what he asked me, it was not so much for his own satisfaction, as for others, whom he could now satisfy:* and he invited me to his house, and said, *I should be welcome:* and he told me, *He would satisfy those that had spoken*

203. An obscure phrase, meaning that the clergy feared losing a source of revenue. *OED* notes that "Diana," alluding to Acts 19:24, meant a "source of gain." In Acts, the Ephesian silversmiths are angry with Paul because his conversion of people to Christianity meant a decline in demand for silver effigies of Diana, and hence a loss of income. Recounting the same courtroom incident in *Legacy*, 59, Trapnel writes of the clergy that, "because I saw their downfal, and told of it, they could not abide me: but that which made them cry out, was their *Diana* Tythe; this gain brought to them by the Rulers, makes them cry up the fourth *Monarchy*, not that they care for them, but its theirs that they are greedy after, and that maketh the Priest take false oaths, or do any thing to ingratiate with the Rulers." Trapnel herself was by some people accounted "the *Diana* of the English, *Acts* 19.34 ['But when they knew that he was a Jew, all with one voice about the space of two hours cried out, Great is Diana of the Ephesians']." Elinor Channel, *A Message From God, by a Dumb Woman* (London: s.n., 1653 [1654]), 7. The identification is pejorative, suggesting that Trapnel is, like Diana, tempting people away from the true religion.

204. The basetext here reads "Haulbow." This is corrected in the Errata: "for Haulbow, read Holse." Untraced, though I have found two possibilities: 1) Richard Hals, rector of Philleigh in 1660: Joseph Foster, *Alumni Oxonienses: The Members of the University of Oxford, 1500–1714,* 4 vols. (Oxford: James Palmer, 1891), 2:636; 2) Joseph Halsey, rector of St. Michael Penkivel, Cornwall, in 1662: "Member of Cornish Association Sept. 1655… . 'Brought into this County by Hugh Boscawen Esq.; and liv'd as Chaplain in his Family, while he preach'd in the Church in this Place … upon the Five Mile Act [1665], remov'd to Filly [Philleigh] with his Family. But that place being farther from Tregavethan than Mr. Boscawen and his Lady could be easie under, he, at their request, remov'd to Merther, the next Parish to theirs." Matthews, *Calamy Revised,* 244. All these parishes are close to Truro.

against me, which were set on by false reports. And all these words, and many other more, amounted to just nothing; it was but clergy-puff, which soon was gone like a puff of wind that is almost at an end, as soon as it riseth, and so was his fair speech to me: for I understand, since he hath reproached me and other friends that are of more worth than I, and yet this man spoke me so fair: but so much shall suffice as to him. I come again to tell you, that this day wherein I expected the warrant for me, it came not: I that day found my timorous, fearful nature work against me, what I should do and say before the magistrate, having never been before any in that kind, to be accused by them; but the Lord seeing me not prepared to go before them, nor strong enough, he would take me first into the mount,[205] and give me the preparations of the sanctuary;[206] and so he did before I was called before them. That night following this day that I have been speaking of, there came about a dozen men and women to see me, and one Mr. Paul,[207] a minister, who had rode ten miles to that town to understand aright concerning me, for that he had heard so many reports; and he desired to be satisfied from my own mouth: so I related the Lord's dealing with me, and what he had freely given me, for my own particular, and for others' benefit: and when I had done speaking, I told him how I was like to suffer through false rumors raised against me; and I desired him to pray with me: but he said, *He would join with me, if I would pray:* I said, *I rather would hear him pray, and have a taste of the cluster he had received of the vine, Christ:*[208] so he prayed very sweetly and spiritually: and when he had ended, it was about twelve o'clock at night: and afterwards I spoke a little by way of discourse, and was a little silent.

Then the Lord made his rivers flow, which soon broke down the banks of an ordinary capacity,[209] and extraordinarily mounted my Spirits into a praying and singing frame, and so they remained till morning-light, as I was told, for I was not capable of[210] that: but when I had done, and was a while silent, I came to speak weakly to those about me, saying *I must go to bed, for I am very weak*; and the men

---

205. I.e., induce in her a visionary state. The reference is to the transfiguration of Jesus on a high mountain, when Peter, James, and John experienced visions: see Matthew 17 and Mark 9. See, too, Trapnel, *Legacy*, 54: "I begun to consult with flesh and blood, but the Lord prevented them that day, that so I might receive strength from the mount before their valleys were presented."

206. On "sanctuary" as indicative of divine revelation, see n36.

207. In *Legacy*, 54, Trapnel describes Mr. Paul thus: "he came out of the west to see me, having heard such various reports of me, for the book had given a report before I came here; and this man after some time spent in discourse, I desired him to pray, the which he did very sweetly; he desired it of me, but I refused."

208. Christ compares himself with a vine in John 15:1–8.

209. See n93.

210. Not able to comprehend, unaware.

and women went away; and my friend that tended me, and some other maids,[211] helped me to bed, where I lay till the afternoon, they said, silent. And that time I had a vision of the minister's wife[212] stirring against me; and she was presented to me, as one enviously bent against me, calling that falsity which she understood not. And I saw the clergyman and the Jurors contriving an indictment[213] against me: and I saw my self stand before them: in a vision I saw this. And I sang with much courage, and told them, *I feared not them nor their doings, for that I had not deserved such usage.*

But while I was singing praises to the Lord for his love to me, the Justices[214] sent their constable[215] to fetch me; who came, and said, *He must have me with him:* and he pulled, and called me, they said that were by, but I was not capable thereof: they said, *He was greatly troubled how to have me to his master:* they told him, *He had better obey God than man: And his hand shook,* they said, *while he was pulling me.* Then some went to the Justices, to tell them I could not come. But they would not be pacified: some offered to be bound for my appearance[216] next day, if I were

---

211. Young women; not necessarily servants.

212. Mr. Powel, whom she calls "a critical-pated man," is the only minister noted to have visited with his wife; see nn175 and 177.

213. A formal charge or accusation: "An Indictment is a Bill or Declaration formally made, containing an accusation of a man for some offence committed, by a Jury to be found of purpose to put the offender to answer to it.... The Indictment or Presentment, is the chief ground-work whereupon the whole trial is afterwards to be built." Sheppard, 2:114–5. See, too, n228.

214. Justices of the Peace (JPs) were local officials appointed to undertake the judicial and administrative government of a county, town, or other district; they could also commit offenders to trial before a judge and jury. County JPs could issue arrest warrants, and (as here) they presided over Quarter Sessions. They were thus an essential and powerful component of local government as well as the judicial system. Stephen K. Roberts has called JPs "the most important single source of prosecuting energy." Roberts, "Juries and the Middling Sort," 189–90. Since the impetus for Trapnel's arrest was political, it seems likely that the warrant for her arrest originated with the JPs rather than a member of the local community. On the issuing of warrants, see Sheppard 1:178–81.

215. An unpaid officer of a parish or town responsible to the JPs; he was the lowliest officer in the system of law enforcement. Wrightson describes constables as "the much tried, sorely abused, essential work-horses of seventeenth-century local administration." Keith Wrightson, "Two Concepts of Order: Justices, Constables, and Jurymen in Seventeenth-Century England," in *An Ungovernable People: The English and their Law in the Seventeenth and Eighteenth Centuries,* ed. John Brewer and John Styles, 21–46 (London: Hutchinson, 1980), 22. See, too, J. A. Sharpe, *Crime in Early Modern England, 1550–1750,* 2nd ed. (London and New York: Longman, 1999. 1st ed. 1984), 49–50; and Joan Kent, "The English Village Constable, 1580–1642: The Nature and Dilemmas of the Office," *Journal of British Studies* 20 (1981): 26–49. For a contemporary account of the duties of the constable, see William Sheppard, *The Offices of Constables, Church-wardens, Overseers of the Poor, Supravisors of the High-wayes, Treasurers of the County-Stock; And some other lesser Country Officers* (London: Ric. Hodgkinsomme, for E. Dod and N. Ekins, 1652).

216. Offered to take legal responsibility for ensuring she appeared in court when next required to do so; offered to act as surety.

in a capacity; but this was refused, they would have me out of my bed, unless some would take their oaths that it would endanger my life to be taken out of my bed: which none could do, without they had loved to take false oaths, like some others in those parts.[217] Then a friend persuaded them to see whether they could put me out of that condition, and told them I was never known to be put out of it; so they came. Justice Launce, now a Parliament-man,[218] was one of them, I was told. These Justices that came to fetch me out of my bed, they made a great tumult, them and their followers, in the house, and some came upstairs, crying, *A witch, a witch;*[219] making a great stir on the stairs; and a poor honest man rebuking such that said so, he was tumbled down stairs and beaten too, by one of the Justices' followers: and the Justices made a great noise, in putting out of my chamber where I lay many of my friends; and they said if my friends would not take me up,[220]

217. Trapnel is condemning as hypocrites those who took oaths of allegiance first to the King and then to the Commonwealth. This might have had particular relevance in Cornwall, which had initially held out as a Royalist stronghold in the Civil War before being secured for Parliament in the late 1640s.

218. James Launce (1630–1688) of Penair, St. Clements, became an MP for Cornwall in September 1654. He was later instrumental in sending a number of Quakers to jail; see Norman Penney, ed., *Record of the Sufferings of Quakers in Cornwall, 1656–1686* (London: Friends Historical Society, 1928). The words "now a Parliament-man" help date the publication of the *Report and Plea* to no earlier than September 1654, the month in which he was elected. In *Legacy*, 56, Trapnel calls Launce "one of *Holland Simpsons* Church people, a very unlovely walker, little sign of membership in him." "Holland Simpson" was probably Sidrach Simpson, an Independent minister who had gone into exile in the Netherlands in the late 1630s, where he had gathered his own church. He returned to London in 1641 and was associated with radical dissent for a number of years before becoming more conservative in the early 1650s, including in 1654 supporting the Cromwellian Protectorate and denouncing the Fifth Monarchists. Liu, "Simpson, Sidrach (*ca.* 1600–1655)," *ODNB*. The Earl of Nottingham includes a "Holland Simpson" as a witness at the trial of the regicides in 1660, testifying against Hugh Peter, among others; but there is nothing to suggest that Trapnel is referring to him. Sidrach Simpson died in 1655, so he and the Holland Simpson at the trial could not have been the same man. Heneage Finch, Earl of Nottingham, *An Exact and Most Impartial Accompt of the Indictment, Arraignment, Trial, and Judgment (According to Law) of Twenty Nine Regicides, the Murtherers of His Late Sacred Majesty of Most Glorious Memory Begun at Hicks-Hall on Tuesday, the 9th of October, 1660* (London: R. Scot, T. Basset, R. Chiswell, and J. Wright, 1679).

219. Trapnel's prophetic trances led to accusations of witchcraft; this is the first charge she seeks to refute later in this text, at the beginning of her "Defiance," 122. The charge was also leveled at other sectaries: in 1652, for instance, George Fox was suspected of being a witch after he and Richard Hubberthorne had safely crossed the treacherous sands of Morecambe Bay on horseback. Fox, *Journal*, 142. The association between witchcraft and trances may have been particularly acute in Cornwall at the time: in 1646 Anne Jefferies' trances had also resulted in allegations of witchcraft. Justice Tregagle, who sat at Trapnel's hearing, also ordered Jefferies' arrest; see Barbara Spooner, *John Tregagle of Trevorder: Man and Ghost* (Truro: A. W. Jordan, 1935), 14–15. On Jefferies, see Diane Purkiss, *The Witch in History: Early Modern and Twentieth-Century Representations* (London: Routledge, 1996), 161–2. See, too, n274.

220. Arrest or apprehend me.

they would have some should take me up: one of my friends told them that they must fetch their silk gowns[221] to do it then, for the poor would not do it. And they threatened much, but the Lord overruled them: they caused my eyelids to be pulled up, for they said I held them fast, because I would deceive the people: they spake to this purpose. One of the Justices pinched me by the nose, and caused my pillow to be pulled from under my head, and kept pulling me, and calling me; but I heard none of all this stir and bustle; neither did I hear Mr. Welstead, which I was told called to the rulers, saying, *A whip will fetch her up:* and he stood at the chamber door talking against me, and said, *She speaks nonsense:* the women said, *Hearken, for you cannot hear, there is such a noise:* then he listened, and said, *Now she hears me speak, she speaks sense.* And this clergyman durst not come, till the rulers came, for then they say the witches can have no power over them: so that one depends upon another, rulers upon clergy, and clergy upon rulers.

And again, after they had made all the fury appear that the Lord permitted them to vent against me, they then went away, saying, *She will fall in a trance, when we shall at any time call for her.* The Lord kept me this day from their cruelty, which they had a good mind further to have let out against me, and that witch-trier woman of that town,[222] some would fain have had come with her great pin which she used to thrust into witches, to try them: but the Lord my God in whom I trust, delivered me from their malice, making good that word to me in the Psalms, *The rage of man shall turn to thy praise, and the remnant of rages thou wilt restrain.*[223] Then further, to tell you how the Lord carried me in singing and prayer after they were gone two hours, as I was told, and then I came to my self; and being all alone, I blessed God for that quiet still day that I had. And the gentlewoman

---

221. Sumptuary laws had earlier dictated that only those of elevated social rank could wear silk; hence Trapnel is here suggesting that people of high rank would have to arrest her, as "the poor would not do it."

222. Woman who gathered evidence against the accused. She would "examine the suspect for unusual bodily marks and then … test these marks by pricking them to find out whether they were insensible." Christina Larner, *Enemies of God: The Witch Hunt in Scotland* (Edinburgh: John Donald, 2000), 110; see, too, Keith Thomas, *Religion and the Decline of Magic* (London: Weidenfeld and Nicolson, 1971), 530–31. It was thought that the devil consummated a pact with a witch by nipping her, and that the mark that this left was insensible to pain and could not bleed. Such a mark was taken as evidence of a pact. Witchcraft was a serious felony, punishable by death, and as such was tried at the Assizes rather than Quarter Sessions.

223. A paraphrase of Psalm 76:10, but closer to the wording of the Geneva Bible ("Surely the rage of man shall turn to thy praise: the remnant of the rage shalt thou restrain") than of the King James version ("Surely the wrath of man shall praise thee: the remainder of wrath shalt thou restrain"). The Geneva Bible (1560) was the English translation favored over the King James version (1611) by many religious radicals because of the Calvinist commentary provided by its marginal notes, though Trapnel's quotations are usually closer to the King James; see nn284 and 285. See Christopher Hill, *The English Bible and the Seventeenth-Century Revolution* (London: Allen Lane, 1993), 56–63.

of the house[224] coming into the chamber, I said, *Have I lain alone all this day? I have had a sweet day:* she replied, and said, *Did not I hear the Justices there, and the uproar that was in my chamber?* I said, *No.* Then she told me, how they dealt by[225] her house, bringing in their followers, and what a noise they made. Then another friend asked me, *Whether I did not hear that stir?* I said, *No.* They wondered, and so did I, when I heard the relation, which is much more than I will write; for I don't take delight to stir in such puddles, it's no pleasant work to me; but that truth engageth me to let the world know, what men have acted against the pourings out of the Spirit in a dispensation beyond their understanding; they hearkened not to Scripture-advice, which would not have any judge that they know not.[226]

After that day's tumult, at night, many came to catch at my words; and it was very probable, that the rulers sent some to watch for what could be had further against me: and there were two women, that they had got their names, who had promised them to swear against me;[227] and of this I shall further speak when I come to it: but now I am telling of what passed that night mentioned: many people spake much to me, asking me questions, the which the Lord helped me to answer. And my friends kept most part of that night in prayer on my behalf. And many watched what they said in prayer, for there were listeners under the window, which fain would have had something to have informed against them. There was great endeavoring to have found a Bill of Indictment[228] against Captain Langdon, but they could not; they could not vent their spleen, though they to the utmost desired it, the Lord would not let them have their evil desires herein; for though they in this would have brought him into contempt, yet they endeavored this that so I might want a surety,[229] and then they had had what they desired, which was, to have cast me into the jail. But to leave that, and to tell you, that I had the presence of the Lord with me that night abundantly, and my sleep was sweeter than at other times; my sister Langdon[230] lay with me that night, and in the morning she told

224. Mrs. Hill.

225. Treated.

226. Perhaps an allusion to 1 Corinthians 4:5: "Therefore judge nothing before the time, until the Lord come, who both will bring to light the hidden things of darkness, and will make manifest the counsels of the hearts: and then shall every man have praise of God."

227. Trapnel is voicing her suspicions that the Justices have sent in two women among the many others who went to hear her prophesy, with the express intent that they would then act as witnesses against her in court.

228. A written accusation presented by the prosecutor to a grand jury, by which they decided whether there was enough evidence for a trial to take place. On indictments, see Sheppard, 2:114–98.

229. Someone who makes himself liable for the appearance of someone else in court for trial; a bail. Trapnel is here arguing that the civic authorities were seeking to make a case against Captain Langdon as well, so that he would be unable to act as surety for her. This would, in turn, have resulted in her imprisonment.

230. Anne Langdon, wife of Francis Langdon. See n133.

me that she could not sleep all night, for thinking of my going to the Sessions[231] that day: she told me she wondered I could sleep so soundly all night: I told her I never had a sweeter night in my life, and as for my going before the rulers, I was no whit afraid or thoughtful; for I had cast my care upon the Lord, which I was persuaded would speak for me: therefore I was not troubled nor afraid; for the Lord said to me, *Fear not, be not dismayed, I am thy God, and will stand by thee.*[232]

Then I rose up, and prepared to go before them at Sessions-house;[233] and walking out in the garden[234] before I went, I was thinking what I should say before the Justices; but I was taken off from my own thoughts quickly, through the word, *Take no heed what thou shalt say; being brought before them for the Lord Christ's sake, he will give thee words: dost thou know what they will ask thee? Therefore look to the Lord, who will give thee answers suitable to what shall be required of thee.* So I was resolved to cast my self upon the Lord, and his teaching: and though I had heard how the form of Bills run, and of that word *Not guilty,* according to the form of the Bill; yet I said, *I shall not remember to say thus, if the Lord don't bid me say so; and if he bids me, I will say it.* And this I thought, I would be nothing, the Lord should have all the praise, it being his due. So I went, the officer coming for me; and as I went along the street, I had followed me abundance of all manner of people, men and women, boys and girls, which crowded after me; and some pulled me by the arms, and stared me in the face, making wry faces at me, and saying, *How do you now? how is it with you now?* and thus they mocked and derided at me,[235] as I went to the Sessions; but I was never in such a blessed self-denying lamb-like frame of Spirit in my life, as then; I had such lovely apprehensions of Christ's sufferings, and of that Scripture which saith, *He went as a sheep, dumb before the shearers, he*

231. Sessions of the Peace were courts presided over by JPs, where misdemeanors were tried; these were lesser offences than felonies, which were punishable by death, and hence referred to a higher court, the Assizes, for trial.

232. A paraphrase of Isaiah 41:10.

233. The building in which the Quarter Sessions were held. In Truro, this was on what is now Boscawen Street (previously Middle Row), in the Coinage Hall (built 1351), which was the building in which tin was weighed and stamped. "The rooms over the Coinage Hall were leased by the [Town] Council and used for a variety of purposes, occasionally for Council meetings, and also for banquets and other entertainments. When the Sessions came it was converted into a courtroom. In May 1789, the Council paid Andrew Stephens for 'putting up the seats at the Coinagehall for the Sessions and fold for the prisoners' etc. Outside the west front were the borough stocks and next to it stood the prison, really little more than a lock-up." Chesher, *Boscawen Street Area, Truro,* 13–14.

234. On gardens, see n89.

235. Compare the accounts of Christ's crucifixion, during which he was frequently "mocked": Matthew 27:29, 31; Mark 15:20; and Luke 18:32, 22:63, and 23:11, 36. In Luke 23:35, when Christ is on the cross, "the rulers" derided him.

opened not his mouth; and when reviled, he reviled not again.[236] The Lord kept me
also, so that I went silent to the Sessions-house, which was much thronged with
people: some said, *The Sessions-house was never so filled since it was a Sessions-
house;*[237] so that I was a gazing-stock for all sorts of people: but I praise the Lord,
this did not daunt me, nor a great deal more, that I suffered that day; for the eternal
grace of Jehovah surrounded me, and kept me from harm; so way was made for me
to draw near to the table,[238] which stood lower than the Justices;[239] and round the
table sat the lawyers and others that attended them, and I with my friends that went
with me, stood by the lawyers, and the Justices leaned over a rail, which railed them
in together; only I espied a clergyman at their elbow, who helped to make up their
indictment,[240] so that he could not be absent, though his pulpit wanted him, it being a fast-day, set apart by authority,[241] which he broke without any scruple, that so
he might keep close to the work of accusation; but though he and the witch-trying-
woman looked steadfastly in my face, it did no way dismay me, nor the grim fierce
looks of the Justices did not daunt me; for soon as I beheld them, I remembered
a dear friend to Christ, who smiled in the face of a great man, that looked fiercely
on him, and sat as a judge to condemn him for the testimony of Jesus;[242] but this
servant of the Lord looked cheerfully all the time of his accusations charged upon
him; so I thinking upon that posture of his before those that acted against him, I

236. Trapnel here conflates Isaiah 53:7 ("He was oppressed, and he was afflicted, yet he opened not
his mouth: he is brought as a lamb to the slaughter, and as a sheep before her shearers is dumb, so he
openeth not his mouth") and 1 Peter 2:23 ("Who, when he was reviled, reviled not again; when he
suffered, he threatened not; but committed himself to him that judgeth righteously").

237. The Coinage Hall in Truro, where the Quarter Sessions were held, was used for many civic purposes; see n233.

238. The basetext omits the words "to the table"; the list of errata specifies that they be inserted here.

239. At Quarter Sessions, "all the Justices of the Peace do sit together, for the general execution of their
authority and commission over all their limits." Sheppard, 2:1.

240. See n228.

241. A day to be observed as a fast, designated as such by the government. This detail makes it possible
to date Trapnel's court hearing to Friday, April 7. Cromwell had ordered that a day of "Solemn Fasting
and Humiliation" be held on March 24 in London and Westminster, and two weeks later (i.e., on April
7) in England and Wales. He gave the reason for it as follows: "The common and notorious sins so
boldly and impenitently practised amongst us, notwithstanding all our Deliverances and Mercies,
together with the present rod of an exceeding and universal Drought, which hath lain upon us for
some years, and still continues and increaseth upon us, threatning Famine and Mortality, are no less
then the voyce of God, calling aloud in our ears to fasting, and Mourning, and great Abasement of
soul before him." *Mercurius Politicus* 197 (March 16–23, 1654): 3353–56 (3353). On Fast Sermons, see
Hill, *The English Bible*, 79–108.

242. This is probably a reference to the trial of the Fifth Monarchist preacher Vavasor Powell, at which
she had been present in Whitehall in January 1654, and during which she fell into a trance and prophesied for eleven days. It may, however, refer to other Fifth Monarchists who had been recently tried,
such as Feake and Simpson, currently in jail in Windsor Castle.

begged[243] the same cheerfulness, and I had the same courage to look my accusers in the face:[244] which was no carnal boldness,[245] though they called it so.

And when I came before them, Lobb,[246] being the mouth[247] of the Court,[248] as he was foreman of the Jury,[249] he represented the whole Court, and he first

243. Desired, or craved.

244. A reference to the principle specified in Acts 25:16, whereby the accused has the right to see an accuser face to face: "It is not the manner of the Romans to deliver any man to die, before that he which is accused have the accusers face to face, and have licence to answer for himself concerning the crime laid against him." Many of Trapnel's contemporaries also cited this principle: see John Lilburne, *The Grand Plea of Lieut. Col. John Lilburne* (London: s.n., 1647), 1; John Crook, *The Cry of the Innocent for Justice* (s.l.: s.n., 1662), 9; and Thomas Ellwood, *A Caution to Constables and Other Inferiour Officers* (London: William Skeate, 1683), 11.

245. William Perkins defined "carnall boldness" as "(not worthy the name of courage; beeing onely a shaddow of true fortitude) arising from ambition, pride, and other fleshly humours," whereas true courage came from God. Perkins, *A Cloud of Faithfull Witnesses, Leading to the Heavenly Canaan* (London: Humfrey Lownes for Leo. Greene, 1607), 428. Agnes Beaumont, another Baptist woman who wrote an account of being wrongly accused, also noted how God gave her "faith and Courage that I might look my Accuser in the face with boldness." Beaumont, "The Persecution of Agnes Beaumont," in Bunyan, *Grace Abounding with Other Spiritual Autobiographies*, 218.

246. Richard Lobb (fl. 1652–1672) was made Sheriff of Cornwall (the chief law-enforcement officer of the county) in 1651. He became MP for St. Michael's, Cornwall, in 1659. Richard L. Greaves, "Lobb, Stephen (d. 1699)," *ODNB*. Lobb was harsh in his treatment of Quakers who appeared before him in 1656, using "much unsavory language." Penney, *Quakers in Cornwall*, 2–3.

247. Spokesman.

248. The court before which Trapnel appeared was a Quarter Sessions, presided over by JPs, who were not trained judges but drawn from the local gentry. These courts sat four times a year, and dealt mainly with minor offences and regulatory matters, referring more serious cases to the Assizes (see n252). It was at Quarter Sessions that "the justices exercised most power. In these courts they sat as judges, assisted in criminal trials by both a grand jury and trial juries.... There were perhaps between 150 and 200 people at any one meeting of the court. These were great public events." John Briggs, Christopher Harrison, Angus McInnes, and David Vincent, *Crime and Punishment in England: An Introductory History* (London: UCL Press, 1996), 27. On the powers of JPs at Quarter Sessions, see Sheppard, 2:8–12.

249. The jury here was a grand jury, not a trial jury. A grand jury consisted of from twelve to twenty-three "good and lawful men of a county" (*OED*). Its job was to assess indictments (formal accusations), deciding whether the evidence was sufficient to refer the case to the Assizes, a higher court, presided over by legally trained judges rather than by JPs. If the grand jury was satisfied that there was sufficient evidence for a case to proceed, they declared it a "true bill"; if not, they threw it out by writing "ignoramus" ("we take no notice of it") on the back of the bill. See Geoffrey Radcliffe and Geoffrey Cross, *The English Legal System* 6th ed., ed. G. J. Hand and D. J. Bentley (London: Butterworth's, 1977), 194–99. Of the constitution and power of the sessions grand jury, Roberts has concluded, "There can be no doubt that of all the institutions of local representation, the sessions grand jury was the closest thing to a mouthpiece for the yeomanry of the county. It was nearly a parliament of the middling sort, but it lacked a vital ingredient, that of self-regulation. Quarter sessions juries were at the beck and call of the class that summoned and dismissed them: the gentry." Roberts,

demanded my name, and I told him; and he said, *Anna Trapnel, here is a Bill of Indictment to be read, for you to give in your answer concerning:* then Justice Lobb said, *Read the Bill:*[250] so it was read to me: and Lobb said, *Are you guilty, or not?* I had no word to say at the present; but the Lord said to me, *Say not guilty, according to the form of the Bill;* so I spoke it as from the Lord, who knew I was not guilty of such an indictment: then said[251] Lobb, *Traverse the Bill to the next Assizes;*[252] so that was done. Then Lobb said, *I must enter into bond for my appear-*

"Juries and the Middling Sort," 184–5. For detailed local histories of grand juries in this period, see J. S. Morrill, *The Cheshire Grand Jury, 1625–1659* (Leicester: Leicester University Press, 1976); and Stephen K. Roberts, "Initiative and Control: The Devon Quarter Sessions Grand Jury, 1649–70," *Bulletin of the Institute of Historical Research* 57.136 (1984): 165–77.

250. The newsbook (an early form of newspaper) *Mercurius Politicus* reported this section of the court hearing: "The Justices of this County have taken notice of her ways and practices; and Mr. *Lobb* giving the charge here this last Sessions, willed the Jury to enquire, 1 concerning Vagrants, 2 such as occasioned unlawful meetings, 3 Such as speak against the present Government. There were two Indictments drawn against her: *Langdon* and *Baudon*, her Compeers and Abettors, endeavoured to make a learned Defence for her, but it was not suffered; only they entered into Bonds of three hundred pounds for her good behaviour and appearance at the next Assizes." *Mercurius Politicus* 201 (April 13–20, 1654): 3430. Sheppard's *Whole Office of the Country Justice of Peace* describes a vagrant thus: "a Rogue, or a wanderer (being all one) is an idle Begger that doth wander and loyter abroad from place to place, without a lawfull Passport, whether he beg or not." Sheppard, 1:107. An unlawful assembly was defined thus: "1. There must be three persons at the least gathered together. 2. Their intent in the first meeting must be evill. 3. Their being together must breed some apparent disturbance of the Peace, either by speech, shew of armour, turbulent gesture, or actuall and expresse violence. … If any divulge any Prophesie with intent to make rebellion, or other disturbance in the Realm." Sheppard, 2:61. The third area of enquiry, concerning such as "speak against the present Government," was the most serious: "The offence of high Treason may be committed (by the Act of Parliament of *May* 14 1649.) to do any of these following things. 1. To print, write, or openly declare that the present Government is tyrannicall, usurped, or unlawfull." Sheppard, 2:42. A new Act against treason had been passed by Parliament on January 19, 1654: see introduction, 9. As a serious felony, treason could not be tried at Quarter Sessions but had to be referred to the Assizes. Prophecy also risked punishment: "False Prophesiers are for the first offence to be imprisoned one year, and for the second, for life." Sheppard, 1:152.

251. The basetext continues here with four pages that are absent from the copies of the *Report and Plea* held in the Haverford College and Huntington Libraries. Those copies break mid-sentence, after "then said," and continue with the words "I now shall declare how God showed me kindness further." Rebecca Bullard suggests these pages were a late addition to the text as it was prepared for the press, resulting in the odd pagination in the copies that include them; see introduction, 35, and n290. For further discussion, see Bullard, "Textual Disruption in *Anna Trapnel's Report and Plea* (1654)," *The Seventeenth Century* 23.1 (2008): 34–53.

252. The Assizes were a higher court, whose periodic sittings were presided over by professional judges rather than JPs. "After consultation with the magistrates and the clerk of the peace jurors could decide to 'traverse' a case; that is, to accept a plea from the accused or his counsel, or suggest themselves, that a case be postponed until the next sessions meeting or reserved to the consideration of the assize jury." Stephen K. Roberts, *Recovery and Restoration in an English County: Devon Local Administration,*

ance at the next Assizes: unto which I agreed: then they demanded sureties:[253] so I desired Captain Langdon and Major Bawden to be my sureties, unto which they were willing: so there were two recognizances[254] drawn, one for my appearance, and the other bound me to the good behavior;[255] and I was entered into both the recognizances £300, and my sureties as much, to both the recognizances. And this being done, they whispered a while: and I thought they had done with me at that time; so they had, if they had gone according to true law, which was not to have brought their interrogatories[256] then; but the report was, that I would discover my self to be a witch when I came before the Justices, by having never a word to answer for my self; for it used to be so among the witches, they could not speak before the magistrates, and so they said, it would be with me; but the Lord quickly defeated them herein, and caused many to be of another mind. Then Lobb said, *Tender her the book which was written from something said at Whitehall:*[257] so the

---

1646–1670 (Exeter: University of Exeter Press, 1985), 67. See, too, Roberts, "Juries and the Middling Sort."

253. See nn229 and 255.

254. Bonds entered into in court, promising the performance of some act or the observation of some condition; here, Trapnel is bound to appear at the next Assizes, in August, and to good behavior: "The condition usually is to keep the Peace or good behaviour against all men; and especially … till the next Sessions, and then to appear: this is the best Form": Sheppard, 1:76–7. A recognizance is the sum of money pledged in surety for such a bond. According to the information she gives here, Trapnel would be liable to pay £300 if she failed to appear at the next Assizes, and if she broke the bond of good behavior, as would Langdon and Bawden, her sureties. The sums she gives in *Legacy*, 50, differ slightly: "Captain *Langdon*, my faithful friend I came down with he, and Major *Bauden*, they were bound for my appearance, 150 l. a piece, and I 200 l." Either way, these were considerable sums of money, though their relative worth is hard to calculate. According to the National Archive Currency Converter, in 1650 £150 had the same spending power as £11,334 (*ca.* US$20,400) in 2005 (http://apps.nationalarchives.gov.uk/currency). According to "Measuring Worth," however, in the 1650s, £150 would have had the purchasing power of *ca.* £20,000 (*ca.* US$33,000), but this sum would have been only as "affordable" to the average person as *ca.* £622,000 (*ca.* US$936,000) would have been in 2011; calculations derived from "Measuring Worth" at www.measuringworth.com/index.php (accessed 08/18/2014) and from private correspondence with the economist Professor John O'Hagan, University College, Dublin.

255. A surety could be required when a JP "doth suspect any one to be inclined to break the Peace." Sheppard, 1:64.

256. Formal questioning. Trapnel is suggesting that since the case had been referred to the Assizes, no further questioning should have taken place. "The general principle that the accused could not be questioned and his offence wrung out of him but that the crime must be proved by other evidence, was very deep seated in English law, and at the trial itself the accused was not competent to give evidence until the Criminal Evidence Act, 1898." Radcliffe and Cross, *English Legal System*, 196.

257. *The Cry of a Stone*, subtitled "a relation of something spoken at Whitehall," had been published in February.

book was reached out to me: and Justice Lobb said, *What say you to that book? will you own it? is it yours?*[258]

A. T. *I am not careful to answer you in that matter.*

Then they said, *She denies her book.* Then they whispered with those behind them. Then spake Justice Lobb again, and said, *Read a vision of the horns*[259] *out of the book:* so that was read: then Justice Lobb said, *What say you to this? is this yours?*

A. T. *I am not careful to answer you in that matter, touching the whole book, as I told you before, so I say again: for what was spoken, was at Whitehall, at a place of concourse of people, and near a Council*[260] *I suppose wise enough to call me into question if I offended, and unto them I appeal.* But though it was said, I appealed unto Caesar, and unto Caesar should I go; yet I have not been brought before him which is called Caesar: so much by the by.[261] *Again,* I said, *I supposed they had not power to question me for that which was spoke in another county:* they said, *Yea, that they had.* Then the book was put by; and they again whispered.

Then Justice Lobb asked me about my coming into that country, *How it came to pass, that I came into that country.*

258. On the punishments for the writing, publishing, and selling of "Scandalous Books and Pamphlets," see Sheppard 1:205.

259. Trapnel, *Legacy*, 56 makes clear that this reference is not to the vision of horns referred to earlier (see n193), but to a later one, directly critical of Cromwell: "They then caused the Vision which mentions the horns; and Cows, and Oxen, to be read, and asked me what I would say to that? was that mine?" This vision had been recounted in Trapnel, *Cry*, 15: "I beheld at a little distance a great company of cattle, some like bulls, and others like oxen, and so lesser, their faces and heads like men, having each of them a horn on either side their heads. For the foremost his countenance was perfectly like unto Oliver Cromwell's; and on a sudden there was a great shout of those that followed him, he being singled out alone, and the foremost; and he looking back, they bowed unto him, and suddenly gave a shout, and leaped up from the earth with a great kind of joy, that he was their supreme. And immediately they prompting him and fawning upon him, he run at me, and as he was near with his horn to my breast, an arm and a hand clasped me round, a voice said, 'I will be thy safety.' He run at many precious saints that stood in the way of him, that looked boldly in his face; he gave them many pushes, scratching them with his horn, and driving them into several houses; he ran still along, till at length there was a great silence, and suddenly there broke forth in the earth great fury coming from the clouds, and they presently were scattered, and their horns broken, and they tumbled into graves." The vision alludes to Psalm 22:12–13: "Many bulls have compassed me: strong bulls of Bashan have beset me round. They gaped upon me with their mouths, as a ravening and a roaring lion."

260. The Fifth Monarchist preacher Vavasor Powell was being tried by the Council of State, the ruling executive body, when Trapnel fell into her prophetic trance.

261. Trapnel is referring to Cromwell as Caesar here—that is, as a temporal authority as opposed to a higher, spiritual one. The biblical allusion is to Acts 25:10–12, where Paul is told that since he has appealed to Caesar for justice, "unto Caesar shalt thou go." In Bridewell, Trapnel complains that she has never been taken before the Council of State, and so has never had the opportunity to vindicate herself before the authority that has condemned her.

I answered, *I came as others did, that were minded to go into the country.*

Lobb.[262] *But why did you come into this country?*

A. T. *Why might not I come here, as well as into another country?*

Lobb. *But you have no lands, nor livings, nor acquaintance to come to in this country.*

A.T. *What though I had not? I am a single person,*[263] *and why may I not be with my friends anywhere?*

Lobb. *I understand you are not married.*[264]

A.T. *Then having no hindrance, why may not I go where I please, if the Lord so will?*

Then spoke Justice Launce, *But did not some desire you to come down?* And this Lobb asked me too: but I told them, *I would accuse none, I was there to answer, as to what they should charge my own particular with.*

Launce said, *Pray Mistress tell us, what moved you to come such a journey?*

A. T. *The Lord gave me leave to come, asking of him leave, whitherever*[265] *I went: I used still to pray for his direction in all I do: and so I suppose ought you,* I said.

Justice Launce. *But pray tell us, what moved you to come such a journey?*

A. T. *The Lord moved me, and gave me leave.*

Launce. *But had you not some extraordinary impulses of Spirit,*[266] *that brought you down? Pray tell us what those were.*

A. T. *When you are capable of extraordinary impulse of Spirit,*[267] *I will tell you; but I suppose you are not in a capacity now:* for I saw how deridingly he spoke: and for answering him thus, he said, *I was one of a bold Spirit; but he soon took me down;* so himself said: but some said, *It took them down:*[268] for the Lord carried me so to speak, that they were in a hurry and confusion, and sometimes would speak all together, that I was going to say, *What are you like women, all speakers, and no hearers?*[269] but I said thus, *What do you speak all at*

---

262. The following section is set as if it were a dialogue or a dramatic text, rather than as a piece of narrative prose, accentuating the adversarial and theatrical quality of the exchanges.

263. In the basetext this is punctuated thus: "*What though? I had not I am a single person.*"

264. "a *Feme covert* [married woman] being a vagrant, is to be accounted a rogue as well as a man"; however, "if a Traveller passe through a Parish," he or she should not be punished as a rogue. Sheppard, 1:108–9.

265. Wherever.

266. The basetext reads "of extraordinary impulses Spirit." In this context, "impulse" means "a strong suggestion supposed to come from a good or evil spirit" (*OED*).

267. The basetext reads "extraordinary of impulse of Spirit."

268. Trapnel is playing on two meanings of "take down": first, "to cause (a speaker) to sit down," and second, "to abase, humble, humiliate, abate the pride or arrogance of" (*OED*).

269. An allusion to the proverb "Dovercourt, all speakers, no hearers." Morris Palmer Tilley, *A Dictionary of the Proverbs in England in the Sixteenth and Seventeenth Centuries* (Ann Arbor:

a time? I cannot answer all, when speaking at once; I appeal to the civillest of you, and I directed my speech to Justice Lobb, who spake very moderately, and gave me a civil answer, saying, *You are not acquainted with the manner of the Court, which is to give in their sayings.*[270] A. T. *But I cannot answer all at once, indeed I do not know the manner of the Court, for I never was before any till now.* Justice Lobb. *You prophesy against Truro.* A. T. *Indeed I pray against the sins of the people of Truro, and for their souls' welfare; are you angry for that?* Lobb. *But you must not judge authority; but pray for them, and not speak so suspiciously of them:* and more to this purpose he spoke to me. A. T. *I will take up your word, in which you said, I was not to judge: you said well; for so saith the Scripture,* Who art thou that judgest another[271] man's servant? to his own master he standeth or falleth; yea, he shall be holden up, for God is able to make him stand:[272] *but you have judged me, and never heard me speak: you have not dealt so well by me as Agrippa dealt by Paul: though Agrippa was an heathen, he would have Paul speak before he gave in his judgment concerning him.*[273] Justice Tregagle:[274] *Oh you are a dreamer!* A. T. *So*

University of Michigan Press, 1950), D575, 171. Tilley cites Thomas Fuller, *History of the Worthies of England* (London: J. G. W. L. and W. G. for Thomas Williams, 1662), 2:124, by way of explanation: "The Proverb is applied to such irregular conferences, wherein the People are all Tongue, and no Eares." Robert Nares cites a slightly different version of the proverb: "But when they clam, the harsh sound spoils the sport, / And 'tis like women keeping Dover-court." Nares, *A Glossary or Collection of Words, Phrases, Names, and Allusions to Customs, Proverbs, &c.* (Stralsund: s.n., 1825), 214. Joseph Taylor gives the following explanation: "This proverb took its rise from a tumultuous court formerly kept at Dover, where was a confluence of many noisy and boisterous seamen, who, by their encroachment upon the woman's prerogative, induced the spectators to remark, they were 'All speakers and no hearers." Taylor, *Antiquitates Curiosae: The Etymology of Many Remarkable Old Sayings, Proverbs, and Singular Customs* (London: T. and J. Allman, 1818), 44.

270. To deliver their remarks to the person officially appointed to receive them (*OED*).

271. The basetext reads "anothers."

272. Romans 14:4.

273. See Acts 25–26. Paul was brought before Festus, procurator of Judaea, and Agrippa II, ruler of Chalcis, to answer complaints made about him by the chief priests of Jerusalem. Agrippa tells Paul that he is allowed to speak for himself in court; after listening to him speak, he tells Paul, "Almost thou persuadest me to be a Christian" (Acts 26:1, 28). See, too, n181.

274. John Tregagle ("Tregegle" in basetext) was foster-brother of, and steward to, John, Lord Robartes, Earl of Radnor, of Lanhydrock House, Bodmin, in Cornwall. Robartes, a supporter of the Parliamentary cause, was from an influential Truro family who had acquired their wealth from tin mining, and still kept a "Great House" in the center of Truro as his town house. It was his association with Robartes that facilitated Tregagle's rise in social status and wealth. A Presbyterian and a supporter of Parliament, Tregagle had some of his property sequestered by Royalist commissioners in the 1640s, and by 1645 he was in exile in London. Here he began to accumulate leases on properties in Cornwall, from which he received rents. It was as a harsh landlord and as a man who "drove an unconsciona-bly hard bargain" that he became extremely unpopular. Spooner, *John Tregagle of Trevorder*, 14. In 1646, Tregagle, already a JP, had been involved in the trial of Anne Jefferies for witchcraft: she had

they called Joseph,[275] *therefore I wonder not that you call me so.* Justice Ceely[276] said, *You knew we were with you yesterday.* A. T. *I did not.* Justice Ceely. *He which is the Major*[277] *said, you will not say so.* A. T. *I will speak it, being it's truth.* He said, *Call the women,*[278] *that will witness they heard you say, You knew we were with you; and he pulled out a writing, and named their names, calling to some to fetch them.* A. T. *You may suborn*[279] *false witnesses against me, for they did so against Christ:*[280] and I said, *Produce your witnesses.* Justice Ceely. *We shall have them for you at next Assizes.*

They put it off long enough, because one was fallen in a sound[281] before she got out of the house where she dwelt; and the other was come into the Sessions-house: and Mrs. Grosse[282] a gentlewoman of the town standing by her that was their false witness, said, *Wilt thou take an oath thus? take heed what thou dost, it's a dangerous thing to take a false oath;* and she ran out of the Sessions-house: this was credibly reported. And here ended their witnesses that they had procured against me as to that. There was a soldier that smiled to hear how the Lord carried me along in my speech: and Justice Ceely called to the jailor to take him away, saying, *He laughed at the Court.* He thought him to be one of my friends: and for his cheerful looking, the jailor had like to have had him: then I said, *Scripture speaks*

---

healing powers, and claimed to speak and dance with fairies (see n219). Tregagle purchased the farm of Trevorder, St. Breock, in 1649 for £1500, where he died, in 1655. His reputation after his death as a harsh, dishonest, and unscrupulous man continued, and legends persisted into the twentieth century of his unquiet ghost being heard in the howling or roaring of the wind. See Spooner, *John Tregagle of Trevorder*; and A. L. Rowse, "Jan Tregagle: In Legend and in History," *History Today* 15.12 (December 1965): 828–34. See, too, Chesher, *Boscawen Street Area, Truro*, 10.

275. Joseph was known for his own prophetic dreams and for his ability to interpret others' dreams; see Genesis 37, 40, and 41.

276. Spelled "Selye" or "Sely" in basetext. In *Legacy*, 56, Trapnel calls him "Major Selly," which suggests that this was Major Peter Ceely, of St. Ives, responsible for the imprisonment of George Fox, and many other Quakers, in Launceston jail; see Fox, *Journal*, 237–38, 246–50, 254, 264; and Penney, *Quakers in Cornwall*, 1–3, 7, 9. Ceely had been mayor of St. Ives in 1650, and was elected to Parliament for St. Ives in 1658 (often recorded as Peter Silly). He was a staunch Puritan and zealous army officer. The other possibility is that this is a reference to Justice Thomas Ceely, who in 1657 committed the Quaker John Rowett to Launceston jail "ffor speakeinge a few words to Joseph allen preist of penryn." Penney, *Quakers in Cornwall*, 7.

277. Major John Bawden; see n157.

278. The women who visited Trapnel while she was in a trance at Mrs. Hill's house; see 81.

279. Bribe or unlawfully procure.

280. See Matthew 26:59–60 and Mark 14:55–58.

281. Swoon, or faint.

282. Spelled "Grose" in basetext. The Grosses were a wealthy and influential Truro family; indeed, Mr. Grosse was "one of Truro's leading citizens." Chesher, *Boscawen Street Area, Truro*, 6. See, too, Palmer, *Truro in the Seventeenth Century*, 68–70, 74–75.

of such who make a man an offender for a word;[283] *but you make a man an offender for a look.* They greatly bustled, as if they would have taken him away; but this was quickly squashed, their heat as to this lasted not long. In the meantime the other, Ceely, was talking to Major Bawden, wondering such a man as he, who had been so well reputed for a judicious, sober, understanding man, should hearken to me: many words were used to him to that purpose: I said, *Why might not he and others, try all things, and hold fast that which is best.*[284] But they still cast grim looks on me; and they had a saying to Major Bawden, and to Captain Langdon then, whom they derided in a letter sent from Truro by some of their learned Court, which wrote, that Captain Langdon and Major Bawden stood up, and made a learned defense. They had indeed such learning from the Spirit of wisdom and of a sound mind, which the Jurors and their companions were not able to contend against, their speech and whole deportment was so humble and self-denying, and so seasoned with the salt of grace,[285] which their flashy unsavory spirits could not endure; those that are raised from the dung-hill, and set on thrones,[286] cannot sit there without vaunting, and showing their fool's coat of many colors, as envy, and pride, and vainglory; these and other colors they show, which delights not King Jesus nor his followers. Justice Lobb told me, *I made a disturbance in the town:* I asked, *Wherein?* he said, *By drawing so many people after me:* I said, *How did I draw them?* he said, *I set open my chamber-doors and my windows for people to hear. A. T. That's a very unlikely thing, that I should do so; for I prayed the maid to lock my chamber-door when I went to bed, and I did not rise in the night sure to open it:* I said, *Why may not I pray with many people in the room, as well as your professing woman*[287] *that prays before men and women, she knowing them to be there; but I know not that there is any body in the room when I pray: and if you indict one for praying, why not another? why are you so partial in your doings?* Justice

---

283. Isaiah 29:21.

284. 1 Thessalonians 5:21. "Try" has the sense of "test" here. The wording Trapnel uses here is closer to that of the Geneva Bible ("Try all things, and keep that which is good") than to that of the King James version ("Prove all things; hold fast that which is good"). This was not always the case: compare the next footnote. Interestingly, the verse preceding this one is "Despise not prophesying," to which the Geneva Bible adds the marginal gloss for prophesying as "The expounding of the word of God."

285. An allusion to Colossians 4:6. Here, Trapnel's wording is closer to that of the King James Bible ("Let your speech be always with grace, seasoned with salt, that ye may know how ye ought to answer every man") than to that of the Geneva Bible ("Let your speech be gracious always, and powdered with salt, that ye may know how to answer every man").

286. This seems to be an allusion to 1 Samuel 2:8 and Psalm 113:7, and yet there it is beggars and the poor who are raised from the dunghill and set on thrones, and the references are instances of God-given reversals of fortune.

287. A woman who testifies publicly to her faith: see n2. It is unclear in the basetext if the word here is "woman" or "women"; the singular form fits best with the subsequent phrase.

Lobb. But you don't pray so as others. A. T. *I pray in my chamber.* Justice Trevill.[288] *Your chamber!* A. T. *Yea, that it's my chamber while I am there, through the pleasure of my friends.* They used more words to me, sometimes slighting and mockingly they spoke, and sometimes seeming to advise me to take heed how I spoke and prayed so again. Many such kind of words Justice Trevill used, and Justice Lobb. And one thing I omitted in telling you, when I told you how I answered Justice Launce; I should have told you how I said to him, *If he would know what the ordinary impulse of Spirit was, that I had to bring me into that country, I would tell him;* so I related the Scriptures, as that in the Psalms, and in the prophet Isaiah, how the presence and Spirit of the Lord should be with me, and he would uphold me and strengthen me with the right hand of his righteousness:[289] he answered, *Such impulse was common, they hoped they had that, they were not ignorant of such impulse of Spirit;* much to this effect was spoken. I seeing they were very willing to be gone, I said, *Have you done with me?* answer was, *I might now go away;* but I said, *Pray what is it to break the good behavior you have bound me over to? I know not what you may make a breaking of it: is it a breaking the good behavior, to pray and sing?* Justice Trevill said, *No, so I did it at the habitation where I abode. It's well,* said I, *you will give leave it shall be anywhere.* I said, *I will leave one word with you, and that is this: A time will come when you and I shall appear before the great Judge of the tribunal seat of the most High, and then I think you will hardly be able to give an account for this day's work before the Lord, at that day of true judgment:* said Tregagle, *Take you no care for us.* So they were willing to have no more discourse with me.

And as I went in the crowd, many strangers were very loving and careful to help me out of the crowd: and the rude multitude said, *Sure this woman is no witch, for she speaks many good words, which the witches could not.* And thus the Lord made the rude rabble to justify his appearance; for in all that was said by me, I was nothing, the Lord put all in my mouth, and told me what I should say, and that from the written word, he put it in my memory and mouth: so that I will have nothing ascribed to me, but all honor and praise given to him whose right it is, even to Jehovah, who is the King that lives forever. I have left out some things that I thought were not so material to be written: and what I have written of this, it's to declare as much as is convenient to take off those falsities and contrary reports that are abroad concerning my sufferings, some making it worse than it was, and some saying, *It was little or nothing.* Now to inform all people's judgments, I have thought it meet to offer this relation to the world's view, and with as much covering as I can

---

288. Justice Andrew Trevill ("Travel" in basetext) was a commissioner for the county of Cornwall and had been High Sheriff of Cornwall in 1651. Samuel Drew, *The History of Cornwall: From the Earliest Records and Traditions* (Helston and London: s.n., 1824), 2:685. Like all the other JPs, he sat at the trials of Quakers in 1657 and 1658: see Penney, *Quakers in Cornwall*, 5, 12, 17, 25.

289. Isaiah 41:10.

of Saints' weaknesses herein, praying the Lord to forgive them; and as for the Lord's enemies, that he would confound them; but as for my enemies, I still pray.[290]

I now shall declare how God showed me kindness further. I rode home with my friends to Tregassow, that day, rejoicing that I was counted worthy to be so reproachfully dealt by, for speaking in the Lord Christ's behalf, in prayer and praises; and I remained very cheerful, continuing in prayer and thanksgiving, and many spiritual songs unto the Lord; but about ten days after, the soldiers of the Fox[291] came to take me, and the day before they came, it being the first day of the week, I went to hear Mr. Frances,[292] who preached hard by where I abode, one whom the clergy would fain have had to have spoke against me, but he said he would not; they then called him my disciple, and laughed and jeered at him when he came among them, on their lecture days. They used to meet at an ordinary[293] where many of the clergy and others dined together: while I was in these parts, the clergy and others made me their table and pulpit talk, and would have had Mr. Frances to have done as they did, but he refused; and hath since, I hear, left the place where he preached when I was in those parts. But I return where I left, in telling you how I was the day before that the soldiers came for me, I was very heavy in my spirit, as I sat at dinner with my friends, and I was very ready to shed tears; and being loath my friends should see me, I held from weeping, as much as I could, for I thought they would think that I took something unkindly, but truly I could not, for I had as much love from every one in the family, as could be desired, but I was very sad, and I rose from the table where I dined, and went and took my Bible, wherein the Lord refreshed me, and in the afternoon I went to hear,[294] and came home, and went into the garden to walk alone; and Captain Langdon coming into the garden, I discoursed a while with him; and I said, sure my London friends pray me up to London, and when I come there, I will write of Cornwell, Cornhell in the West. He said you might have suffered at London, but not as here said I; for here they deal very uncivilly, and unchristian like by me: well said I, the Lord send me to London, for I shall count it a great mercy to see their

---

290. The pagination in the basetext is faulty at this point. Page 28 concludes at the end of this paragraph, but the next page is numbered 25; this numbering then continues through to the end of the text. Bullard makes the case that this was not the result of a mistake but of the late insertion of additional material; see Bullard, "Textual Disruption."

291. Captain John Fox was the Deputy Governor of Pendennis Castle in Falmouth, some twelve miles south of Truro. Pendennis had been one of the last Royalist garrisons to surrender to the Parliamentary forces, following a lengthy siege in 1646. The Parliamentary forces maintained the castle as a garrison. In the following year the Quaker leader, George Fox, encountered Captain Fox in Falmouth; he thought him a "light, chaffy man." Fox, *Journal*, 262.

292. Untraced, though perhaps the minister of St. Erme at this time; see n307.

293. An eating house or inn.

294. I.e., went to hear Mr. Frances; see n292.

faces again, I had said a Bridewell[295] among them shall be sweet to me, and so the Lord made it: I that night was persuaded, my work was done in Cornwall, and that I should ere long see London, yet being I was bound over to the Sessions, which was not to be till August, so that I was to have tarried many weeks by the Justices' order, but they could not bear so much praying, so long a time to be in their parts, therefore they hasted their letters to the Council at Whitehall,[296] to send their order[297] down for me, having a Governor's troop[298] so near, to agitate[299] their business. And the Governor[300] was afraid of his soldiers, he commands them to their colors:[301] and Ensign Raundle, he must be cast out of his place, for inviting his old friend Captain Langdon, and his wife, and his mother and me, to come with them to his house. And the soldiers were charged to keep me out of Tregony,[302] that is, three miles from Tregassow, where a poor tempted soul was, that would fain have entertained me at her house, and this work the Fox made in his fortified places; but the poor who are rich in faith, prayed for me in those parts, and some I never saw, about ten miles from the place where I was, who hearing of my trouble, improved their interest with the Lord for me; their faith and prayer, did me more good than all the gold, or silver, or favors of great men could have done me.

I shall relate now further concerning that night before the soldiers took me; I saw in my sleep soldiers come to take me, and I rode towards London with them very joyfully, and in the morning I made me ready, and went downstairs; and there was a friend came to see Captain Langdon, so I went up into my chamber, to write to London,[303] and I was thinking of that I saw in my sleep, that I was riding from the house towards London; and I also was marveling, that my spirit was so

295. House of Correction in London intended for the reform of the poor, vagrants, and the destitute. The latter part of this text, and her *Legacy*, recount her incarceration in Bridewell following her enforced return to London from Cornwall. See n378.

296. The Council of State at Whitehall was the governing body at this time.

297. I.e., for her arrest: see nn324, 374, and 375.

298. Fox's troop, garrisoned at Pendennis Castle.

299. To act as an agent for (*OED*).

300. The officer in command of the fortress and the troops garrisoned there.

301. "Colors" refers to the flag of a regiment or troop, here invoked for its symbolic importance. Captain Fox is reminding the soldiers of their duty to regimental loyalty, discipline, responsibility, and their place in a hierarchy that is symbolized by their regimental flag. He is thus reminding them of their "station" in the sense of place, and simultaneously their "station" in relation to his authority. My thanks to Professor Simon Barker for his help with this reference.

302. Spelled "Tregny" in basetext; this spelling is indicative of the pronunciation. The village of Tregony is east of Truro, and southeast of Tregassow. It is actually about six miles from Tregassow. The Fifth Monarchist John Carew (see n122) had sat as MP for Tregony since 1647.

303. Trapnel, *Legacy*, 49–52, includes a letter written from Tregassow on April 15, addressed to the church of Allhallows in London. The letter, Trapnel writes, had been sent as an enclosure in one to "brother Gardner." Trapnel, *Legacy*, 53–57, includes what is almost certainly the letter to Gardner,

heavy the day before, and this saying I had in my heart, Christ was heavy before the hour; before they came to take him he was in an agony: said I, Lord, what manner of saying is this? and as I was pondering upon it, my sister Langdon came up into my chamber, very sad, and said, sister, pray thee do not be frighted. Why? said I, what is the matter? There is, said she, half a troop of horse[304] come to take thy body, or my husband's; there was half a dozen soldiers, and they made such a clutter, she thought they had been a greater number, but there was a number great enough to take a poor silly maid. So I rejoiced, and said I am not troubled, for I shall see my friends at London; she said to Mistress Frances, her mother's maid, Pray thee Mistress Frances, take my sister, and escape into the wood hard by the house,[305] they cannot find her there; but I said, I will not make my self guilty by flying away, for I have not broke any law, whereby man should do thus, and as long as God is on my side, said I, men nor devils shall not affright me; and the Lord gave me that word of Nehemiah, who said, *Shall such a man as I flee?*[306] So said I to them, *Shall such a one as I flee?* who have lived with the Lord, all my days, and have been courageous for Christ hitherto, I will not now flinch through the strength of the Lord keeping me, and I know he will keep me: then many in the family came, and the neighbors, and wept about me, but I was no whit daunted. The minister of the parish[307] came, and said he would not wish me to go down, without they would show an order, I answered, what order have they brought? None but Captain Fox's letter, they told me; That, said I, is enough; for there is the Fox's claws to bring[308] me to Plymouth, so notwithstanding their[309] persuasions, I run downstairs, where I heard the soldiers very rough in their words, and they said they would not tarry a moment for me, and they would have me by foul means, if I refused to go; they threatened much what they would do, the Quartermaster[310] was very high in his words. So when I had heard them bluster

---

addressed to "a Friend" and written at Tregassow on April 14. These letters both include accounts of her recent experiences in Truro.

304. A subdivision of a cavalry regiment.

305. Tregassow Wood is still to be found just to the east of the house.

306. Nehemiah 6:11.

307. The minister of St. Erme has not been definitively identified. He may have been the Mr. Frances previously mentioned, who preached "hard by" where she was staying. However, one of the daughters of John Jago, Anne Langdon's brother (see n133), married the minister of St. Erme, "Mr Carthew," but there is no indication when this marriage took place: see Davies Gilbert, *The Parochial History of Cornwall* (London: J. B. Nicholls and Son, 1838), 1:398. According to George Leyden Hennessey's unpublished "Devon and Cornwall Incumbents," held at Devon Record Office, John Carthew was rector of St. Erme until 1672, when Robert Flavell took over from him.

308. The basetext reads "pin." The list of errata corrects this: "for pin, read bring."

309. The basetext reads "through." The list of errata corrects this: "for through, read notwithstanding their."

310. The regimental officer responsible for accommodation, ammunition, and supplies.

thus a while, I stepped among them, many of my friends being with them, I coming into the room, stood by them, and said, friend, whom do you seek? speaking to the Quartermaster: he said, is this the lady? I said, I do not know what you mean by lady, but that is a soldier's compliment: I pray, whom do you seek? So he asked whether my name was Anna Trapnel, I said, I suppose that is my name; then he said, I demand your body; said I take it, if it will do you any good, I am ready to go with you: then he was very respectful, and said, he would show me all the courtesy and civility that lay in his power, I thanked him and said, they could not harm me; for my God would not suffer them; then they said, they would wait till I was fitted to go, and they tarried till the afternoon: And when we had dined, I took my leave of my dear loving friends, and departed, riding behind a friend that came to see Captain Langdon, who put off his journey that he was riding, and offered to carry me, and Captain Langdon's man, and his mother's maid, they sent with me, and I went filled with the joy of the Lord: and that day, some two or three miles off, I met with some dear friends, who bore me company a while, but I had so much of the refreshings of God, which quickly overcame my ordinary capacity, and I felt not the trotting of the horse, nor minded anything but the spiritual communion, that I was in with the Lord; and so I rode praying, all the first day's journey, till I came to Fowey-town,[311] where they took me down off the horse, and set me in a chair, but I came not to my capacity to speak a great while, and when I looked up, and saw many men, women and children about me, and sitting on a high wall, right over where I sat, I was amazed to see so many people, and not knowing where I was, but at length I spake to them in Scripture language, the which they listened to, and when I went away, they gave a great shout; the people said, they used to do so at some strange sight: so they led me into the boat, for we went over a passage,[312] and many men and women went over with us from that town, and the room was full of people, where I lodged, some came to gaze on me, and some came in love to the Lord Jesus, to hear experiences, and some tempted souls were much refreshed, and rejoiced much to see me there, though not as I was, a prisoner; they wept for me as to that condition, and I sat up most part of the night at Fowey, and begged those that came to jeer at me, that they would consider the wrong they did to their poor souls, and had Scripture very suitable to those I spoke; I asked them what they came to see, I was but as a reed shaken with the wind; I was a simple creature, only divine wisdom was pleased to make use of the simple, and to call them to him, to show them his love, to choose such to do him service, and I said, I am a poor sorry reed, but divine power, and

---

311. Fowey (pronounced "Foy," and spelled thus in the basetext) is on the south coast of Cornwall, about twenty miles from Tregassow.

312. Fowey is on the western bank of the estuary of the River Fowey, which has to be crossed by boat.

the wind that Christ told Nicodemus, in the 3rd of John the 8th[313] which bloweth where it listeth, that wind, said I, hath taken a silly creature, and hath made her understand its sound, that which Nicodemus, a great rabbi, could not tell what to make of; so that I prayed them that derided, that they would have a care, and that they therein would consider the saying of Christ in the 25th of Matthew, who said, what they did to his, they did to him,[314] though I be one of the worst of Christ's little ones, yet said I, he will own me, where ever I am: I beseech sinners to love Christ, who was the chiefest of ten thousands, and I spoke how the church set him out in the Canticles;[315] and I told them, though they made me a byword, and a reproach, yet I would pray for their souls: I told them I came not into the country to be seen, and taken notice of, but I came with my friends. I desired Christ and the beauty of holiness might be taken notice of, so that others thereby might be taken with Christ; and that I might be only a voice, and Christ the sound; I spake much to profane sinners, and to the civilized ones that they would eye the new Covenant,[316] which admits of no condition, nor qualification, nor preparation, but is a free Covenant to sinners, as sinners, that if they venture their souls thereupon, it will at the moment change, and make them hate sin, and all manner of evil, and cleave to that good[317] the Scripture makes mention of; then to the tempted was spoken from Hebrews 2.18.[318] for in that Christ suffered being tempted, he is able to succor them that are tempted, and unto them were experiences spoken, how greatly Christ was sensible of the temptations of his people, and his succorings were great, and his sympathizing much: So I related what bowels of compassion from the Lord I found herein, though when I was murmuring against the Lord, who I thought dealt roughly by me, I said with Jonas, I do well to do thus, as he said, *I do well to be angry:*[319] So I was very peevish, thinking that Satan would have

313. John 3:8–10: "The wind bloweth where it listeth, and thou hearest the sound thereof, but canst not tell whence it cometh, and whither it goeth: so is every one that is born of the Spirit. Nicodemus answered and said unto him, How can these things be? Jesus answered and said unto him, Art thou a master of Israel, and knowest not these things?" Nicodemus was a Pharisee and Jewish religious leader who, in John 3, visits Jesus in prison to listen to his teachings.

314. Matthew 25:40: "And the King shall answer and say unto them, Verily I say unto you, Inasmuch as ye have done it unto one of the least of these my brethren, ye have done it unto me."

315. In the Christian tradition, Canticles (also known as the Song of Songs or the Song of Solomon) is read as an allegory of the relationship of Christ and the church: see Longfellow, *Women and Religious Writing*, 24–31.

316. See Hebrews 8:6-13. The New Covenant refers to the replacement of the old Mosaic covenant between God and his people by a new and better one, as promised by the prophet Jeremiah (Jeremiah 31:31–34). This was to reside in the heart rather than consisting in outward symbols and institutions.

317. Romans 12:9.

318. Hebrews 2:18: "For in that he himself hath suffered being tempted, he is able to succour them that are tempted."

319. Jonah 4:9. Jonas and Jonah are versions of the same name.

made an end of me. I said with Jonah, *I do well to be angry to the death.* I prayed tempted souls to hearken to Christ, and not to Satan; some tempted souls there wept bitterly, and the next day came again, and accompanied me out of that town: So I took my leave, they begging to hear from me, and desired my welfare.

Then I rode to a place called Looe,[320] where I desired to stay an hour, but it was hard to be obtained of the Quartermaster, though he had promised Captain Langdon that I should see some friends there; yet when I came there, he was afraid I should have broke out into prayer there, and so have stayed him longer than he would, but I and my friends did so entreat him, that he gave me leave to go with a soldier with me, to bring me quickly back to him again, he staying a little way off, and said that I should have nobody come into the house that I went to; this he charged the soldier, so that coming to that house I went to, there I was entertained with much love, and some few did hear of my being there, and came to see me, and watched for my coming out. I had some discourse with a blind man there, who had much of the light of the Lord in his soul, and his words were so savory, that my heart was quickened by the Lord in that discourse I had with this seeing soul, though blind outwardly; and I stayed among them a while, till I was full of joy in the sight of these dear friends; so that being hurried away by the soldiers, I brake forth into tears, and said, the time will come that spiritual communion shall not be interrupted; and indeed the thoughts of eternity melted my heart, that I said, I weep not for sorrow, but my tears flow from apprehensions of communion with the Lord, and those glorified Saints there; if Saints on earth did so take up my heart, I said, what will that company be to me, in heaven, sure it will be joy to the full: So those dear souls went with me out of the town, and then bid farewell, saying, they were sorry, I could stay no longer with them, so I parted, and rode towards Plymouth[321] with very much of the Lord's presence.

And when I came to Plymouth, after the Quartermaster had been to inform that I was coming, he came and had me up to the fort,[322] two of the other soldiers going with me, and four others who were my friends, these bore me company to the fort, and when I came into the Lieutenant's house, I sat down a while, and he told me I was committed to his charge as his prisoner, for that Major Sanders[323] was not there unto whom the letter was sent concerning me; so after a few words

---

320. A small coastal town, ten miles east of Fowey.

321. An important port city seventeen miles east of Looe, on the boundary between Cornwall and Devon. A Puritan city, loyal to Parliament, it had been besieged by Royalist forces between 1642 and 1646, during the Civil Wars.

322. Built in 1596 on the western side of the harbor, Plymouth Fort was replaced by the Royal Citadel in the latter part of the 1660s in response to the threat posed by the Second Anglo-Dutch War (1665–1667). For the history of fortifications in Plymouth, see R. N. Worth, *History of Plymouth, From the Earliest Period to the Present Time* (Plymouth: W. Brendon & Son, 1871), 294–306.

323. Major Thomas Sanders was Commander of Plymouth Fort. *CSPD*, 7:86.

had passed between us, I desired him to let me hear the order[324] read; so he read it, wherein was expressed that I was to be sent from thence in the first state's ship[325] that went to Portsmouth, and so to be sent from thence to the Council; and when this was read, after a little while spent in discourse, Lieutenant Lark,[326] in whose house I was a prisoner; he asked me whether I would go upstairs and see my chamber, unto which I was willing, and my four friends went up with me, and I bless the Lord, I never was in so blessed a frame in my life, being in an ordinary capacity, the which I was in a while, but at length the Lord wound me up higher; and as I was telling you, that coming into my chamber, I found the Lord Christ opening his love to me from that Scripture, in Hosea the 2.19.[327] I have betrothed thee to my self in mercy and loving kindness for ever. And I had some enlargement upon that, and likewise from Scripture expressions in the Canticles, and in Habbakuk, but I omit writing what sweet unfoldings I had therein from the Lord, because I intend if the Lord will give me opportunity to write down the cordials of the Lord, which I had in my confinement by man, in a book wherein I shall set out Satan's prison, the which I was in a year before man's prison, that very month that I was set at liberty from Satan's confinement, men confined me, which was the second month called April, which was a year after that horrible pit of Satan's, the which I lay in, from the beginning of February, till the beginning of April, about nine weeks,[328] but I have been in man's prison fifteen weeks, yet that was to me much easier, than a shorter time in Satan's clutches.

But I return to the relation of my first coming into prison, I was exceedingly transported in my spirits, and I was as if I had been to die presently, nothing was in my thoughts but divine bosom, which made me bid farewell to all creatures: I thought I could have embraced death, though it should be never so ghastly, and cruelly tendered to me, I never had such joy in the thoughts of death, and I said to Lieutenant Lark, pray Sir, let me have the liberty to be private a while with

---

324. On April 11, Henry Lawrence, the President of the Council of State, sent a letter to Major Sanders at Plymouth: "Council having directed Capt. Fox to apprehend Anna Trapnell, and deliver her to you, you are to send her to Portsmouth, to be there disposed of as the enclosed order directs." *CSPD*, 7:89. Sanders was clearly vexed by his charge, writing to General Desborough on April 28, "Coming here lately, I find Anna Trapnell sent prisoner from Cornwall, and by order of Council to be sent to Portsmouth in the first State's vessel for her trial, but there is none likely to go for a long time except commanded, and that I cannot do without order. Should I send one of those here with her and some prisoners of war that are in the castle, to Portsmouth? they are a great trouble to us, being forced to keep a guard of 16 men every night on account of the weakness of the place." *CSPD*, 7:134.

325. I.e., a navy ship, as opposed to a merchant vessel.

326. Lieutenant Samuel Larke of Plymouth Fort. *CSPD*, 7:585.

327. Hosea 2:19: "And I will betroth thee unto me for ever; yea, I will betroth thee unto me in righteousness, and in judgment, and in loving kindness, and in mercies."

328. In *Cry*, 10, Trapnel records being assailed by Satan, from "the first of the twelfth month [February], 1653, till the latter end of the second month, called April."

my friends, who came with me, the which he granted, and he went down from us, then I said, this is the greatest preferment as ever I had, to be honored with a prison for Christ, this is honor said I indeed, I now can take my leave of all things under the sun, and see all things vanity,[329] and poor empty nothings; and I said farewell all creatures, and welcome Christ, then I desired my friends that we might pray together before they departed; for I said it was the best work to begin my imprisonment in spiritual communion, then we prayed, and after some time spent in prayer, the Son of righteousness shone so hot on my spirits, that I could not forbear singing forth his praise; and my friends told me, that I was three hours on my knees, praying, and praising, that I felt no pain nor wearisomeness, though I had journeyed so far. They took me off my knees, and set me in a chair, where I sat some hours after in singing, and then was silent, and some women put me to bed, where I lay praying and singing the other part of that night, while morning: and the maid that tended me said, she sat in the bed, wiping away the tears from my eyes, which she said came exceeding fast all night, as I sung and prayed. And truly the Son from on high had very much thawed my heart, and I prayed and sung after that night, four days, and sometimes wrapped up in silence with the Lord, beholding his glory in visions, and on the last day of that week, I spoke to some seamen and others that came to visit me, telling them the Lord's kindness to me in my troubles in Cornwall, and other experiences I related to them, and the Lord knows I did speak of these things to them that they might be more in love with Christ, who let out himself to a poor creature so extraordinarily. And the next day after, it was the first day of another week, some would fain have had me gone to have heard the word preached that day, but it could not be granted that I should go out of the fort; and indeed I was very weak, having lain four days and five nights, and came not out of my bed, nor took no refreshing creature, save a draught of small beer or cider, and sometimes ate a little piece of toast out of it, and this was but once at a night, and not every night neither; and this was for six days: and this first day that I rose out of my bed, I lay down again quickly, and I took a Bible, and read the 11th chapter of Luke, and the 12th chapter, and my heart was much taken with the words there that Christ spoke to them, and the Lord applied much to me of what Christ spoke concerning their calling of him Beelzebub:[330] and if they dealt so with Christ, I thought it was but as Christ was dealt with, to be called devil, and that saying I was possessed with a lying spirit, but this was made very easy, when I conceived Christ bare[331] a great deal more, and after that these chapters were fastened and knit to my heart, the Lord making them mine. I admiring at the sufferings of Christ, and at his patience, and I continued singing most

---

329. Ecclesiastes 1:14: "I have seen all the works that are done under the sun; and, behold, all is vanity and vexation of spirit." Variations on these words are repeated many times throughout Ecclesiastes.

330. See Matthew 12:24–28.

331. Archaic form of past tense of "bear."

part of that day, concerning the resurrection, and my interest therein, and I sang as to the conditions of many who lived in the fort, and concerning my passage on the sea that I should have; speaking of the Lord's appearances that I should have there, and the joy and triumph I should be in, in all my imprisonment time, and the next day after this, it being the second day of the week, I had been a prisoner seven days, and this was the eighth day from the soldiers taking me, so I that day at night, after the hours spent with my friends at London, which I knew kept that day in part, in prayer, so did I, though absent in body from them; and at night as I said before, I went down and discoursed with Lieutenant Lark a while, and after I had showed him two letters which I had written to London,[332] that he saw there was none of that which is called treason in them, then I wished him a good night, and I went to bed, and he the next day rode out of town to fetch his wife, who was with her friends in the country, and in his absence, Ensign Owen was my keeper, and he was very careful to fulfill his office, and was loath to let in my friends to see me, but charged them at the gate with trespass, if they let in any of my friends, saying, they had best to be traitors too; so that[333] he was as severe, as if I had been a traitor; yet he spake me very fair to my face, but I saw he endeavored to catch my words, and to ensnare me, putting his own sense upon them, but the Lord kept me out of his ensnarements, but he watched for my halting, and when my friends came a great way to see me, they had much ado to get into the fort, and then my jailer sat by, and heard what I said to my friends, but this severity was not many days, for Major Sanders came, and then my jailer departed, who told me the order did not make mention of my going to the Council, but Major Sanders read that I should, and so did the Lieutenant, but my jailer it may be had a mind to affright me, but he could not; and he told me I dreamed that the order run so; I am sure, I said, I was not asleep, but he jeered me, and he told Major Sanders, that I would not have so many people come to me: indeed he would have had nobody come, if he could have bore sway, but the Lord ordered all for my good: and when Major Sanders came, he gave me leave with a keeper, which was a friend, to go to hear the first day's; and he was very courteous, and so was Lieutenant Lark, who came home with his wife before I was gone: I stayed there for the wind, and a state's ship to carry me: I stayed five weeks; the Lord made it but as a few days to me, I had so much of his presence and power from him, he made kindness flow from strangers

---

332. Trapnel, *Legacy*, includes two letters written from Plymouth: one is to Feake and Simpson in prison at Windsor Castle, written on Saturday, May 6, the other to the church meeting at Allhallows, dated Monday, May 8. The latter may have been one of the letters she refers to here, as it was addressed to London. Even though in *Legacy*, 64, she signs the letter off with the words "in haste, going strait with Captain Kendal a States Ship to Portchmouth," she seems to have remained some time longer in Plymouth, as she reports here spending five weeks in Plymouth, which suggests she must actually have left Plymouth on May 16 or 17. For Captain Kendall, see n342.

333. The catchword "that" at the end of page 32 in the basetext is not followed by this word at the top of page 33, which starts with "he."

in the family, and in the fort; these were strangers, and yet they were fellow citizens, and I bless the Lord, they are not now strangers, but acquaintance, and they are a company that are written in my heart, they and their teacher; for they were not ashamed of my chain, they owned me in my bonds, and were a succor to me in a strange country: my soul was administered to by them, and the pastor over them; they every way administered to my necessity in what I stood in need of; I wanted not their help, and the people of the parish showed me love in visiting me, and some of them when they had heard me pray, and in singing, they wept that they had taken up hard thoughts of me.

Their teacher Mr. Hughes[334] was very bitter against me, and would not come and talk with me, though some of his auditory[335] desired him; but he writ to one of his friends at Cornwall, that he had read my book, and he from that drew that I was an impostor and he called the book nonsense, so that he confirmed his friend in her judging of me; and so he continued judging me for the sake of that dispensation he never saw, nor came not to try it by the word, but he endeavored to incense others against me, and his sometimes scholar (R.V.[336]) was afraid to displease his Father Hughes, else he would have come according to his promise, but it may be had forgot that he promised a young man whom I sent the first night I came, to tell him I was come to the fort a prisoner and I knew not how little a while I should stay; therefore I should be glad to see him: and he told the messenger that he would come next day, but he came not; and yet was much in the town most part of my stay there, and many wondered he came not to see me, having been acquainted with me above seven years, the which they understanding, said sure, he knew some evil by me: thus it bred a jealousy among strangers, concerning me, but some said, he would not suffer evil to be spoken of me; for he said, sure, the root of the matter was in me; he was much urged by my friends to come, but would not see me, though in

---

334. George Hughes had been Vicar of St. Andrew's, Plymouth, since 1643. In 1654 he was also made assistant to the commissioners of Devonshire, and in 1655 was instrumental in the foundation of the Exeter Assembly, which drew together ministers regardless of their particular religious allegiance. Hughes was born in Southwark, London, educated at Oxford, and became a lecturer at Allhallows in Bread Street, London. Later, having occasioned Archbishop Laud's displeasure, he left London and became Rector of Tavistock in Devon in 1638, moving to Exeter at the outbreak of the Civil War. Hughes was a leading Presbyterian minister and Puritan divine, who published a number of his sermons as well as collections of aphorisms and exegetical texts. Matthews, *Calamy Revised*, 281–82; and Mary Wolffe, "Hughes, George (1603/4–1667)," *ODNB*.

335. Audience; here, congregation.

336. Ralph Venning of Tavistock in Devon, was George Hughes's first convert. He had a lectureship at St. Olave's, in the borough of Southwark, London, where he gained a reputation as a great preacher. Venning published many texts: sermons, exegeses, and other devotional works. Stephen Wright, "Venning, Ralph (ca. 1621–1674)," *ODNB*; and Matthews, *Calamy Revised*, 501–2. In *Cry*, 6, Trapnel had named Venning as one of a number of reputable people to whom she was well known; he could, she wrote, "give testimony of me, and of my walking in times past."

bonds; and this use I was taught by the Lord, to make of that unkindness of a friend, who I hearing, when I was coming to Plymouth, that such an one was come there, I leaned upon him as a prop to me in my suffering, and I rejoiced much, saying to my friends, that he would vindicate me, who had been known to him so long, and one whom I was always ready to vindicate, when aspersed; but my God learned me to know, that all flesh was grass, and a fading flower,[337] and like an Egyptian reed:[338] and by this unkindness from a friend, my God drew me the more to rest upon himself alone; and what unkindness I relate from any received, my end hereby is not to reproach or seek revenge on any, but the Lord my God knows, had there not been so many several reports passed far and near, I would not have set pen to paper in this kind, but it is that truth may silence falsity; and though I fail in an orderly penning down these things, yet not in a true relation, of as much as I remember, and what is expedient to be written; I could not have related so much from the shallow memory I have naturally, but through often relating these things, they become as a written book, spread open before me, and after which I write.

Now I shall come again to the relation, and tell you that I had much kindness at Plymouth, from many, and great labor of love showed me until my departure, and some went with me a shipboard, and were sorry to have me go from their quarters, not that I was anything, but the Lord did their souls good through a worm; and when we had been a day and a night tossing on the sea, the wind being against us, drove us back into the harbor again: Some at Dartmouth[339] reported that I had bewitched the winds, that the ships could not go to sea, and they cursed me there, but the Lord blessed me the more; many reproaches he helped me to bear, and though we were beating on the waves against the wind, yet I was not sick; for the Lord had there much for me to declare to seamen of free grace,[340] and of the vileness of man's nature, and the excellent work of redemption. And I spake this unto them, and prayed and sang in the cabin where I lay; and the seamen were much affected: the Lord made some of them declare how the Lord refreshed them, and that they knew if I had stayed longer, much good their souls would have reaped, they were very respectful to me, though there were few that had any relish of good, the Lord made much to be relished by them, through a poor nothing creature: the Scripture the Lord enlarged amongst them, in the 73rd Psalm, verse 1. *Truly, God is good to Israel, and to them that are of a clean heart;*

---

337. See Isaiah 40:6 and 1 Peter 1:24.

338. 2 Kings 18:21: "Now, behold, thou trustest upon the staff of this bruised reed, even upon Egypt, on which if a man lean, it will go into his hand, and pierce it: so is Pharaoh king of Egypt unto all that trust on him"; see, too, Isaiah 36:6 and Ezekiel 29:6.

339. Dartmouth is a port town in the county of Devon, some thirty miles east of Plymouth. Its deepwater harbor, able to accommodate large ships, made it of longstanding strategic importance in the defense of the coast and English Channel.

340. On free grace, see nn65, 146, and 186.

the new Covenant[341] the Lord made known amongst them very much: so that it was a blessed passage, though as from man it was bitter to be tossed upon the sea four days, and the maid that came with me, lying vomiting grievously by me, and sick, even ready to die, she thought her heart would have broke, and I hurt my leg against the ship-side, that it raged greatly a day and a night; and lying in a little cabin sweating much, the maid and I together, which lodge was very little, it being in the master's cabin, which was a little lodge: But though I met with much difficulty, as flesh and blood, yet I murmured not, only I was once a little troubled, and said, Lord, why is man thus cruel to deal thus with me? they never considered whether my nature could bear the sea: but I said, Father, lay not this evil usage to their charge. I was brought up among the pirates,[342] that had robbed upon the sea, and were taken prisoners, and sent in the ship with me, but the Lord preserved me from all hurt, and carried me safe to land, and all in the ship; both Captain and Master, and men gave me civil respect while I was with them: So the Lord made good his promise to me, that nothing should harm me, neither on the sea, nor the land.

---

341. See n316.

342. The pirates were "Wm. Hebditch, John Dorrell, and Paul Roch … enemies to the commonwealth." *CSPD*, 7:487. Dorrell is also referred to as William Doran in this volume. The pirates were returned to London "by Wm. Kendall, captain of the Sunrise frigate," and imprisoned in the Marshalsea prison (the usual prison for pirates) from June to September. On September 2, the Governor of the Marshalsea received an order from the Council of State for their release, on condition that they "depart within 20 days, not to return without leave." *CSPD*, 7:191, 200, 359, 436, 441. Since the three men are referred to as "enemies of the commonwealth," they may have been Royalist privateers rather than pirates; this might also account for the leniency of their punishment. I am grateful to John Appleby for these suggestions, which are supported by references to Doran and Roche in Elaine Murphy, ed., *A Calendar of Material Relating to Ireland from the High Court of Admiralty, 1641–1660* (Dublin: Irish Manuscripts Commission, 2011), 99, 209, 244, 303. Other references to Kendall's ship at this time name it as the *Success*: see C. T. Atkinson, ed., *Letters and Papers Relating to the First Dutch War, 1652–1654* (s.l.: Navy Records Society, 1912), 5:17, 273, 275–76; 376; Bernard Capp, *Cromwell's Navy: The Fleet and the English Revolution, 1648–1660* (Oxford: Clarendon, 1989), 274, 276–77; William Laird Clowes, *The Royal Navy: A History from the Earliest Times to 1900*, 7 vols. (London: Chatham, 1996; first edition 1898), 2:188; and Elaine Murphy, *Ireland and the War at Sea, 1641–1653* (Woodbridge: Boydell and Brewer, 2012), 84, 170. For histories of seventeenth-century piracy, see John C. Appleby, "Jacobean Piracy: English Maritime Depredation in Transition, 1603–1625," in *The Social History of English Seamen, 1485–1649*, ed. Cheryl A. Fury, 277–99 (Woodbridge: Boydell, 2012); David Loades, "The English Maritime Community, 1500–1650," in *The Social History of English Seamen*, ed. Fury, 5–26; C. M. Senior, *A Nation of Pirates: English Piracy in its Heyday* (Newton Abbot: David and Charles, 1976); Peter Earle, *The Pirate Wars* (London: Methuen, 2003); and Margarette Lincoln, *British Pirates and Society, 1680–1730* (Aldershot: Ashgate, 2014).

And the Captain with some of his men, came with me ashore, and we landed at Portsmouth,[343] and the Governor[344] not being in town, I went with the Captain to Major Murford's, the Deputy Governor,[345] who receiving the order from the Captain of the ship, after some discourse with him he departed; and the Deputy Governor told me, I was committed to his charge, until such time that he could dispose of me with conveniency: so he lovingly entertained me, and those two friends that came with me, and his daughters showed me much kindness: and in the afternoon the Deputy Governor having no lodging in his house for me, he procured me lodging at Ensign Baker's, in the town, and he went with me thither, it being not far off; and there he left me, desiring the Ensign's wife to be kind to me, but she heard I was a frenzy-headed[346] creature, and she looked very sour upon me, and all the while I was there, she offered me no drink, nor anything else; but one day when the Governor sent his servant to see what I had, then she sent to me, and I had newly eaten a piece of pie, that I had brought with me from Plymouth, so that was all my food I ate from the second day to the fifth day, that I came away; then she seemed to be very kind, and said, she heard such a clamor concerning me, which made her afraid of me, but after she heard me, she was of another mind. I prayed and sang there a night and a day for the most part, and so departed from thence the next morning after, and came in a coach to London, and a Lieutenant came with me to convey me to Westminster;[347] and he brought a present of eggs that was sent from Guernsey to the great man at Whitehall,[348] they were partridge eggs of the largest kind, I was told; and if they were not well

343. An ancient and important port city on the south coast, and the chief base of the Parliamentary naval forces.

344. From 1649 to 1659, the Governor of Portsmouth, responsible for the safety of the town and the ships in the harbor, was Colonel Nathaniel Whetham (1604–1688). A baker by trade, Whetham had fought in the Parliamentary armies during the Civil War and had been Governor of Northampton, holding the town for Parliament for several years in the 1640s, before being made Governor of Portsmouth, the chief naval base and most important garrison town in the country. Whetham was elected to Parliament for Portsmouth in September 1654. See Catherine Durning Whetham and William Cecil Dampier Whetham, *A History of the Life of Colonel Nathaniel Whetham* (London: Longmans, Green and Co., 1907), and http://www.zoominfo.com/p/Nathaniel-Whetham/1085526583 (accessed November 20, 2015).

345. Major Peter Murford (Moreford in basetext) became Lieutenant-Governor of Portsmouth in 1656, taking over responsibility for the town during Whetham's absence with General Monck in the campaign in Scotland from 1655 to 1657. See http://www.zoominfo.com/p/Nathaniel-Whetham/1085526583 (accessed November 20, 2015).

346. Deranged, crazed.

347. The distance from Portsmouth to Westminster is about seventy-five miles. This would have been a two-and-a-half to three-day journey, perhaps longer, since the coach broke twice and overturned once.

348. A reference to Cromwell.

put up,[349] they could not be kept whole, for the coach broke twice by the way, and overturned once: it was a great mercy that we had no hurt, the dealings of man being unjust, everything will make them manifest, and discover their breakings, where they or their presents be: If such that hold forth King Jesus be near, one danger or other they will be liable to meet withal.

I was through divine power brought safe in the coach to Fox Hall,[350] where we lighted, and the coachman and Lieutenant told me, I must bear all my charges both by the way and the coach hire, so I did, and I was brought from Fox Hall by water, to Westminster, and stayed a while at the George[351] in King Street,[352] and then, one of the messengers came, and carried me in a coach to Titon's,[353] but my friends paid the coach hire; and at Titon's house in Covent Garden,[354] there that messenger left me, which brought me thither; it was that messenger that took hold of Vavasor Powell,[355] and carried him before the Council, I told him it was

349. Stored, packed, or stowed away for safe keeping (*OED*).

350. Fox Hall Manor, also known as Fulke's Hall, Faukeshall, and Vauxhall, was in Kennington, South London, near the site of the present Vauxhall Bridge. At this time the river could only be crossed here as Trapnel does, by boat. Popular pleasure gardens (originally known as New Spring Gardens) were added to the manor shortly before the Restoration, and remained open to the public until 1859. Weinreb and Hibbert, *The London Encyclopædia*, 909, 910–12.

351. A coaching inn in George Yard, King Street. It was demolished in about 1750, "when George Yard and other slum alleys were swept away for the creation of Great George Street, as an approach road for Westminster Bridge." Westminster City Archives Research Group, *One on Every Corner: The History of Some Westminster Pubs* (London: Westminster City Archives, 2002), 7.

352. A narrow street in Westminster, between Whitehall and Westminster Abbey, no longer extant. "King Street … was notorious for the number of its taverns, which were considered snares for unwary travellers… . In his Diary, Pepys identifies at least 12 taverns on King Street, all of which he frequented… . He also describes the traffic congestion in King Street by this time, a picturesque street with overhanging gables and at least half a dozen celebrated inns: the Swan, the Boar's Head, the Bell, the Dog, the Antelope, the George and the Angel." Westminster City Archives, *One on Every Corner*, 2.

353. Edward Titon (spelled "Titon" and "Tyton" in basetext) was Deputy Serjeant-at-Arms throughout the 1650s. The Serjeant-at-Arms is responsible for keeping order in debates in the House of Commons in Parliament, and used also to be responsible for its general security. He also, along with his deputies, undertook a range of administrative tasks on behalf of the Commons and was able to make arrests, without a warrant, if asked by the Commons to do so. In the 1650s, Edward Dendy was Serjeant-at-Arms; he had (in 1651) fourteen deputies: see *CSPD*, 4:80.

354. The first residential public square or *piazza* in London, developed at the expense of the Earl of Bedford in the 1630s to a design by architect Inigo Jones. It had arcaded houses to the north and east, St. Paul's Church to the west, and the Bedford's family mansion to the south. A small fruit and vegetable market started in the square in 1649 but did not become London's main one until after the Great Fire of 1666, which destroyed the older markets in the city. See Weinreb and Hibbert, *The London Encyclopædia*, 204–5, and http://www.coventgardenlife.com/info/history.htm

355. A prominent Welsh Baptist/Fifth Monarchist preacher, who had been a chaplain in the Parliamentary army and, in the early 1650s, a key figure in the Commission for the Propagation of the

no good office to be so employed to lay hold of the Saints in that kind, but I said, though I was troubled at him for his taking Mr. Powell, yet for taking me, and conducting me into custody, I was no whit troubled at him, but I told him his office was not good, this I said, as I was riding to Titon's; and there I was had to my chamber, which was Mr. Feake's prison first,[356] so that I was quickly raised in my joy, in thinking of that prayer, which had been put up in that room, for the coming of King Jesus to reign on the earth, and to throw down Babylon, for this did that dear servant of Christ[357] cry earnestly, and the Lord made an unworthy handmaid to second those cryings, and to ring a peal to Whitehall ward,[358] but they had not a mind to hearken, though the cry of a stone[359] was brought near them again, occasioned by their own doings, thinking to silence *allelujahs* triumphing over the beast, and the false prophet,[360] but they could not do it. The secret voice of thunder[361] hath a louder report, than men's great cannons. The Lord renewed my joy much at the sight of my friends, and in the thoughts that I was brought, near Whitehall to be a witness against their black doings, the which I hope I shall witness against unto the death: that time at Titon's was spent much in prayer, and singing forth Babylon's fall, and the ruin of those which endeavored to be nurses and rockers[362] to Babylon's brats;[363] the Lord will cut off those breasts that give Babylon milk; for the whore of Rome,[364] the Lord will not have nourished by any, high or low, rich or poor, much was sung to this purpose at Titon's; and I often told of a present from heaven, which was much better than the present of

---

Gospel in Wales. Like Trapnel, Powell had been a supporter of the Barebone's Parliament, and, in the days following the declaration of Cromwell as Lord Protector, he preached frequently against the new turn of events and in particular against Cromwell, for which he was repeatedly arrested and released. It was at his examination in Whitehall by the Council of State following one such arrest in January 1654 that Trapnel had fallen into a trance and spoken the prophecies published in *The Cry of a Stone*. See introduction, 17; *BDBR*, 3:55–57; and Stephen K. Roberts, "Powell, Vavasor (1617–1670)," *ODNB*.

356. Woolrych, *Commonwealth to Protectorate*, 364, notes that Feake and Powell were both held by the Serjeant-at-Arms for a few days following their arrest.

357. A reference to Christopher Feake; see n59.

358. District.

359. A reference to *The Cry of a Stone*, the title of one of Trapnel's texts already published that year, recounting her prophecies delivered in Whitehall.

360. A reference to Trapnel herself, from the perspective of her detractors.

361. The voice of God is frequently associated with thunder in the Bible; see for example 2 Samuel 22:14; Job 37:4–5; 40:9; Psalms 18:13, 29:3; 77:18; 104:7; and Revelation 14:2. Psalm 81:7 speaks of a "secret place of thunder."

362. Those who rocked the cradles.

363. See n34.

364. For Protestants, the whore of Rome was the Roman Catholic Church. This identification was based on their interpretation of Revelation 17:4–6 as a reference to the perceived iniquities of the Roman Catholic Church. See n32.

partridge eggs;[365] yea, it was costlier than the gold of Ophir,[366] or rubies and pearls from a far country. I would fain have had the great Council, and their Protector,[367] to have received a present sent from the great Protector,[368] which is indeed, a Protector of the faithful, who makes use of silly[369] handmaids to carry his present sometimes; and I said this, O great ones of the earth, is the present from the great Jehovah to you, even his son Christ?[370] In that you[371] profess yourselves to be builders, the great God hath presented to you a cornerstone elect and precious, a sure foundation,[372] an excellent platform for those that are willing to build to purpose; now therefore said I unto you, that love rarities for presents, here are rarities indeed, not like those things that will fade in their beauty, nor like that which soon loseth its scent, though never so well perfumed, nor like that which in time will be wasted and gone, nor like eggs that are subject to rot or to break before they come to be large partridges, or any at all; but it was said, oh that Protector, and his Council, and clergy, would all agree to receive such a present that fades not,[373] nor cannot waste, nor be broken, nor rot, nor is not subject to any casualty. And for presenting them with the Lord's present, they sent their messengers with a Bridewell reward to me, for all my pains and good will, and love to their welfare.

I was eight days at Titon's house,[374] expecting to be sent for before the Council every day, according to their orders, declaring that I was to come be-

365. A reference to the eggs carried in the coach (see 105) but also alluding to Jeremiah 17:11, where the futility of unmerited wealth is compared with the partridge that "sitteth on eggs, and hatcheth them not."

366. In the Old Testament, Ophir is a region renowned for its wealth; its exact location remains unknown.

367. The Council of State, and Cromwell, who had recently been made "Lord Protector of the Commonwealth of England, Scotland and Ireland" by the Instrument of Government that had ended the Barebone's Parliament. This title was seen as moving Cromwell closer to the position of a monarch, and was thus the source of great anger among Fifth Monarchists.

368. God.

369. Unlearned or humble, rather than foolish.

370. Christ is understood as God's gift to humanity: "For God so loved the world, that he gave his only begotten Son, that whosoever believeth in him should not perish, but have everlasting life" (John 3:16); "the gift of God is eternal life through Jesus Christ our Lord" (Romans 6:23).

371. The punctuation is the basetext is "Jehovah to you? even his son Christ, in that ..."

372. St. Paul writes of faith as built upon "the foundation of the apostles and prophets, Jesus Christ himself being the chief corner stone" (Ephesians 2:20). See, too, Matthew 21:42: "Jesus saith unto them, Did ye never read in the scriptures, The stone which the builders rejected, the same is become the head of the corner: this is the Lord's doing, and it is marvellous in our eyes?" See, too, Mark 12:10; Luke 20:17; Acts 4:11; and 1 Peter 2:7.

373. Christ, as God's gift to humanity.

374. Trapnel was held at Edward Titon's house (see n353), therefore, from May 25 to June 2, at which point she was moved to Bridewell. "Hannah Trapnell sent in custody from Cornwall according to an

fore them;[375] but they had no time to hear the truth, from such a silly[376] nothing creature; and they sent an order honored with President Lawrence's[377] hand to it, which was brought by two messengers late at night, unto which I have already spoken something of; the hour they came for me, and of their loathness to show me the order, for my removal, but they did show it me before my departure from thence.

And now I am further to tell you, how I fared at my last prison, which was in Bridewell,[378] unto which I was brought at 11 of the clock in the night, the

---

order of Council, and now under charge of the serjeant-at-arms, to be sent to Bridewell, and kept there till further order." On the same day, June 2, a warrant was issued to the Keeper of Bridewell "To receive Hannah Trapnell and keep her till further order." *CSPD*, 7:197, 436.

375. The Council's order for Trapnel's arrest specified that she should appear before them: Major Sanders, commander of "the fort at Plymouth," was told she should be "sent up to Council." *CSPD*, 7:86. A newsbook reported that she "is for some seditious words brought up from *Cornwal* by Order of the Council." *The Weekly Intelligencer* 243 (May 30–June 6, 1654), 280.

376. Insignificant, unlearned, lowly.

377. Henry Lawrence sat as MP for Hertfordshire, was appointed to the Council of State in December 1653, and made its Lord President in January 1654. He was close to and trusted by Cromwell. "A man of integrity and forceful political moderation, respected by intellectual heavyweights such as Milton and Oldenburg, Lawrence was both a serious theologian and a capable administrator who bore much of the weight of day-to-day government business under the protectorate." Timothy Venning, "Lawrence, Henry (1600–1664)," *ODNB*. See, too, *BDBR*, 2:175–76.

378. Situated between Fleet Street and the Thames, Bridewell Palace had been built by Henry VIII but soon abandoned as a royal residence in favor of the new palaces of Whitehall and Hampton Court; it was then briefly a residence for French and Imperial ambassadors; see L. W. Cowie, "Bridewell," *History Today* 23.5 (1973): 350–58 (351). It was established as a House of Correction in 1553 for the reform of "the thriftless poor": vagrants, the idle, the destitute, or the disorderly. The intention was "that those sent there would be deterred from leading a life of wantonness and idleness through corporal punishment and work at hard and disagreeable tasks." Although it was originally intended as a workhouse and reformatory, over time it also came to be used as a prison: "Though primarily intended to reform the vagrant, Bridewell was also a necessary department of the state. It came to be used as a convenient place of confinement for religious prisoners who, by the nature of their offense, could not or would not be reformed.... . Religious offenders were generally subjected to simple confinement, and were not required to work with or live in the company of common criminals." Women inmates were kept separately from men; the women's accommodation was in the center of the western side of the northern quadrangle, and had room for about thirty prisoners. William G. Hinkle, *A History of Bridewell Prison, 1553–1700* (Lewiston, NY: Edwin Mellen Press, 2006), 37, 44, 187, 191, 60, 115. The Quaker Thomas Ellwood wrote a detailed account of his confinement in Bridewell in 1662; Ellwood, *The History of the Life of Thomas Ellwood* (London: J. Sowle, 1714), 161–87. See, too, Joanna Innes, "Prisons for the Poor: English Bridewells, 1550–1800," in *Labour, Law, and Crime: An Historical Perspective*, ed. Francis G. Snyder and Douglas Hay, 42–122 (London: Tavistock Press, 1987). In his history of Bridewell, Edward Geoffrey O'Donoghue includes a colorful if dismissive account of Trapnel's work and her sojourn in Bridewell: O'Donoghue, *Bridewell Hospital, Palace, Prison, Schools* (London: John Lane, 1923), 1:98–101. For a

Matron[379] received me off the messengers. And being brought by the messengers of the Council, she thought I was some exceeding guilty person; and her words declared as much, for she said, I warrant you are one of the plotters:[380] It's my portion, said I, to be dealt so with, as if I were one of them, but I am sure that I am none; then she said, I don't think but I have had in my keeping such as you are before now; then she looked steadfastly in my face: And asked me, whether I did not know one Mistress Cook,[381] I said, I had heard of such a one, but I had no knowledge of her: I warrant you are one of that crew she said; there is a company of ranting[382] sluts of which I have had some in my house, who have spoken a great many good words like you; but they had base actions: This discourse passed from her, and much more that night. And I said to her, It's no hurt to me to be ranked among such vile ones, which she likened me to; but I bless the Lord, said I, that I am no such, but do abhor such evil practices; much was spoke while we waited for my friends'[383] coming, whom I had sent for to take care for the maid that came out of Cornwall with me, the Matron[384] was loath to have sit up till my friends came, for it was almost twelve o' clock at night; but at last my friends came, who said; this our sister is no vagabond, it's well known by many in the city, her civil manner of life from a child, though the Council is pleased to deal thus with her,

---

newsbook account of Trapnel in Bridewell, see *The Faithful Scout* 184 (June 16–June 23, 1654): 1449 (mispaginated).

379. The matron was responsible for the supervision of the female prisoners; she lived on site and was available twenty-four hours a day. Hinkle, *History of Bridewell Prison*, 98.

380. Perhaps a reference to the "Gerard Plot." In May 1654 a plot by the Royalist John Gerard to assassinate Cromwell as he traveled in his coach from Whitehall to Hampton Court had been discovered. Gerard and five co-conspirators were arrested, and in June were tried before the Court of High Justice. All were found guilty, and Gerard and one of the other conspirators, Peter Vowell, were executed on July 10. Stephen Porter, "Gerard, John (1632–1654)," *ODNB*.

381. "Mistress *Cook* she went to *Westminster* Church to shew the Minister a sign, she stript her self stark naked, and went into the Church; so some threw a cloak over her to cover her nakedness, and she was committed to *Bride-well*, and there she was clothed all in white linnen like the Queen of Heaven." Lodowick Muggleton, *A Looking-Glass for George Fox the Quaker, and other Quakers; Wherein They May See Themselves to be Right Devils* (London?: s.n., 1667), 87. Muggleton himself was in Bridewell, with his fellow prophet John Reeve, from September 1653 to April 1654. William Lamont, "Muggleton, Lodowick (1609–1698)," *ODNB*.

382. The Ranters were antinomians, who claimed that no act, if undertaken in the love of Christ, was sinful; consequently, Ranterism was seen "a mystically justified practice of swearing and free love—though many reports of Ranter activity were invented." Nigel Smith, *Perfection Proclaimed: Language and Literature in English Radical Religion, 1640–1660* (Oxford: Clarendon Press, 1989), 8. See, too, Christopher Hill, *The World Turned Upside Down: Radical Ideas During the English Revolution* (Harmondsworth: Penguin, 1975), chapters 9 and 10. "Ranter" became a general pejorative for licentious and disorderly people.

383. The basetext reads "freinds."

384. The basetext reads "matrons."

to send her to such a place, among harlots and thieves; much to this purpose they spoke that night: and they desired to see my lodging, so she had me upstairs into a large room,[385] but it was very close,[386] there being but a little window at one corner of the room, and the common shore[387] running under the window-place, which sink[388] smelt grievously, and there was such a filthy smell with the rats that abode much in that room, so that at the first coming in, these scents entered much into my nice[389] stomach, and having been newly fetched out of the country too, and my friends that lived there hard by, were not able to endure the scent of the room, without stopping their nostrils, but they said nothing to me that night of what offended them, because they would not discourage me: so the bed was made for me, which was a hard flock-bed,[390] and my friends saw it, and were much grieved to see my hard usage, but they saw it was in vain to find fault that night: so they departed, and I was left alone. The Matron would not admit of the maid's being with me, who came from Cornwall with me, but said, she would tend me, I should not have a maid to wait on me there: so my friends departed from me, leaving me in the Lord's protection, and the Matron bid me make haste to bed, for she must fetch away the candle, for she said, she did not trust her prisoners to put it out.

And when she was gone down, as I was making my self unready,[391] I was much assaulted by Satan and my own heart; who said, to be so forward for God, see what thou hast got by it, thy mother little thought this would have befallen thee, when she prayed that God would double his spirit on thee,[392] now thou mayst see what her prayer is come to; I then was tempted to murmur at that prayer, and the tempter bid me speak against that prayer, and the tempter said to me that I

385. Since Bridewell had been built as a palace, not a prison, it did not have cells. Most inmates were held in wards, each of which was subdivided into smaller rooms; "single rooms or suites of rooms … were used for the solitary confinement of important state prisoners." Hinkle, *History of Bridewell Prison*, 116.

386. Airless, stifling.

387. Sewer. The Fleet river, which ran into the Thames along the east side of Bridewell, was increasingly polluted by the residents of Holborn upstream, such that in 1582 John Howes suggested that this was one reason why Henry VIII had occupied it for such a short time, calling the Fleet "a filthy ditch which did so continually annoy the house that the King had no pleasure in it." Cowie, "Bridewell," 351.

388. Sewer, cesspool.

389. Delicate.

390. A mattress stuffed with flock, "a material consisting of the coarse tufts and refuse of wool or cotton, or of cloth torn to pieces by machinery, used for quilting garments, and stuffing beds, cushions, mattresses, etc." (*OED*). Most Bridewell prisoners "slept in boxes with a little rye-straw on the floor to serve as bedding; fresh straw was provided once a month." Hinkle, *History of Bridewell Prison*, 123. The fact that Trapnel had a bed is indicative of her higher status, her friends, and her greater means.

391. Undressing.

392. In *Cry*, 6, Trapnel recounts how her mother, on her death-bed, uttered three times, as her final words, "Lord! Double thy spirit upon my child."

should be a byword and a laughing stock while I lived, and that everyone would point at me as I went up and down the streets, when I came out, they would say, there goes a Bridewell bird,[393] and then many will gather about thee, to mock and deride thee; and as for thy kindred, they will be ashamed of thee, and will not care to hear thy name mentioned in their ears, because of Bridewell reproach, and therefore said Satan wilt thou still retain thy faith concerning Christ as King and Governor in the earth; And I was tempted to let go my confidence as to this, but my Father kept me, and gave me a discovery of my Savior, as he was hung between two thieves, and also brought those scriptures to my thoughts which makes a report of Christ, as he was ranked among transgressors;[394] and how he that knew no sin[395] was dealt with, so as to endure the contradiction of sinners.[396]

And now the Lord talked with me about my Savior's suffering much for me, and therefore do not hearken to Satan said the Lord, but look unto him that suffered the contradiction of sinners for thy sake, then was my heart cheered, and I went unto the unlovely lodging, and the Matron locked me in, or bolted me in, I know not well which, but there I was shut in alone, and yet not alone, for Christ was with me; and when I had lain a while, I grew very sick, for the hard damp bed struck much into my stomach, and the cold sheets; so that all this set me into an ague,[397] and I shook much, and my limbs smarted with cold, and I smelt such a strong scent about the bed, that my heart panted, and lay beating, and my stomach working, and my head aching exceeding much, most part of my being in that lodge this first night; and at break of the day, I threw off the clothes from my stomach, for I was almost spent, being very sick, and in much pain some hours: and I said, dear Father, hast thou brought me to Bridewell to die; the Lord and my Father answered me presently, and said no; thou shalt not die but live, and declare the works of the Lord; and he further told me, that though my heart and my strength failed me, the Lord was the strength of my heart, and my portion for ever,[398] and he would never leave me nor forsake me; the Lord said, he would be my safety from the horn of men[399] and devils; and I then recovered a little strength, and I sang forth allelujahs song of thanksgiving, and I out of that fell in a

393. Either prisoner, or whore, or both; see Gordon Williams, *A Dictionary of Sexual Language and Imagery in Shakespearean and Stuart Literature*, 2 vols. (London: Athlone Press, 1994), 1:150.

394. Luke 22:37.

395. 2 Corinthians 5:21.

396. Hebrews 12:3.

397. A violent fever.

398. Paraphrase of Psalm 73:26.

399. See n259 on her vision of cattle, in which Cromwell, in the figure of a bull, runs at her "with his horn."

little slumber; and my friends came,[400] and waked me presently, against their wills they did it, for they were very tender of me, and it grieved them greatly, when they heard what a night I had; they then spake a while to me, and soon after I rose, and made me ready, and then went to prayer with some of my sisters that came that morning, and after prayer I received much reviving in my outward man,[401] but was not well, yet I walked about the house all that day, and was in the lower room with my friends, who came that day many of them, whom I walk in fellowship with,[402] and many others; for they thought I was put in a place that would daunt me, if the Lord did not much appear to me; and they came to express their tender love and care that they had of my welfare, and they pleaded very much with the Matron, and fetched out the order that brought me there,[403] and procured a copy of it, which cost them sixteen pence,[404] a few words copying out; and this copy of the order was showed to the Matron, how that nothing was laid to my charge, and that I was only to be kept there, till further order; and my friends prayed her to let me have another bed, and other sheets, the which they offered me of theirs, but that she would not grant, but they prevailed at length with her after much persuasion, to lay me on one of her beds, and to let me have other sheets, the which I had the second night, and they procured one to be with me, for they said, I was not fit to be alone, for that I was oft-times weak in body, and required help: so they also obtained, that, some engaging to the Matron, that they would bear her harmless[405] in her giving way to this: many that day so sweetened my chamber with several perfumes, and strewed it with herbs, and flowers, that it much altered the smell, yet it smelled very offensive all the time of my being there, though I every day sometimes was burning many several things in the room for the first week, and several times while I was there, and after this day, I was very sick; yet the Matron urged me with the first day of the week to go hear their minister at Bridewell,[406] but I told her, I was very ill, she said, she thought I dissembled at the first, but afterward she thought it was a judgment from the Lord, my sickness, because I

---

400. Prisoners received visits from family and friends, who delivered food, money, and clothing to them. Hinkle, *History of Bridewell Prison*, 2.

401. Body: "though our outward man perish, yet the inward man is renewed day by day"(2 Corinthians 4:16).

402. With whom I worship; i.e., from the congregation of Allhallows the Great.

403. See nn324, 374, and 375.

404. Sixteen pence was one shilling and fourpence, now equivalent to around £10 (US$17). "Measuring Worth": see n254. Until 1971, English currency had twenty shillings to the pound and twelve pence to the shilling.

405. Maintain her innocence.

406. Bridewell had its own church, originally the palace chapel, "into which every Sabbath (through a bye or backward passage) [the prisoners] were brought from their several lodgings to hear divine service." Hinkle, *History of Bridewell Prison*, 57, quoting John Stow, *Survey of the Cities of London and Westminster, and the Borough of Southwark* (London: W. Innys and J. Richardson et al., 1754–55), 264.

was unwilling she said, to hear their minister: and she said, she saw by my high color, that I was not well, and indeed I was much in a fever that day only, I had the ague a little while in a cold fit, and I lay, not desiring to be spoken to, because it was painful for me to speak, or to turn my self in my bed: and the next day the ague and fever was much upon me, so that my heart even sunk within me, I being so burning and in so close a room, and friends had a great ado to get to see me, the Matron was so strict, and would hardly let them in, but some friends came, who made the plasters[407] to lay to my wrists, and posset drink,[408] to drink the next fit.

But that second day in the night, I was pleading with the Lord, and asked of the Lord a removal of that sickness, and saying, Lord, it's very grievous to lie sick in this place; the Lord answered me, and said, I have taken away thy sickness, thou shalt be sick no more, while thou art here in Bridewell, for I will fill thee with more triumph here, than ever thou hadst in thy life, so the Lord did I am sure; and it was further said to me, thy friends have provided means to take away thy ague, but the Lord hath been thy Physician aforehand; and he further said, he would take me into the mount[409] that day, for the perfect cure of my sickness, and so the Lord did, and I spake by way of prayer and singing from morning till night, and felt no sickness nor pain, nor faintness, not all that day, nor at night when I came to my self, to be capable[410] of a body; for truly, all that day I was wrapped up, so that I could not tell, whether I was in the body or out: and yet I sung with understanding, as to the things the Lord was doing among the sons and daughters of men; and at night, I had sweet rest all night, and in the morning, it being the fourth day the Matron came and told me, that it was a Court day, and I must rise and go to the Court,[411] I have been sick I said, and I prayed her to tell them so; she came the second time, and bid me rise to go before the Court, I told her I was weak, and had lain in my bed three days, only I rose the second day, and could hardly endure up[412] while my bed was made, and I thought it not safe to rise up,

407. Solid medicinal or emollient substance spread on a bandage or dressing and applied to the skin, often becoming adhesive at body temperature (OED).

408. A drink made from hot milk curdled with ale, wine, or other liquor, flavored with sugar, herbs, spices, etc., and often drunk for medicinal purposes (OED).

409. Induce in her an "extraordinary spirit" of singing and praying, a visionary state. This is a reference to the transfiguration of Jesus on a high mountain, when Peter, James, and John experienced visions; see Matthew 17 and Mark 9. See, too, n93.

410. Able to be affected by (OED).

411. Bridewell had its own courtroom, over which presided its governors; "it served not only as a police-court with a whipping room attached, but also a boardroom where the committee met weekly to transact the business of the prison." Hinkle, *History of Bridewell Prison*, 95. "The minutes from the Court of Governors chronicle the commitments and discharges of inmates, but they are combined with the court's other mission to put the poor to work." Hinkle, *History of Bridewell Prison*, 178. See, too, n413.

412. Being up.

being I was in a sweat, and go presently into the air; she came the third time, and said, if you will not rise, I must send the man to call you up, that was an old man, that called up the harlots and thieves, every morning betimes to beat hemp,[413] he was to slap them up to work; and she threatened to send him to fetch me up, but I said, tell the Court I have been sick, and am not fit to rise out of the bed; but many of my friends came who persuaded me to strive to rise and go to the Court, so I did, my sister Ursula Adman,[414] helping me, and other of my sisters, and they led me up to the Court,[415] for I was very weak, so that the Court gave me leave to sit down before them, they were very courteous to me, and they spoke not much to me, only said, it was the custom they had to see all their prisoners at their first coming in; I told them, truly, gentlemen, I would have waited on you sooner, but I have been sick and therefore I stayed so long before I came before you, there was through some words spoken an opportunity given me to tell them of my sickness, the Matron finding fault with so many people coming to see me, I told them, that if I had not been put into such a place, it was probable so many would not have come; but further I said to them, I being put into such a close room, coming out of the fresh air it was very offensive to me, the room and the bed had such a strong scent, and damp, that it set me into an ague, and a fever; one of them said, they did not use to[416] have their beds smell where their prisoners lay, for they were looked well to;[417] I said, but the scent was grievous to me, and the bed was damp having not been laid upon, not lately it may be; I said truly Sir, if you had been there, you might have smelt it, the scent was very grievous to me and others who smelt it as well as I; I am sure, I told them it was a cause of my sickness; for I was well when I came there: Then the Matron said I spoke to wrong her, but I did not: only I would have it known what was the reason of my sickness. I am certain I had no revenge any way towards her, then she told them that I would have men come to me, and that word went to my heart, I knowing my bashful nature, and my civil[418] life was known to many; and I said to them truly, gentlemen, my delight is not nor never was in men's company, but in all people as they are godly, I delight in their

413. The tough stems of the hemp plant were beaten with mallets (or "beetles") to produce fibers for rope-making or for weaving into canvas. This was a standard part of the hard labor required of prisoners in Bridewell; in 1732 William Hogarth produced an engraving of women prisoners beating hemp as a part of his series *A Harlot's Progress* (Plate IV: "The Harlot Beating Hemp in Bridewell"). See Hinkle, *History of Bridewell Prison*, 203–6.

414. Active in Fifth Monarchist circles in the 1660s, Ursula Adman was arrested in June 1669 for holding a Fifth Monarchist meeting in her home in Hillingdon, Middlesex, and for not attending church; she was found not guilty. Capp, *Fifth Monarchy Men*, 239 and *BDBR*, 1:3. See, too, n54.

415. The Bridewell Court Book records this as taking place on Wednesday, June 7. Bridewell Court Minute Book, June 7, 1654, 661; Bcb-09 Series Box Number C04/3 Series BCB.

416. Were not accustomed to.

417. Basetext reads "too."

418. Decent, respectable.

company: And I said, that the officers of the church was to look after the members of the church,[419] they said it was reason they should, and they were not against it: They asked me how many was of them officers, I said about ten I thought: they asked me how many I would have come to see me of my sisters at a time, I said, six, so it was granted;[420] but some would have had their names penned down, that so only those half a dozen might have come; but it was procured otherwayes[421] by friends. And after this the Lord gave health and strength and stomach to my food, and a better digestion than ever I had since I can remember.

The Lord also filled me with joy unspeakable, and full of glory in believing, and many visions and hallelujah songs[422] I had there; and more frequent they were than they ever had been: I was at Bridewell Court,[423] once more only to be gazed on; for little was said to me, only they asked me, why I lay there still; And I said, I waited upon the pleasure of the Council: And they asked me, why my friends did not seek to get my liberty? I said, I know not, they know what they have best to do themselves; one said, but they come every day to see you, do not they tell you what they will do? I said, I do not ask them, I leave it to them; Something more was said, and I came away, and retired to my chamber, wherein I kept most of

---

419. Trapnel explains that she is being visited by the elders of her congregation, whose duty it is to look after their church's members.

420. Bridewell's "Court of Governors" met every two or three weeks to conduct the institution's business, and to take decisions about offenders currently in their keeping. The Bridewell Court Book records Trapnel's appearance before the court on Wednesday, June 7: "This Courte being informed of many disorders by greate numbers of people resorting dayly to Hanna Trapnell in the custody of the Matron of this Hospitall being committed hither by the Councell of state soe that the Matron & other Officers & Servants within this Hospitall cannott perform their services for this Hospitall as they ought to doe And the saide Hanna Trapnell here present alleadged that shee was much troubled herselfe thereby being weake and sickly And desired that the Officers of of [sic] the Church whereof shee was a member being about 10: or 12 might only bee permitted to come vnto her to take care of her and divers of her freinds here present desired that not above five or Sixe might come vnto her att a tyme to bring her necessaryes And promised to give to the Porter of this Hospitall the names of such as shee & they desired might come vnto her that hee might give a note thereof to the Matron that she might knowe their names to permitt them quietly to come vnto her Mr Treasurer Mr Holloway Mr Butler Mr Church & Mr Hooper or any two of them are intreated to attend the Councell of State to acquainte them herewith & to desire the significación of their further pleasure concerning the said Hanna Trapnell & the great number resorting her that the services of this Hospitall may not bee hindered & disturbed as lately they have beene." Bridewell Court Minute Book, June 7, 1654, 661; Bcb-09 Series Box Number C04/3 Series BCB. The men requested to attend the Council of State were all governors of Bridewell.

421. Otherwise.

422. Songs in praise of God.

423. The Bridewell Court Book records Trapnel's continuing presence (but with no further details) on June 28, July 5, and July 26. Bcb-09 Series Box Number C04/3 Series BCB.

those eight weeks, paying five shillings a week for it;[424] It cost forty shillings, and I bless the Lord that I had friends, and some means of my own, else I must have lain in the jail upon straw: The Matron told me so,[425] the first night, and when some said, If I must beat hemp,[426] they would beat for me; She said, I should beat it my self: and for ought she knew I was to beat hemp, but she did not know me; and so spoke as she used to speak to those that deserve harshness; for after she had knowledge of me, she was very loving, and respectful both to me, and to my sister Ursula Adman, who kept me company seven weeks of my being there: She was a friend born for the day of adversity, as Solomon speaks;[427] and indeed she, night and day, showed her tenderness to me, and helped to bear my burden. And therein she fulfilled the law of Christ,[428] and she did this as a freewill offering,[429] love constraining her thereunto, so that it was thereby made easy to her to bear and endure that which few would, especially so freely without reward; yet I am confident the Lord will reward her double for that prison kindness she let out to me[430] without any fainting,[431] or being troubled, that the time was long, or the noises burdensome; there was many difficulties to undergo night and day; but little quiet sleep to be had, there was such scolding[432] among the prisoners near our lodging: and they were brought in often a nights which made a great noise, and the rats run about our bed, and made a great noise, like dogs and cats in the

---

424. Five shillings (25 pence, or 40 US cents) had the purchasing power of about £32 in 2011, but was about as affordable as £1000 (US$1660) is now (see "Measuring Worth" http://www.measuringworth. com/index.php using average earnings calculation and a range of years from the 1650s). It was usual to be expected to pay accommodation and subsistence costs while imprisoned. The matron and other warders were paid a wage, although it was understood that they might also "exact various fees from their prisoners according to the scale sanctioned by the court." The amount paid determined their access to accommodation and privileges. In 1649, the matron "was paid a regular salary of 20 pounds a year with various allowances. However, as in all other prisons, she had to supplement an inadequate salary by the fees that she could extort from prisoners who had money or friends. She was authorized to charge 2d. a night for a separate bed; pauper women slept on the straw. As a matter of fact, however, she was in the habit of charging 4d. for the first night, and 2d. for every succeeding night." Hinkle, *History of Bridewell Prison*, 96, 118, 190.

425. The basetext is punctuated thus: "matron told me, so the ..."

426. See n413.

427. See Proverbs 17:17.

428. A reference to the so-called Golden Rule: "And as ye would that men should do to you, do ye also to them likewise" (Luke 6:31). See, too, Matthew 7:12.

429. A spontaneous gift or voluntary sacrifice; see Exodus 35:29; Leviticus 22:18; Numbers 15:3; and Ezra 3:5, 7:16.

430. Gave vent to, showed me (*OED*). The basetext is punctuated thus: "that prison kindness, she let out to me without any fainting."

431. Losing heart or becoming depressed.

432. Quarrelling, brawling.

room; and this was no pleasant prison sure to such that were brought up tenderly, and never knew any hardship as to the outward man: And truly the Lord made this and many more annoyances, received in Bridewell prison, to be very pleasantly embraced by divine love appearing in the midst of all trials; my God made this smarting scourge (as from man it was so) but God I say made it easy; for his tenderness was much, he made foes become friends, and the harsh to be kind, and overcame the rough and hasty spirits; the Lord is worthy of all praise. I had but a little while affliction in my spirits, which was occasioned by a friend, and that made it grievous, but the Lord made that little storm, to work abundance of good to me many ways: and all things that were afflictive, the Lord quickly broke such fetters. I said not, O when will there be an end of this or the other affliction, but I often said, and desired a purging out of my corruptions, before a removal of sufferings, that so I might come out more holy and more humble, and more self-denying and self-debasing, and abhorring them when I went into prison: That so I might all my days be willing to take up the cross of Christ, and follow him, whithersoever[433] he would have me, either to do or suffer: I shall begin to shorten my relation, lest I should be too tedious to the reader, and leave the visions and opening of Scriptures, that the Lord brought to my soul, while I was in Bridewell for my own benefit, and for others that are his little flock, with whom he hath made an everlasting covenant, well ordered in all things and sure.

At the time near my coming out, some came and desired me to petition,[434] I told them I had not offended man, whereby to seek to him; And they knew that I was in prison by their order; but some said they may forget: I said, that they could not, for many of their friends still told them: The Protector[435] said, he did not know that I was put in Bridewell, till I had been there above a week, that one went and informed him: but it was a strange thing that servants should do such an act without their master, and great Governor's knowledge; surely, if he had not liked of it, he would have reproved them: but said I, now he knows it, and yet he doth not send for me out. Again, some others came and said, they knew they could quickly procure my liberty: I told them, I would not come out upon base terms: said one to me, what are your terms, let us hear them? I said, they shall acknowledge the reproach and odium they have brought upon me, through this their prison: said one, is that your terms? then you may lie long enough; but surely all rational men will say, this was but equity:[436] Then after this, some spoke great matters, what they would do for my liberty: and they went to the Council and spoke to them, and President Lawrence,[437] said, if that I would, or any for me

433. The basetext reads "whether so ever."

434. Petition the Council for her release.

435. Cromwell.

436. Fair and right.

437. See n377.

engage,[438] I might come out; but said Captain Kettlebeator,[439] none can engage, for she herself cannot engage as to a dispensation, that she is so taken up in, that she knows not what is done about her at that time, nor capable[440] of any being with her in the room: And he told him, that he had known me many years: And my whole deportment of life had been, and was very civil and religious; he spake more to that purpose: And the President said, so he had understood; some more speech they had, and they came to tell me that, nay[441] what they had spoke in my behalf: I said, I will never engage to that which lies not in me to perform, for what the Lord utters in me, I must speak: so one said, he would go again to the Council, I told him I desired no favor of them but justice and equity: and if he could procure my coming before them to hear what they have against me, that's all I desire of you I said; and what he said or did, it was of his own offering: so he said, he would not leave them so, but he would go again and try what they would do; but I heard no more concerning him, he was forgetful it may be, like his master: After this some others undertook this business, and came to hear what I would say to it. And one asked me upon what account I suffered imprisonment, whether it was for Christ, and if so then I had a great deal of comfort in my sufferings; for he said, he had found it so, having been imprisoned for the testimony of Jesus; I told him the Council never sent for me, to tell me upon what account they imprison me here for; and I said, the recognizances[442] are taken off concerning Cornwall business, so that I was merely upon the pleasure and wills of the Council, and of Lord Lawrence; for indeed I will call him my Bridewell Lord, for that his hand was in chief to the order: but I told them, I was sure I suffered for Christ. And I enjoyed his presence abundantly; and I gave them some account of my sufferings, and of the Lord's comforts therein, then after some further discourse, they asked me whether, I would be willing to go out, if an order should come for my liberty? I told them, I would never engage:[443] they said, that was not desired; I said, yes but it was, for my Lord Lawrence told some if I would engage, I might come out: then they said, but if the order come, and give you liberty freely, will you accept of it? I

438. To pledge oneself; to enter into a covenant or undertaking (*OED*); here, she is being asked to pledge that she will desist from her prophetic trances.

439. In February 1642 (1643 by the modern calendar: see "Editorial Principles and Practices," 38–39), "Henry Kettlebeater of Ratcliffe highway Cutler" had married "Margaret Jones of Mileend," in St. Dunstan's, Stepney: see Thomas Colyer-Fergusson, ed., *The Marriage Registers of St. Dunstan's, Stepney, in the County of Middlesex, 1640–1696* (Canterbury: Cross and Jackman, 1899), 2:33. Trapnel grew up in Poplar, a hamlet in the parish of St. Dunstan's, Stepney, so it is conceivable that this was Captain Kettlebeator, since she says he had known her "many years."

440. Able to perceive.

441. The sense is that they had been refused what they had asked for. "To have nay" is to receive a refusal (*OED*).

442. See n254.

443. See n438.

was silent, only my sister said, if we can have liberty, we will choose it rather than bonds?[444] so after a little while these departed.

And the next week after, upon the sixth day of the week, I rose early in the morning and walked about my chamber, putting up[445] requests to the Lord secretly for purging grace, that I might go out of prison much more purified from the dross of corruptions, than when I went into prison fire; that so others might see it had been a purifying furnace[446] to me: And after I had been up some hours, I said to my sister that abode with me, I think said I to her, everyone that I hear coming to the door, comes from the Council with an order for my liberty; come let us pray before it comes, and ask counsel of God concerning it, and the Lord indeed counseled me, and took me into the mount of heavenly rapture that day, so that my friends were fain to take me off my knees and lay me upon my bed, where I lay praying and singing more than ever I did in my life unto many public concernments, the which I am sure will be accomplished in due time: and I often desired that they in high places had some of the dainties with me at Bridewell; and that day the order[447] was brought, and I lay silent when they came with it; but I was talking with the Lord who showed me many things, which I know shall come to pass, and the Lord told me that my freedom out of that place was near, the which I saw three weeks before, and sang it forth, so I did now; one of them tarried that brought the order, I was told so afterwards; but I knew not that any was by me, when I thus lay, either silent or speaking. That day I spake to some that said, he would choose imprisonment for gain, he spoke of an outward gain, but if he got by his imprisonment formerly; I am sure I cannot say, nor those that are imprisoned upon this account for the Fifth Monarchy, cannot say so: we would not gain for our outward man, if we might, by robbing others, to enrich ourselves; I can say, I have refused what hath been tendered me freely: I took nothing save for my necessity, unto which I had enough supply, had not the rulers put me to such charges through their imprisonment, and bringing me from place to place, and making me pay for it. So that I have been robbed, but I have robbed none: I had rather go in a canvas[448] coat, or any mean garb, than so do; and eat any mean

---

444. The basetext is punctuated here with a question mark. In early modern usage, the question mark was also used, as here, as an exclamation mark; see Percy Simpson, *Shakespearean Punctuation* (Oxford: Clarendon Press, 1911), 85–86.

445. Offering a prayer, especially a petition for help, to God (*OED*).

446. Psalm 12:6.

447. The order for her release from Bridewell was made by the Council of State on Wednesday, July 26. *CSPD*, 7:438.

448. A strong or coarse unbleached cloth made of hemp or flax (*OED*).

kind of food, than to fare[449] dainty and go in brave[450] robes with that cost, which is others' right inheritance.

I shall further relate in the close of this relation, how the next day I came forth, for I came not into a capable frame, to speak to anybody, till late at night, on the sixth day; and when I spoke that night, my friends said, do you know you are set at liberty? you sang as if you had known; I said, the Lord hath given it me, I will thank him for it; so you told us today in your singing, said my friends: And the next morning the keeper of Bridewell came, and said, I was free by order from the Council, and I might go out when I pleased: I told him they should fetch me out that put me in; had they put me among thieves and whores, and now did they send for me out without acknowledging the reproach they had brought upon me? He said, the same order with the same hands that puts you in fetches you out: I desired to see my order, so I should he said, if I would pay sixteen pence[451] for a copy of it: so I sent for it, and read it. And seeing I might go out upon no dishonorable terms, and the Lord having instructed me beforehand, he being my guide and Counselor, in my imprisonment, and in my coming out. And I said to a friend, go tell your masters, though they will not see me they shall be sure to hear from me, and so they have: for I sent letters to them, that so they might not say, they had not heard of the injustice acted under their dominion: Now I have given a declaration, through the assistance of the Lord, and not to set up my self and throw down others; but to throw down lies, and exalt truth; the Lord would not have cities nor countries, nor Whitehall Council, a refuge for lies: For his people are recorded in the 63rd of Isaiah verse 8 to be children that will not lie, so he became their Savior: I desire that truth may be written in buff[452] and sent through Europe; I would have the whole world taste the sweetness of truth, that all people may know, and see, and consider, and understand together, the hand of the Lord, and what he is doing, and will do for his, that trust in him; And sure wisdom is justified of her children:[453] Come, O you children of wisdom, observe that you may understand, and seek after Christ's reign, and say with me,[454] *Come Lord Jesus come quickly, according to thy saying, Even so come Lord Jesus;*[455] Let those that wait on the Lord's coming say, *Amen, even so be it.*

---

449. "fair" in basetext. To behave, act, or conduct oneself; or to eat (*OED*).

450. Fine.

451. See n404.

452. That is, be naked, unrefined: see "buff" (*OED* a. 2).

453. Matthew 11:19 and Luke 7:35.

454. Comma replaces basetext's period.

455. Revelation 22:20.

A Defiance to all reproachful, scandalous, base, horrid, defaming speeches, which have been vented by Rulers, Clergy, and their Auditors, and published in scurrilous Pamphlets[456] up and down in Cities and Countries, against Anna Trapnel, late prisoner in Bridewell for the Testimony of Jesus the Lord.

I am forced out of my close retired spirit, by rulers and clergy, who have brought me upon the world's stage of reports, and rumors, making me the world's wonder, and gazing stock; and as some have said, they thought I had been a monster, or some ill-shaped creature,[457] before they came and saw, who then said, they must change their thoughts, for I was a woman like others, that were modest and civil, and many commending words they uttered; which (because it's of my own particular) I forbear to mention; and what I do mention is to advance free grace[458] showed me, in making gainsayers to receive a check in their own consciences, and to be ashamed that they took up reports: Truly rulers and clergy, I will bid defiance to all the words and actions which have undeservedly and unjustly been by you or others vented against, and inflicted upon me; I speak this (the Lord my God knows) not vauntingly,[459] but humbly: For I am conscious to my self, that I have abundance of infirmities, and am sure the worst of all the Lord's flock,[460] indeed a sorry worthless creature; and as from the Lord I deserve nothing save hell

---

456. While references to Trapnel's prophecies and travels survive in some newsbooks of the day (see, for example, nn122, 250, and 375), the "scurrilous pamphlets" she refers to here do not; ephemeral and topical, they are likely to have formed part of the body of contemporary pamphlets and broadsheets that were not preserved.

457. It was commonly believed that behaviors that were perceived to be disorderly or unnatural would be matched by, and apparent in, a deformed body. Such phenomena might then, in turn, be read as indicative of religious, political, or social disruption. On the popular representation and interpretation of monsters, see Julie Crawford, *Marvelous Protestantism: Monstrous Births in Post-Reformation England* (Baltimore: Johns Hopkins University Press, 2005).

458. See nn65, 146, and 186.

459. Boastfully, vaingloriously.

460. It was conventional among Puritans to claim oneself as the worst of sinners; the title of John Bunyan's spiritual autobiography, *Grace Abounding to the Chief of Sinners* (1666), is only the best known instance. The biblical source is 1 Timothy 1:15: "This is a faithful saying, and worthy of all acceptation, that Christ Jesus came into the world to save sinners; of whom I am chief."

and eternal destruction,[461] yet he loves me, and hath loved me with an everlasting love; and will you, oh men, condemn and pass your sentences upon me?

First, for a witch; Pray, wherein can you make this appear? Oh you inhabitants of Truro,[462] and clergy there or in any other place, or at Court; Can any ruler there make good their words? I am sure, I may defy this their speech, and will.

Further, they call me impostor; Pray which of the ways and ordinances or statutes of the Lord have I perverted through deceit? Canst thou, oh man, or woman, lay anything of this nature to my charge? Do then; but through grace you cannot: Therefore I can defy this saying also.

Again, you call me vagabond;[463] but how will you make that good? All the art, skill, or policy that any politician hath among you, cannot make this saying true, not in the least: I lived with my mother till she died, which was about twenty years, then I kept house with the means my mother left me, and paid taxes towards maintaining of the army then in the field;[464] and this I did not grudgingly, but freely and willingly; I sold my plate and rings, and gave the money to the public use; you did not call me vagabond then; I am compelled, as I told you, to bring my private Spirit forth to the view of the world, and to declare my free-will-offering, yet not boastingly, but so as that the world may judge whether this term of vagabond will hold good concerning me; the sum of money my mother left me, I freely gave for the army's use, and I wrought many nights hard to get money, the which I cheerfully bestowed, not on my own back[465] nor belly cheer,[466] but fared hard,[467] that so I might minister towards the relief of the nation; and if that little

461. A reference to the Calvinist doctrine of salvation as the unmerited gift of God, rather than something earned, deserved, or affected by the actions of fallen humanity.

462. The type is indistinct in the basetext; however, it appears to read "Fruroir." It seems likely that this was intended to read "Truro," since this was where the witch-trying woman was called on to testify in court; see 83.

463. Itinerant sectaries, and in particular Quakers, were frequently accused of being vagabonds, and hence vulnerable to arrest and banishment from the place in question, as the civic authorities were concerned that they might become an expense by drawing on parish relief. This seems to have been one of the charges faced by Trapnel in the court in Truro; see n250.

464. Parliament struggled to raise revenue throughout the Civil War and Commonwealth period; it did so principally through the introduction of two new taxes: an assessment tax (a tax on property owners) and excise duty (a tax on certain commodities, such as ale, beer, and spirits, certain textiles, meat, and salt). Excise duty, introduced in 1643 for the first time, was very unpopular and led to a number of riots in England and Wales in the 1640s. The Barebone's Parliament had considered a proposal to end excise duty, but it was too important a source of revenue by then for this to be agreed. On the history of the excise, see William J. Ashworth, *Customs and Excise: Trade, Production, and Consumption in England, 1640–1845* (Oxford: Oxford University Press, 2003), 94–116.

465. Not on clothing.

466. Gluttony, luxurious eating.

467. Ate poorly (*OED*).

means which I have left had been in money, I could not have kept it from you; Oh army, and rulers, that then would not have defamed me; I pray why are you so unchristian-like in your carriages to me now? you have taxes from me still; and am I a vagabond for this? Ask your lawyers, will they not say you were much to blame herein? Let all that knew me, speak, when they saw or knew me a vagabond: After the time was over of my keeping house, I was desired by Mrs. Spenser,[468] a minister's widow, to abide with her, and her daughters, who were sober, holy, humble walkers with God, and not of a frothy,[469] wanton, light, giddy[470] carriage and deportment,[471] as many professors in those days appeared in; I lived among these, taking up my abode with Mrs. Harlow, daughter to the aforementioned Mrs. Spenser,[472] who lived near her mother in the Minories;[473] She, her maid, and I lived together a while, and they are my witnesses, whether I was then idle, and others beside them can witness for me; I kept close to the Word, and fasting, and prayer, and so observing times for civil employment; was I a vagabond then? Then I was desired by Mrs. Wythe[474] my kinswoman, a merchant's wife in Fenchurch Street, to live with her, with whom I lived six years; could I be a vagabond there? They shall be my judges in this, I lived with them in city and country[475] till rulers were displeased at a dispensation above their understanding, and therefore gave

468. Untraced.

469. Vain, trifling.

470. Frivolous, flighty.

471. Behavior and conduct.

472. Untraced. There was, however, a Dorothy Harlow living in the nearby parish of St. Mary Staining or St. Olave, Silver Street in 1662; see http://www.british-history.ac.uk/report.aspx?compid=118426& strquery=Dorothy Harlow.

473. Street running from Aldgate High Street to Tower Hill in London. The street took its name from "an abbey of nuns of the order of St. Clare," the *Sorores Minores*, or Little Sisters, established in this location in 1293. Weinreb and Hibbert, *The London Encyclopædia*, 521.

474. Two possibilities have been identified for Mrs. Wythe: 1) Martha Smith, who married Thomas Wythe on February 3, 1630, at St. Olave, Hart Street, which is very close to Fenchurch Street; see W. Bruce Bannerman, ed., *The Registers of St. Olave, Hart Street, London.* Publications of the Harleian Society. (London: s.n., 1916), 265; or 2) the wife of the John Wythe, who had been living in the parish of St. Benet Fink in 1638 (http://www.british-history.ac.uk/report.aspx?compid=31997&strquery=wy the). St. Benet Fink was less than half a mile from Fenchurch Street, which, also in the City of London, runs between Aldgate and Gracechurch Street. In 1733, Seymour's revision of Stow's *Survey* noted Fenchurch Street as "a Street of good Account, being large, well built, and inhabited by Merchants, and others." John Stow, *A Survey of the Cities of London and Westminster, Borough of Southwark, and Parts Adjacent* (London: J. Read, 1733–35), 1.430. Trapnel's London addresses, in the Minories, Mark Lane (where she was living in 1654), and Fenchurch Street, are all within a half mile of each other.

475. In *Cry*, 10, Trapnel notes that she lived with her kinsman, Mr. Wythe, in Hackney. Hackney was still a small rural village at this time, a recreation ground for Londoners wanting to get out of the city, and a place where wealthy Londoners were building houses: see introduction, 15. Mr. Wythe seems to have been a successful merchant, therefore, with houses in both the city and countryside.

out threatening speeches, that my relation and friend where I lived was afraid to receive me for losing his place: And now I have related my places of abode from my childhood, until the 11th month 1653,[476] all which time I suppose no rational man will say I was a vagabond: And as for the time since, as soon as I was rejected of[477] my kinsman for the rulers' sake, many friends would have let me into their houses, which are very grave, godly, conscientious, wise, sober, persons, that are unwilling to entertain vagabonds; but to this day I have a settled habitation,[478] and pay assessments,[479] therefore stand convinced from this day, and hereafter all you rulers, clergy, and people in all places and countries, that I Anna Trapnel am no vagabond, nor runagate[480] person, though I have and may sometimes live in the city, and sometimes in the country, as yourselves do, and why should I be accounted a vagabond more than you?

Let me yet further, bid defiance to those that have called me whore, which language hath proceeded from Court, I hear so; and will any that have said so, stand to their words without blushing? Truly, I would try them, were there any law up, save the wills of men; you may peradventure say, this savors of revenge; I answer, It doth not, for Solomon saith, *The name of the righteous is as a precious ointment,*[481] and therefore dead flies are to be cast out, which would putrefy it,[482] and it's to be carefully preserved because costly and precious for use, so that if it be putrefied it's not of use; so Christ's flock are for his use, and he keepeth them, that nothing can putrefy them in that new-born state they are in; yet as to that usefulness for the benefit of Saints and sinners, herein they may be hindered, through the dead flies' stinking scent, brought on their names, that all people may have no knowledge of: And as to this charge, being I do not suffer as an evil-doer, I will triumph and give glory to the Lord my God, who hath kept me from open profaneness, and from secret sins,[483] and in a great measure hath freed me from my iniquity, which is the sin of my disposition, which doth not run out, nor incline to lustfulness, neither of the flesh nor eye, nor pride of life; but my iniquity

---

476. That is, January 1654 (by the modern calendar: see "Editorial Principles and Practices," 38–39), when she spoke her Whitehall prophecies.

477. By.

478. In *Cry,* 79, 10, Trapnel writes that, following her Whitehall prophecies in January 1654, she walked first to Hackney and then to Mark Lane. She had been living at "Widow Smith's, glazier" in Mark Lane at the end of 1652.

479. Taxes based on the assessment of the value of one's property or income.

480. Wanderer, vagabond.

481. An allusion to Song of Solomon 1:3: "Because of the savour of thy good ointments thy name is as ointment poured forth, therefore do the virgins love thee."

482. Ecclesiastes 10:1: "Dead flies cause the ointment of the apothecary to send forth a stinking savour: so doth a little folly him that is in reputation for wisdom and honour."

483. Psalm 90:8: "Thou hast set our iniquities before thee, our secret sins in the light of thy countenance."

is passion, apt to be hasty, it's more within than appears without; this I speak to my shame, and the advancement of free grace not to[484] prompt any, or my self to boast of sinful infirmities, though God heals my backslidings, and loves me freely; I will not sin that grace may abound,[485] but I will confess my sins to him who is just and faithful to forgive, and he that covers his sin cannot prosper; it's written, he that saith he hath no sin is a liar;[486] yet I can say, they are liars that have thus reported of me, as I have penned down, and having this boldness which is not of a carnal form, I may look my enemies in the face with cheerfulness,[487] and yet with sobriety, and so I can through mercy and divine goodness, and oh that all my adversaries would take the pains, as David did to find out their iniquity,[488] which dogs them at the heels, so that they may cry against it, and be humbled before the Lord: I would fain be comfortable to[489] the death and resurrection of Christ, though I fall short, indeed I do, I am not unwilling to confess it; yet oh, yet I can with a face unveiled contend with my adversaries, whether they be men or devils, and bid defiance to them for Christ's sake: As for me, truly I am not worth mentioning, nor regarding by any, none can sure think viler of me than I think of my self: yet I bless the Lord, and my Father, as unto men's reports I am not guilty, nor a transgressor in their sense, for the which I praise Jehovah, and still I will advance him who is my all in all.[490]

I have a further word with the Cornwall jurors, who say they are for the Lord Protector of the Commonwealth of England, Scotland, and Ireland, etc. and upon their oaths present Anna Trapnel to be a dangerous seditious person, not only, say they, imagining, but devising and maliciously intending the peace, tranquility and felicity of the good people of this Commonwealth of England to disturb, but, say they, to move, stir up, and raise discord, rebellion and insurrection among the good people of England, as aforesaid; this they affirmed upon oath, in their indictment; all which I bid defiance to as false; and likewise those sayings of theirs, which were, that I would cause authorities' just and righteous actions to be brought into contempt, disgrace, and hated with the good people, calling me one of a devilish mind, and wicked imaginations; and saying, I uttered with a loud voice malicious, scandalous, horrible, and seditious words in the hearing of

---

484. The basetext reads "so "; emended to "to."

485. See Romans 6:1: "What shall we say then? Shall we continue in sin, that grace may abound?"

486. 1 John 1:8: "If we say that we have no sin, we deceive ourselves, and the truth is not in us."

487. See nn244 and 245.

488. 2 Samuel 24:10: "And David's heart smote him after that he had numbered the people. And David said unto the Lord, I have sinned greatly in that I have done: and now, I beseech thee, O Lord, take away the iniquity of thy servant; for I have done very foolishly."

489. In conformity with.

490. See 1 Corinthians 15:28: "And when all things shall be subdued unto him, then shall the Son also himself be subject unto him that put all things under him, that God may be all in all."

diverse people: Can you tell what you say? Oh jurors, when you say you are for the Lord Protector, I am sure you do not mean the great Lord Protector[491] of heaven and earth, sea, and dry land, who hath indeed all dominions belonging unto him: And as for him you call your Protector, you do not give him that tithe in love[492] to him more than to another, nor so much as to old King Charles, and to his son,[493] who is in your hearts, you love a king dearly, Oh that you did love King Jesus, he would never fail you, he would teach you to make your indictments truer, and not upon persons undeserving, he would teach you not to use his children as witches, and vagabonds when they come into your parts: I pity you, oh you envious jurors, you have not injured me, nor indicted me, but yourselves, and though I could say, when before you examined, *Not guilty*, I could say so with a clear conscience, yet I am sure you cannot say so, at the Lord's judgment seat, when he shall read the Bill of Indictment against you, can you say to him, you are not of a devilish mind, nor of a wicked imagination, nor seditious, not maliciously bent against the great Lord Protector and his subjects, against whom you imagine, devise, stir up, and raise discord, rebellion and insurrection against the great Lord Protector, and his good people aforesaid, endeavoring to bring his righteous and just actions into contempt, disgrace, and hatred amongst all sorts of people, good and bad;[494] And be it known unto you, that the Jehovah Protector is my King, Priest, and Prophet, whose Kingly power I obey, and all government consonant to it, and whose Priesthood, and also deny that which shall offend it, and make it of no effect; and I love to listen to that great Prophet, who teaches like him; and though I say thus, yet I love the Gospel found in and through the Lord's trumpeters; I do not despise true prophecy from any, I love to read what the Lord spake through a Balaam, who was a sorcerer yet spoke excellently of Christ,[495] that blessed star of Jacob, and redeemer of Israel; This I speak, to give you to understand my delight, and love to all the Lord's ordinances and speakings; so that I must take leave to mention another defiance to your letter you sent against me to London, wherein you reported that I denied ordinances, which hundreds of people can and will witness to the contrary; Thus you may see your folly, Oh, you Cornwall clergy, and Justices; and indeed I should be glad, if you saw your evil, and repented, and humbled your

---

491. I.e., God.

492. See Luke 11:42: "But woe unto you, Pharisees! for ye tithe mint and rue and all manner of herbs, and pass over judgment and the love of God: these ought ye to have done, and not to leave the other undone."

493. A reference to Charles I, executed in 1649, and his son, the future Charles II, currently in exile in France.

494. Comma in basetext.

495. Balaam was a prophet who was asked by Balak, king of Moab, to curse Israel. Balaam, however, declares he can only speak the word of God, and three times utters a prophecy blessing Israel. See Numbers 22–24.

souls before the Lord, against whom you have sinned: what you have done to me is small, when compared with your trespass against the living God, whose appearing is as devouring fire, and everlasting burnings;[496] who can dwell with God and stand before him, when he thus appears? The prophet Isaiah tells you, 33.15. *He that walketh righteously, and speaketh uprightly, he that despiseth the gain of oppressions, that shaketh his hands from holding of bribes, that stoppeth his ears from hearing of blood, and shutteth his eyes from seeing evil, they shall dwell on high;*[497] their place of defense shall be not only a Rock, but munitions of rocks,[498] like the strength of many rocks, that are many times doubled, and trebled one within another, and one a top of another, which maketh it an high and a strong place that none can enter, or reach the upright; the upright shall see him in his glory, which is a sight worth the making after, and preparing for: Who will withhold no good thing from those that love his appearing, he will give them salvation for walls and bulwarks,[499] as it is written, and he taketh them as he did Moses, when he showed him Canaan afar off,[500] so the Lord will take all his faithful ones, and show them the lovely land, wherein no dragon can cast his floods;[501] nor wolf can catch the sheep into their prison-paws, nor lion can cast into their Bridewell-den; there shall be no Fox[502] to inform, and lay hold with their soldiers, the children and Saints of the most high God; this land is a safe place, where no ravenous beast shall molest the Saints; and the beauty of King Jesus shall take so with them, that they shall forget all their hard measure, that they have had from the sons and daughters of men. And then who shall be so deep-speeched,[503] as Saints now who are counted novices, and shallow fellows, and frantic[504] handmaids, not fit to stand to speak to the learned wise rabbis[505] of these times, which call such that speak plainly frantic, and under the administration of evil angels and seditious whimsical-headed ones; but the time is coming which will discover the King in his

---

496. Isaiah 33:14: "The sinners in Zion are afraid; fearfulness hath surprised the hypocrites. Who among us shall dwell with the devouring fire? who among us shall dwell with everlasting burnings?"

497. Isaiah 33:15–16.

498. Isaiah 33:16.

499. Isaiah 26:1.

500. In Deuteronomy 34:1–5, the Lord shows Moses the promised land; he dies, however, without setting foot in it.

501. Revelation 12:16: "And the earth helped the woman, and the earth opened her mouth, and swallowed up the flood which the dragon cast out of his mouth."

502. A reference to Captain Fox, Deputy-Governor of Pendennis Castle, in Cornwall, who arrested Trapnel; see n291.

503. A reference to Isaiah 33:19: "Thou shalt not see a fierce people, a people of a deeper speech than thou canst perceive; of a stammering tongue, that thou canst not understand."

504. Insane.

505. Priests (used derogatorily).

beauty[506] to his, that are so slighted, and then they shall be the only scribes who are the Lord's chosen Baruchs,[507] he will employ them to write his rolls;[508] and truly he now makes use of them, to meditate terror, and to count the towers;[509] they are not deceived in their accounts, concerning the beast and the false prophets, and those that adhere to them, which shall feel the terror of the Lord; and they, their scribes, receivers, and towers shall fall before him whose name is a strong tower, into whom the righteous run and are safe,[510] and therefore let not any wonder at those that pleadeth praise for the name of King Jesus, which is so blasphemed, and set at naught by self-seekers; the name of the Lord is worth suffering for, and they that have suffered for it, and do still suffer for it may joy in the Lord as their portion (Lamentations 3:24, 25, 26[511]), which the church rejoiced in, though in great afflictions, that God was her portion, and she would hope in him, and saith, *The Lord is good to those that wait for him, and to the soul that seeketh him, it's good, saith she, to hope, and quietly wait for the salvation of the Lord;*[512] they that hope aright to see the King in his beauty, they quietly wait, they wait without murmuring: But not without prayer, and earnestly contending[513] for the faith of Christ, touching any of his concernments;[514] not a passionate contending is approved, but a zealous contending is allowed by the Lord, recorded by the apostle;[515] therefore hold fast your zeal for God, little remnant,[516] who have given up your hearts and hands, and foreheads to his mark and stamp,[517] abhorring that

---

506. Isaiah 33:17: "Thine eyes shall see the king in his beauty: they shall behold the land that is very far off."

507. Baruch was a loyal scribe to Jeremiah, who read the prophet's warnings to the people when Jeremiah was in hiding: see Jeremiah 36.

508. Papers, books.

509. Isaiah 33:18: "Thine heart shall meditate terror. Where is the scribe? where is the receiver? where is he that counted the towers?"

510. Proverbs 18:10: "The name of the Lord is a strong tower: the righteous runneth into it, and is safe."

511. See n7.

512. Lamentations 3:25–26.

513. A reference to Jude 1:3: "Beloved, when I gave all diligence to write unto you of the common salvation, it was needful for me to write unto you, and exhort you that ye should earnestly contend for the faith which was once delivered unto the saints."

514. Concerns, matters in which one takes an interest.

515. A reference to Galatians 4:18: "But it is good to be zealously affected always in a good thing, and not only when I am present with you."

516. A small number (originally of Jews) who survive persecution and in whom future hope is vested. See Isaiah 10:20–23.

517. Revelation 13:16–17, 14:1, and 20:4.

of the beast, the Lord would have you let go passion, but love zeal,[518] and hold it fast, whatever men say of it, or do against you for it, yet let the zeal of the Lord[519] eat you up, David saith, *The zeal of thy house hath eaten me up:*[520] Where are such now? There are many that their pride and lustfulness, and vainglory hath eaten them up, and swallowed what they seemed to hold forth, for others' benefit, even for those that are the Lord's household, but now self hath devoured all, and the Lord's heritage must wait for their right, till their King Jesus comes, whose right all power and dominion is, and will take his great power and reign; who then shall gainsay him? Then there shall be no mockers, nor deriders to scoff at the Fifth Monarchy, where then shall be the table-scoffers,[521] and the pulpit-deriders, and such that make a sport and jeer at those that are for Christ's reign, and cry, Raze them; raze, even to the ground, their persons, estates, and whatever is theirs; but the Lord laughs such enemies to scorn, and hath them in derision, and will require and recover all from them that have defrauded; a fierce people shall not overcome the Lord's anointed, fierce looks, nor deep speech[522] gathered up and fetched from both Cambridge and Oxford Universities[523] shall not affright the Lord's flock, though they stammer, they shall be understood, no dark saying shall be concealed from the faithful, they shall understand fierce looks, and deep subtle speeches, though they be brought forth with a Latin tongue, and in Greek expressions, yet the wise-observing-spirited ones shall understand the cunning works of the politic sophister;[524] glorious things spoken of the City of God:[525] And the Lord encourageth the afflicted to hope and take confidence in him, who will bring

---

518. Passionate eagerness; a word strongly (and disparagingly) associated with Puritans, as with Ben Jonson's character Zeal-of-the-Land Busy, in *Bartholomew Fair* (1614).

519. The phrase is used in 2 Kings 19:31; Isaiah 9:7; and Isaiah 37:32.

520. Psalm 69:9.

521. Obscure; perhaps a variation on "table-gospeller": "a person who treats the gospel as merely a subject for table talk; one whose religion is mere talk" (*OED*).

522. See n503.

523. The only two English universities at the time, and the objects of sectarian opposition. Fifth Monarchists "stressed that ministers were made by God, not by education, and denied that university-trained men were true ministers unless also called by a congregation." Capp, *Fifth Monarchy Men*, 188. This was largely because the universities' main function was to train the "national clergy"—the ministers of the Church of England—to whose privileges and doctrines the sects were opposed. Both universities and clergy were seen as cornerstones of the system that they were striving to change; and both were funded, directly or indirectly, by tithes—a much-resented tax and one of the main targets of all the radical sects, but which were, in the end, never abolished. The full title of *The Cry of a Stone* had claimed that Trapnel's Whitehall prophecies related to "the Governors, Army, Churches, Ministry, Universities, and the whole Nation"; in the same text, 54, she berates the clergy for speaking "their university language, their headpiece language, their own sense."

524. One who uses specious or fallacious arguments.

525. Psalm 87:3.

judgment unto victory; faithful is he that hath promised, who will do it; then Saints may look upon Sion[526] as the city of their solemnities, their eyes shall see Jerusalem a quiet habitation, a tabernacle[527] that shall not be taken down, not one of the stakes thereof shall ever be removed, neither shall any of the cords thereof be broken, but there the glorious Lord will be unto us, a place of broad rivers, and streams wherein shall go no galley with oars, neither shall gallant ship pass thereby: For the Lord is our Judge; the Lord is our Law-giver, the Lord is our King, he will save us, thy tackling are loosed, they could not well strengthen their mast, they could not spread the sail, then is the prey of a great spoil divided, the lame take the prey, and the inhabitants shall not say I am sick: the people that dwell therein shall be forgiven their iniquity, this time is coming wherein the spoiler shall be spoiled,[528] in the restoration of the kingdom to Israel, then shall quietness and peace that passeth all understanding[529] be in their habitation, and round about them, no dealing of men shall make them afraid, their tabernacle no politician shall take down, if any Assyrian[530] or others shall stretch out their tongue or hand against the Lord's prophets, and servants, they shall wither and shrink up with leprosy: For they that are true to the Lord, he will be a tabernacle unto them for a shadow in the day time from the heat, and for a place of refuge, and for a covert from storm, and from rain, Isaiah 4:6. The tabernacle spoken of in Leviticus,[531] and in other places typed[532] out Christ to come excellently, as the great refuge and holy center for his people, who bring their sacrifices to him, they shall have admittance to enter in, being his priests, they shall not stand at the door of the tabernacle, but have liberty to come into this tabernacle, and find acceptance, and welcome, what need they then matter whether men bid them welcome to their thrones and houses or no, their welcome oftentimes is but a compliment; for the most part not real, but the Lord's welcome and invitation is always real: Oh what strong stakes and cords hath this tabernacle,[533] which is a stability of those

526. A close paraphrase of Isaiah 33:20–24. Sion, or Zion, is a synonym for Jerusalem.

527. In the Old Testament, the tabernacle contained the Ark of the Covenant and other holy objects. It served as the portable sanctuary of the Israelites while they were in exile.

528. Isaiah 33:1.

529. Philippians 4:7.

530. In Old Testament times, Assyria was a powerful neighboring nation and one of Israel's oppressors. Isaiah prophesies God's vengeance against the Assyrians repeatedly.

531. The account of the construction of the tabernacle had concluded the previous book, Exodus. Leviticus sets out the place of the tabernacle in rituals of worship and holiness.

532. The Old Testament was frequently read as offering prophecies, analogues, or "types" of the later Christ; these included (among many others) Adam, Isaac, and David. The tabernacle is, similarly, read as a "type" of Christ, as a place of sanctuary in which to encounter God. See n17.

533. Isaiah 33:20: "Look upon Zion, the city of our solemnities: thine eyes shall see Jerusalem a quiet habitation, a tabernacle that shall not be taken down; not one which of the stakes thereof shall ever be

glorious times of Zion, none of her strength or fortifications shall be broken or taken down by Belial[534] or any of his crew: for their cords are not like those green withs,[535] which the Philistines brought to Dalilah to bind Sampson, Judges 16th chapter.[536] For the Lord hath made them abhor their Dalilah sins, and cut off such right hands, and pluck out such right eyes,[537] those sins that were so near and delightful to them, they say, get you hence, they hate folly, and vain thoughts, and say with David in the 119th Psalm, *O how I love thy Law;*[538] unto such will the glorious Lord be a place of broad rivers;[539] not a narrow channel, nor a marshy ditch, where the flags and rushes cover the water springs, nor a narrow winding creek, where boats cannot pass along, neither is it shallow, but deep and broad, a place of broad rivers and streams, it's indeed an ocean, it comprehends all rivers, and streams, and this may be said of it, Oh, the height and depth, length and breadth; these are rivers that the waters rise up to the ankles, yea to the knees, and so to the loins, and at length they become a flowing high spring, that runs over banks and fills the meadows, and Ezekiel gives a report of these high spring waters in his prophecy (Ezekiel 47:3, 4, 5[540]), it's good to be dipped or plunged in this Jordan river,[541] which takes away all deformity, and cleanseth from all leprosy,[542] and it's a comforting refreshing river, this is water of life, it recovers the dying vitals,[543] and fainting Spirits, the which none of men's strong liquors of arts and

---

removed, neither shall any of the cords thereof be broken." See, too, Isaiah 54:2.

534. The basetext reads "Bolial." Belial was a demon identified in the New Testament with Satan: see 2 Corinthians 6:15.

535. More commonly spelled "withes"; these were bands, ties, or shackles consisting of a tough flexible twig or branch, or of several twisted together (*OED*).

536. Dalilah (or Delilah) was bribed by the Philistines to find out the source of Sampson's supernatural strength. His first (false) answer to her said that if the Philistines bound him with green withes, he would lose his strength. See Judges 16.

537. An allusion to Matthew 5:29–30: "And if thy right eye offend thee, pluck it out, and cast it from thee: for it is profitable for thee that one of thy members should perish, and not that thy whole body should be cast into hell. And if thy right hand offend thee, cut it off, and cast it from thee: for it is profitable for thee that one of thy members should perish, and not that thy whole body should be cast into hell."

538. Psalm 119:97.

539. Isaiah 33:21.

540. See n7.

541. Crossing the River Jordan marked the final stage of the Israelites' journey from captivity to freedom, and Jesus was baptized by John the Baptist in its waters. The River Jordan is thus symbolic of liberation and spiritual cleansing. See Joshua 1 and Matthew 3:13–17.

542. Naaman is cured of leprosy when, on Elisha's advice, he dips himself seven times in the River Jordan; see 2 Kings 5:1–14.

543. Those organs or parts of the body essential to life (*OED*).

sciences[544] can do, neither can any compounded water of human invention be so effectual, though they still[545] it in the limbeck[546] of brain-study, draining it through the long pipe of curious witty phrases, yet such liquors will soon lose their spirits; but as for the water that the soul draws out of the well of salvation,[547] through faith's bucket, which retains the scent and fragrant smell, and operative nature, and the soul swims in the broad rivers that are promised Zion; which rivers will admit no galley with oars[548] to row therein, no troublers shall come there, none of men's gallantry, nor ships of merchandise shall sail there, no Turkish, nor English galley of power and strength and device,[549] managed with soldier oars shall appear to take the free-born captive; that river will presently sink such galleys and oars too; and if so be gallant Council ships,[550] and great numerous Parliament ships, which are made of wood; and pitch, and rosin, and tar, and oakum,[551] such stuff as will burn to ashes when the fire comes, which Scriptures speaks of,[552] it's not the clergy nails that can fasten such ships together, and make them sail, which are heavy lumpish bottoms,[553] that have no nimble swift motion at all, whereby to do service for King Jesus and his subjects: But the broad river is preparing, it's making its path thorough[554] all opposition, and its ships are all making ready and preparing to swim:[555] The great Ship-Wright, I speak this with reverence and holy awe of God, and say that the great artificial[556] Ship-Wright, and carpenter's son so called by the Jews, which was the glorious Messiah, this mighty God is fitting his ships for this time, these are the Zion spoken of, Micah 4:13,[557] whose horns are

---

544. Trapnel is here contrasting the intoxicating but ultimately useless properties of human learning with the life-sustaining ones of divine knowledge.

545. Distil (*OED*).

546. Alembic: in chemistry, an apparatus used for distilling.

547. Isaiah 12:3: "Therefore with joy shall ye draw water out of the wells of salvation."

548. Isaiah 33:21.

549. Contrivance.

550. Trapnel is here moving from the biblically originating "galley with oars" to the idea of "the ship of state," a longstanding metaphor for governance and statecraft.

551. All these are materials that were used in ship-building: pitch and rosin are sticky resinous substances used for the sealing of ships; oakum was hemp fiber used to caulk ships' seams. On shipbuilding, see introduction, 12.

552. See, e.g., Revelation 12:9.

553. Ships.

554. I.e., through.

555. Float.

556. Skilled in an art or craft, adept (*OED*).

557. Micah 4:13: "Arise and thresh, O daughter of Zion: for I will make thine horn iron, and I will make thy hoofs brass: and thou shalt beat in pieces many people: and I will consecrate their gain unto the Lord, and their substance unto the Lord of the whole earth."

iron, and hoofs brass, who are exhorted to arise and thresh, and beat in pieces many people, and these will not waste the gain, neither will they feast it away, but they will consecrate it unto the Lord of the whole earth, they will serve his interest with it, not their own ends, and selfish interests.

This is a time longed for by the new nonconformists,[558] who are Christ's little flock, whom he bids not to fear, for it pleased his Father to give them a Kingdom.

Therefore get you to your strong holds, oh Israel, and prisoners, for you are prisoners of hope,[559] you seek not great things for yourselves, but for the Lord's anointed ones; you cry to the Lord, and not for earthly palaces, nor Whitehall garden walks, nor kitchen-belly-cheer,[560] nor lardery-dainties,[561] nor banquet sweetmeats, nor Council-robes, nor Parliament tithes, nor Emperor advancement, nor great attendance, nor for Colonels' and Captains' silken buff,[562] and garnished spangled[563] coats, and gilded cloaks, and brave[564] London and country houses; I say, fellow-prisoners and sufferers for Christ, seeing we have none of this in our eye nor desires, let us bid defiance to all reproaches, and vilifyings and derisions against us; this defiance have I presented to Cornwall clergy and Justices with their auditories[565] or agents[566] joining with them, whether they be devout men or women, great gifted and learned, or ignorant; I bless the Lord, I can send defiance to all your reports, and reproachful language there, and so I can to all such here, and to their harshness, which say, it is pity but[567] I should be hanged, and that would commend a whip to my back; and to all base terms and names, and to Bridewell usage too, I will write defiance, and say, Who can lay any thing

558. Dissenters; those who had separated from the Church of England. Early in the century, the term "nonconformist" had meant those who continued to subscribe to the doctrines of the Church of England, but not its practices, but it was increasingly used for those who separated from it, including Baptists and Fifth Monarchists. Christopher Feake had recently published *The New Non-Conformist*, in May 1654, written in his cell in Windsor Castle and addressed to "his Little Flock at W.L. [Warwick Lane]." The text is dated May 24 by Thomason, but the preface, written by Feake, is dated "28 of 6 Moneth [sic], 1654": that is, August 1654, or, at the earliest, June (if he is taking the New Year to begin in January: on the early modern calendar, see "Editorial Principles and Practices," 38–39).

559. Zechariah 9:12: "Turn you to the strong hold, ye prisoners of hope: even to day do I declare that I will render double unto thee."

560. Feasting, luxurious eating.

561. Dainties or delicacies from the larder.

562. Military attire (*OED*).

563. Glittering.

564. Fine, grand.

565. Audiences.

566. Representatives.

567. It would be regrettable unless.

to my charge, worthy of such reproach, indictments, or binding over to the good behavior, or of three or four prisons, or of sending to Bridewell?[568]

And now in this defiance let all take their share; Enemies take yours, and don't be offended at true speaking, but be humbled and repent, that your evil words, and unjust actions, and thoughts of your heart may be forgiven you, and for you I shall pray.

And to friends, I have this word, do not you find fault with oppressions, but labor to amend them with candid and charitable constructions, and spiritual application of those Scripture-observations which are your due; and that we may all practice that which is good, and escape the evil, is the desire and earnest request of

Your praying Friend
ANNA TRAPNEL

---

568. The basetext ends this sentence with a period.

An Errata.[569]

In page 17. line 26. for horrible fit, read horrible pit. In page 19. line 15. for Haulbow, read Holse. In page 24. line 9. read draw near to the table. page 27. line 13 for pin, read bring, and for through, read notwithstanding their.

569. Used thus, "errata" meant "a list of errata" (*OED*). These errata are noted in the text: see nn192, 204, 238, 308, and 309.

Bibliography

Achinstein, Sharon. "The Politics of Babel in the English Revolution." In *Pamphlet Wars: Prose in the English Revolution*, edited by James Holstun, 14–44. London: Frank Cass, 1992.

Ancestry. http://www.ancestry.co.uk.

Anonymous. *Literary and Critical Remarks, on Sundry Eminent Divines and Philosophers*. London: B. Crosby, 1794.

Anonymous. *Reasons Humbly Offered in Justification of the Action, of Letting a Room in London-House unto Certain Peaceable Christians, called Anabaptists*. London?, s.n., [1642?].

Anonymous. *The World's Doom; or, The Cabinet of Fate Unlocked*. 2 vols. London: B. Crosby, 1795.

Appleby, John C. "Jacobean Piracy: English Maritime Depredation in Transition, 1603–1625." In *The Social History of English Seamen, 1485–1649*, edited by Cheryl A. Fury, 277–99. Woodbridge: Boydell, 2012.

Ashworth, William J. *Customs and Excise: Trade, Production, and Consumption in England, 1640–1845*. Oxford: Oxford University Press, 2003.

Atkinson, C. T., ed. *Letters and Papers Relating to the First Dutch War, 1652–1654*. S.l.: Navy Records Society, 1912.

Aughterson, Kate, ed. *The English Renaissance: An Anthology of Sources and Documents*. London: Routledge, 1998.

Baker, Naomi. "'Break Down the Walls of Flesh': Anna Trapnel, John James, and Fifth Monarchist Self-Representation." In *Women, Gender, and Radical Religion in Early Modern Europe*, edited by Sylvia Brown, 117–38. Leiden, Boston: Brill, 2007.

Bannerman, W. Bruce, ed. *The Registers of St. Olave, Hart Street, London*. Publications of the Harleian Society. London: s.n., 1916.

Beaumont, Agnes. "The Persecution of Agnes Beaumont." In John Bunyan, *Grace Abounding, with other Spiritual Autobiographies*, edited by John Stachniewski with Anita Pacheco, 191–224. Oxford: Oxford University Press, 1998.

Berg, Christine, and Philippa Berry. "'Spiritual Whoredom': An Essay on Female Prophets in the Seventeenth Century." In *1642: Literature and Power in the Seventeenth Century*, edited by Francis Barker et al., 37–54. Colchester: University of Essex, 1981.

Birch, Thomas, ed. *A Collection of the State Papers of John Thurloe, Esq., Secretary, First, to the Council of State, and Afterwards to the Two Protectors, Oliver and Richard Cromwell*. 7 vols. London: Woodward and Davis, 1742.

The Book of Common Prayer. 1571. Reprint, London: Eyre and Spottiswoode, n.d.

Bradstock, Andrew. *Radical Religion in Cromwell's England: A Concise History from the English Civil War to the End of the Commonwealth.* London: I.B. Tauris, 2011.

Bridewell Court Minute Book. Bcb-09 Series Box Number CO4/3 Series BCB.

Briggs, John, Christopher Harrison, Angus McInnes, and David Vincent. *Crime and Punishment in England: An Introductory History.* London: UCL Press, 1996.

British History Online. "Hearth Tax: City of London, 1662, Farringdon within Ward." http://www.british-history.ac.uk/report.aspx?compid=118426&strquery=Dorothy Harlow.

_____. "Inhabitants of London in 1638: St Benetts Finke." http://www.british-history.ac.uk/no-series/london-inhabitants/1638/pp38-39.

Brockett, Allan. *Nonconformity in Exeter, 1650–1875.* Manchester: Manchester University Press, 1962.

Brothers, Richard. *Wonderful Prophecies.* London: M. Ritchie for B. Crosby, 1795.

Bullard, Rebecca. "Textual Disruption in *Anna Trapnel's Report and Plea* (1654)." *The Seventeenth Century* 23, no. 1 (2008): 34–53.

Bunyan, John. *Grace Abounding, with Other Spiritual Autobiographies.* Edited by John Stachniewski with Anita Pacheco. Oxford: Oxford University Press, 1998.

Burrage, Champlin. "Anna Trapnel's Prophecies." *English Historical Review* 26 (1911): 526–35.

Calamy, Edmund. *The Nonconformist's Memorial: Being an Account of the Ministers, Who Were Ejected Silenced after the Restoration, particularly by the Act of Uniformity.* Edited by Samuel Palmer. 2 vols. London: W. Harris, 1775.

Capp, B. S. *Cromwell's Navy: The Fleet and the English Revolution, 1648–1660.* Oxford: Clarendon, 1989.

_____. *The Fifth Monarchy Men: A Study in Seventeenth-Century English Millenarianism.* London: Faber and Faber, 1972.

Cary, Mary. *A New and More Exact Mappe or Description of New Jerusalems Glory.* London: W. H., 1651.

Channel, Elinor. *A Message From God, by a Dumb Woman.* London: s.n., 1653 [1654].

Chapman, Henry. *A Catalogue of Near Twenty Thousand Volumes of Curious Books.* London: s.n., 1785.

Chesher, Veronica. *The Boscawen Street Area, Truro.* Truro Civic Society and Buildings Research Group with the University of Exeter Extra Mural Department, 1980.

Clarke, Elizabeth. *Politics, Religion, and the Song of Songs in Seventeenth-Century England.* Basingstoke: Palgrave Macmillan, 2011.

Clowes, William Laird. *The Royal Navy: A History from the Earliest Times to 1900.* 7 vols. London: Chatham, 1996; first edition, 1898.

Coate, Mary. *Cornwall in the Great Civil War and Interregnum, 1642–1660.* Oxford: Oxford University Press, 1933. Reprint. Truro: D. Bradford Barton, 1963.

_____. "An Original Diary of Colonel Robert Bennet of Hexworthy (1642–43)." *Devon and Cornwall Notes and Queries* 18 (1934): 251–59.

Cockburn, J. S. *A History of English Assizes, 1558–1714.* London: Cambridge University Press, 1972.

College of Arms, Great Britain. *The Visitations of Cornwall, Comprising the Heralds' Visitations of 1530, 1573, & 1620.* With additions by J. L. Vivian. Exeter: William Pollard, 1887.

Colyer-Fergusson, Thomas, ed. *The Marriage Registers of St. Dunstan's, Stepney, in the County of Middlesex.* Vol. 2: 1640–1696. Canterbury: Cross and Jackman, 1899.

Comber, Thomas. *Christianity No Enthusiasm; or, The Several Kinds of Inspirations and Revelations Pretended to by the Quakers.* London: T. D. for Henry Brome, 1678.

Comenius, Johann Amos. *Prophetical Extracts. No IV. Relative to the Revolution in France, and the Decline of the Papal Power in the World.* London: G. Terry, [1794?].

Como, David R. *Blown by the Spirit: Puritanism and the Emergence of an Antinomian Underground in Pre-Civil-War England.* Stanford: Stanford University Press, 2004.

Cornwall Record Office, Truro. Thrall, Llewellyn and Pearce, solicitors, of Truro. Mortgage for £400, Trelassick, Ladock, May 16, 1696. TLP/343.

Covent Garden Life. http://coventgardenlife/com/info/history.htm.

Cowie, L. W. "Bridewell." *History Today* 23, no. 5 (1973): 350–58.

Crawford, Julie. *Marvelous Protestantism: Monstrous Births in Post-Reformation England.* Baltimore: Johns Hopkins University Press, 2005.

Crook, John. *The Cry of the Innocent for Justice.* S.l.: s.n., 1662.

Davies, Thomas. *A Catalogue of a Large Collection of Curious and Scarce Pamphlets.* London: s.n., 1771.

Drew, Samuel. *The History of Cornwall: From the Earliest Records and Traditions.* Helston and London: s.n., 1824.

Earle, Peter. *The Pirate Wars.* London: Methuen, 2003.

Early English Books Online (EEBO). http://eebo.chadwyck.com/home.

Eco, Umberto. *The Search for the Perfect Language.* Translated by J. Feutress. Oxford: Blackwell, 1995.

Edwards, Thomas. *Gangraena; or, A Catalogue and Discovery of Many of the Errors, Heresies, Blasphemies, and Pernicious Practices of the Sectaries of this Time.* London: printed for Ralph Smith, 1646.

Ellwood, Thomas. *A Caution to Constables and Other Inferiour Officers.* London: William Skeate, 1683.

_____. *The History of the Life of Thomas Ellwood*. London: J. Sowle, 1714.

English Heritage. "Hexworthy." List Entry Number 1219191. http://www.english-heritage.org.uk.

English Short Title Catalogue. http://estc.bl.uk.

Erbery, William. *The Bishop of London*. London: s.n., 1653.

Ezell, Margaret J. M. "Performance Texts: Arise Evans, Grace Carrie, and the Interplay of Oral and Handwritten Traditions during the Print Revolution." *ELH* 76 (2009): 49–73.

The Faithful Scout 184 (June 16–June 23, 1654).

Feake, Christopher. *A Beam of Light, Shining in the Midst of Much Darkness and Confusion*. London: J. C. for Livewell Chapman, 1659.

_____. *The New Non-Conformist; Who Having Obtained Help of God, Doth Persist unto This Very Day*. London: Livewell Chapman, 1654.

Feroli, Teresa. *Political Speaking Justified: Women Prophets and the English Revolution*. Newark: University of Delaware Press, 2006.

Finch, Heneage, Earl of Nottingham. *An Exact and Most Impartial Accompt of the Indictment, Arraignment, Trial, and Judgment (According to Law) of Twenty Nine Regicides, the Murtherers of His Late Sacred Majesty of Most Glorious Memory Begun at Hicks-Hall on Tuesday, the 9th of October, 1660*. London: R. Scot, T. Basset, R. Chiswell, and J. Wright, 1679.

Firth, C. H., and R. S. Rait, eds. *Acts and Ordinances of the Interregnum, 1642–1660*. 3 vols. London: Stationery Office, 1911.

Floyd-Wilson, Mary, et al. "Shakespeare and Embodiment: An E-Conversation." *Literature Compass* 2 (2005): 1–13.

Foster, Joseph. *Alumni Oxonienses: The Members of the University of Oxford, 1500–1714*, 4 vols. Oxford: James Palmer, 1891.

Fox, George. *The Journal of George Fox*. Edited by John L. Nickalls. Cambridge: Cambridge University Press, 1982.

Fuller, Thomas. *History of the Worthies of England*. London: J. G. W. L. and W. G. for Thomas Williams, 1662.

Gascoyne, Joel. *A Map of the County of Cornwall, 1699*. Reprinted in facsimile; introduction by W. L. D. Ravenhill and O. J. Padel. Exeter: Devon and Cornwall Record Society, 1991.

Gilbert, Davies. *The Parochial History of Cornwall*. London: J. B. Nicholls and Son, 1838.

Gill, Catie. "'All the Monarchies of this World Are Going Down the Hill': The Anti-Monarchism of Anna Trapnel's *The Cry of a Stone* (1654)." *Prose Studies* 29, no. 1 (2007): 19–35.

Gillespie, Katharine. *Domesticity and Dissent in the Seventeenth Century: English Women's Writing and the Public Sphere*. Cambridge: Cambridge University Press, 2004.

Graham, Elspeth, Hilary Hinds, Elaine Hobby, and Helen Wilcox, eds. *Her Own Life: Autobiographical Writings by Seventeenth-Century Englishwomen*. London: Routledge, 1989.

Great Britain. Public Record Office. *Calendar of State Papers: Domestic Series; The Commonwealth, 1649–1660*. 13 vols. London: Longman, Brown, Green, Longmans, & Robert, 1856–72.

Great Britain. Public Record Office, Mary Ann Everett. *Calendar of the Proceedings of the Committee for Compounding &c., 1643–1660*. 5 vols. London: H. M. Stationery Officer, 1889.

Great Britain. Public Record Office. Records of the Prerogative Court of Canterbury. PRO Prob/11/281.

Greaves, Richard L., and Robert Zaller, eds. *Biographical Dictionary of British Radicals in the Seventeenth Century*. 3 vols. Brighton: Harvester, 1982–84.

Guibbory, Achsah. "England's 'Biblical' Prophets, 1642–60." In *Writing and Religions in England, 1558–1689: Studies in Community-Making and Cultural Memory*, edited by Roger D. Sell and Anthony Johnson, 305–26. Farnham: Ashgate, 2009.

Hammons, Pamela S. *Poetic Resistance: English Women Writers and the Early Modern Lyric*. Aldershot: Ashgate, 2002.

Harvey, Sir Paul. *The Oxford Companion to English Literature*, 4th ed., revised by Dorothy Eagle. Oxford: Clarendon Press, 1967.

Hathorn, Humphrey. *The Old Leaven Purged Out*. London: s.n., 1658.

Hayes, Tom. "Diggers, Ranters, and Women Prophets: The Discourse of Madness and the Cartesian *Cogito* in Seventeenth-Century England." *Clio: A Journal of Literature, History, and the Philosophy of History* 26, no. 1 (1996): 29–50.

Heath, James. *A Chronicle of the Late Intestine Wars in the Three Kingdoms of England, Scotland and Ireland*. 2nd ed. London: J. C. for Thomas Basset, 1676.

Hill, Christopher. *Antichrist in Seventeenth-Century England*. London: Oxford University Press, 1971.

_____. *The English Bible and the Seventeenth-Century Revolution*. London: Allen Lane, 1993.

_____. *God's Englishman: Oliver Cromwell and the English Revolution*. London: Weidenfeld and Nicolson, 1970.

_____. *The World Turned Upside Down: Radical Ideas During the English Revolution*. 1972. Reprint, Harmondsworth: Penguin, 1975.

Hill, L. M. "The Two-Witness Rule in English Treason Trials: Some Comments on the Emergence of Procedural Law." *American Journal of Legal History* 12, no. 2 (1968): 95–111.

Hinds, Hilary. "Anna Trapnel, *Anna Trapnel's Report and Plea*." In *A Companion to Early Modern Women's Writing*, edited by Anita Pacheco, 177–88. Oxford: Blackwell, 2002.

_____. *God's Englishwomen: Seventeenth-century Radical Sectarian Writing and Feminist Criticism.* Manchester: Manchester University Press, 1996.

_____. "Sectarian Spaces: The Politics of Place and Gender in Seventeenth-Century Prophetic Writing." *Literature and History* 13, no. 2 (2004): 1–25.

_____. "Sectarian Writing." In *A New Companion to English Renaissance Literature and Culture*, edited by Michael Hattaway, 2 vols. 1.464–77. Oxford: Wiley-Blackwell, 2010.

_____. "Soul-Ravishing and Sin-Subduing: Anna Trapnel and the Gendered Politics of Free Grace." *Renaissance and Reformation* 25, no. 4 (2001): 117–37.

_____. "The Transvaluation of Body and Soul in the Spiritual Autobiographies of Anna Trapnel." In *Paradigms, Poetics, and Politics of Conversion*, edited by Jan N. Bremmer, Wout J. van Bekkum, and Arie L. Molendijk, 107–21. Leuven: Peeters, 2006.

Hinkle, William G. *A History of Bridewell Prison, 1553–1700.* Lewiston, NY: Edwin Mellen Press, 2006.

History in Portsmouth. "Colonel Nathaniel Whetham, Governor of Portsmouth (1604–1668)." http://history.inportsmouth.co.uk/people/whetham.htm

The History of Parliament Online. "Vincent I, Walter (1631–80), of Truro, Cornw." http://historyofparliamentonline.org/volume/1660-1690/member/vincent-walter-i-1631-80.

Hobbes, Thomas. *Behemoth; or, The Long Parliament.* Edited by Ferdinand Tönnies. 1679. Reprint, London: Simpkin, Marshall, and Co., 1889.

Hobby, Elaine. *Virtue of Necessity: English Women's Writing, 1649–88.* London: Virago, 1988.

Hodgson-Wright, Stephanie, ed. *Women's Writing of the Early Modern Period, 1588–1688: An Anthology.* Edinburgh: Edinburgh University Press, 2002.

Holstun, James. *Ehud's Dagger: Class Struggle in the English Revolution.* London: Verso, 2000.

Hughes, Ann. *Gender and the English Revolution.* London: Routledge, 2011.

Hutton, Ronald. "The Experience of the Civil War in the West." In *Somerset Archaeology and Natural History: The Proceedings of the Somerset Archaeological and Natural History Society* (1995): 1–6.

Innes, Joanna. "Prisons for the Poor: English Bridewells, 1550–1800." In *Labour, Law, and Crime: An Historical Perspective*, edited by Francis G. Snyder and Douglas Hay, 42–122. London: Tavistock Press, 1987.

Jonson, Ben. *Bartholomew Fair* [1614]. In *Jonson, Four Comedies*, edited by Helen Ostovich. London: Longman, 1997.

Kent, Joan. "The English Village Constable, 1580–1642: The Nature and Dilemmas of the Office." *Journal of British Studies* 20 (1981): 26–49.

King, Matthew, and Alasdair Middleton. "On London Fields." http://www.hmdt.org.uk/hmdt_downloads_1.html

Lake, Peter, with Michael Questier. *The Antichrist's Lewd Hat: Protestants, Papists, and Players in Post-Reformation England*. New Haven and London: Yale University Press, 2002.

Langdon, A. T. "A Cornish Royalist Family in the Seventeenth Century." *Devon and Cornwall Notes and Queries* 25–26 (1953): 89–93, 116–120.

Larner, Christina. *Enemies of God: The Witch Hunt in Scotland*. Edinburgh: John Donald, 2000.

Lees-Jeffries, Hester. "Literary Gardens, from More to Marvell." In *A New Companion to English Renaissance Literature and Culture*, edited by Michael Hattaway. 2 vols. 1.379–95. Oxford: Blackwell, 2010.

Lilburne, John. *The Grand Plea of Lieut. Col. John Lilburne*. London: s.n., 1647.

Lincoln, Margarette. *British Pirates and Society, 1680–1730*. Aldershot: Ashgate, 2014.

Loades, David. "The English Maritime Community, 1500–1650." In *The Social History of English Seamen, 1485–1649*, edited by Cheryl A. Fury, 5–26. Woodbridge: Boydell, 2012.

Loewenstein, David. *Representing Revolution in Milton and his Contemporaries: Religion, Politics, and Polemics in Radical Puritanism*. Cambridge: Cambridge University Press, 2001.

Longfellow, Erica. *Women and Religious Writing in Early Modern England*. Cambridge: Cambridge University Press, 2004.

McGregor, J. F., and Barry Reay, eds. *Radical Religion in the English Revolution*. Oxford: Oxford University Press, 1984.

Mack, Phyllis. "The Prophet and her Audience: Gender and Knowledge in the World Turned Upside Down." In *Reviving the English Revolution: Reflections and Elaborations on the Work of Christopher Hill*, edited by Geoff Eley and William Hunt, 139–52. London: Verso, 1988.

_____. *Visionary Women: Ecstatic Prophecy in Seventeenth-Century England*. Berkeley: University of California Press, 1992.

Magro, Maria. "Spiritual Autobiography and Radical Sectarian Women's Discourse: Anna Trapnel and the Bad Girls of the English Revolution." *Journal of Medieval and Early Modern Studies* 34, no. 2 (2004): 405–37.

Marshall, I. Howard. *The Acts of the Apostles: An Introduction and Commentary*. Leicester: InterVarsity Press, 1980.

Mastnak, Tomaž. "Introduction: The Ways of *Behemoth*." In *Hobbes's Behemoth: Religion and Democracy*, edited by Tomaž Mastnak, 1–37 (Exeter: Imprint Academic, 2009).

Matthews, A. G. *Calamy Revised: Being a Revision of Edmund Calamy's Account of the Ministers and Others Ejected and Silenced, 1660–2*. Oxford: Clarendon Press, 1934.

Measuring Worth. http://www.measuringworth.com/index.php.

Mercurius Politicus 197 (March 16–March 23, 1654).

Mercurius Politicus 201 (April 13–April 20, 1654).

Mercurius Politicus 312 (May 29–June 5, 1656).

Milton, John. "Areopagitica." In *Prose Writings*, edited by K. M. Burton, 145–85. London: Dent, 1958.

Mintz, Susannah B. "The Specular Self of *Anna Trapnel's Report and Plea.*" *Pacific Coast Philology* 35, no. 1 (2000): 1–16.

Monroe, Jennifer. *Gender and the Garden in Early Modern English Literature.* Aldershot: Ashgate, 2008.

Moore, Rosemary. *The Light in their Consciences: The Early Quakers in Britain, 1646–1666.* University Park: Pennsylvania State University Press, 2000.

Morrill, J. S. *The Cheshire Grand Jury, 1625–1659.* Leicester: Leicester University Press, 1976.

Morris, Christopher, ed. *The Journeys of Celia Fiennes.* London: The Cresset Press, 1947.

Muggleton, Lodowick. *A Looking-Glass for George Fox the Quaker, and other Quakers, Wherein They May See Themselves to be Right Devils.* London?: s.n., 1667.

Munro, Lucy. *Archaic Style in English Literature, 1590–1674.* Cambridge: Cambridge University Press, 2013.

Murphy, Elaine, ed. *A Calendar of Material Relating to Ireland from the High Court of Admiralty, 1641–1660.* Dublin: Irish Manuscripts Commission, 2011.

——————. *Ireland and the War at Sea, 1641–1653.* Woodbridge: Boydell and Brewer, 2012.

Nares, Robert. *A Glossary or Collection of Words, Phrases, Names, and Allusions to Customs, Proverbs, &c.* Stralsund: s.n., 1825.

National Archives Currency Converter. http://apps.nationalarchives.gov.uk/currency.

Nevitt, Marcus. "'Blessed, Self-denying, Lambe-like'? The Fifth Monarchist Women." *Critical Survey* 11, no. 1 (1999): 83–97.

——————. *Women and the Pamphlet Culture of Revolutionary England, 1640–1660.* Aldershot: Ashgate, 2006.

Norden. John. *Speculi Britanniæ Pars: A Topographical and Historical Description of Cornwall.* London: William Pearson, 1728.

O'Donoghue, Edward Geoffrey. *Bridewell Hospital, Palace, Prison, Schools.* London: John Lane, 1923.

Ostovich, Helen, and Elizabeth Sauer, eds. *Reading Early Modern Women: An Anthology of Texts in Manuscript and Print, 1550–1700.* London: Routledge, 2004.

Otten, Charlotte F., ed. *English Women's Voices, 1540–1700.* Gainesville: University Press of Florida, 1992.

Oxford Dictionary of National Biography: In Association with the British Academy: From the Earliest Times to the Year 2000. Edited by Matthew H. C. G. Harrison and Brian Howard. Oxford: Oxford University Press, 2004. http://www.oxforddnb.com/.

Oxford English Dictionary. 2nd ed. Oxford: Oxford University Press, 1989. http://www.oed.com/.

Palmer, June. *Truro in the Seventeenth Century: A Pattern of Place and People*. Truro: June Palmer, 1989.

Pelling, Margaret. "Skirting the City? Disease, Social Change, and Divided Households in the Seventeenth Century." In *Londinopolis: Essays in the Cultural and Social History of Early Modern London*, edited by Paul Griffiths and Mark S. R. Jenner, 154–75. Manchester: Manchester University Press, 2000.

Penney, Norman, ed. *Record of the Sufferings of Quakers in Cornwall, 1656–1686*. London: Friends Historical Society, 1928.

Pepys, Samuel. *The Diary of Samuel Pepys: A Selection*. Edited by Robert Latham. London: Penguin, 1987.

Perkins, William. *A Cloud of Faithfull Witnesses, Leading to the Heavenly Canaan*. London: Humfrey Lownes for Leo. Greene, 1607.

Peters, Kate. *Print Culture and the Early Quakers*. Cambridge: Cambridge University Press, 2005.

Philip and Harold Mernick Online. "The Church of St. Matthias, Poplar." http://mernick.org.uk/thhol/stmatthi.html.

Plomer, Henry R. *A Dictionary of the Booksellers and Printers who were at Work in England, Scotland, and Ireland from 1641 to 1667*. S.l.: Bibliographical Society, 1968.

Prineas, Matthew. "The Discourse of Love and the Rhetoric of Apocalypse in Anna Trapnel's Folio Songs." *Comitatus* 28 (1997): 90–110.

Public Record Office. Records of the Prerogative Court of Canterbury. PRO Prob/11/281.

The Publick Intelligencer 13 (December 24–December 31, 1655).

Purkiss, Diane. "Anna Trapnel's Literary Geography." In *The Intellectual Culture of Puritan Women*, edited by Johanna Harris and Elizabeth Scott-Baumann, 162–75. Basingstoke: Palgrave Macmillan, 2011.

_____. *The English Civil War: A People's History*. London: Harper Perennial, 2007.

_____. "Producing the Voice, Consuming the Body: Women Prophets of the Seventeenth Century." In *Women, Writing, History, 1640–1740*, edited by Isobel Grundy and Susan Wiseman, 139–58. London: Batsford, 1992.

_____. *The Witch in History: Early Modern and Twentieth-Century Representations*. London: Routledge, 1996.

Radcliffe, Geoffrey, and Geoffrey Cross. *The English Legal System*. Edited by G. J. Hand and D. J. Bentley. 6th ed. London: Butterworth's, 1977.

Ravenhill, W. L. D. and O. J. Padel, "Introduction." In Joel Gascoyne, *A Map of the County of Cornwall, 1699*. Exeter: Devon and Cornwall Record Society, 1991.

Raymond, Joad. *Pamphlets and Pamphleteering in Early Modern Britain*. Cambridge: Cambridge University Press, 2003.

Roberts, Stephen K. "Initiative and Control: The Devon Quarter Sessions Grand Jury, 1649–70." *Bulletin of the Institute of Historical Research* 57, no. 136 (1984): 165–77.

_____. "Juries and the Middling Sort: Recruitment and Performance at Devon Quarter Sessions." In *Twelve Good Men and True: The Criminal Trial Jury in England, 1200–1800*, edited by J. S. Cockburn and Thomas A. Green, 182–213. Princeton: Princeton University Press, 1988.

_____. *Recovery and Restoration in an English County: Devon Local Administration, 1646–1670*. Exeter: University of Exeter Press, 1985.

Rogers, John. *Sagrir; or, Doomes-Day Drawing Nigh*. London: R.I., 1653.

Rohr, John von. *The Covenant of Grace in Puritan Thought*. Atlanta, GA: Scholars Press, 1986.

Rowse, A. L. "Jan Tregagle: In Legend and in History." *History Today* 15, no. 12 (1965): 828–34.

Saint Dunstan and All Saints, Register of Baptisms, September 1608–January 1637/8. P93/DUN, Item 256. London Metropolitan Archives.

Seaver, Paul S. *The Puritan Lectureships: The Politics of Religious Dissent, 1560–1662*. Stanford: Stanford University Press, 1970.

Senior, C. M. *A Nation of Pirates: English Piracy in its Heyday*. Newton Abbot: David and Charles, 1976.

Severall Proceedings of State Affaires in England, Scotland, and Ireland 225 (January 12–January 19, 1653 [1654]).

Sharpe, J. A. *Crime in Early Modern England, 1550–1750*. 2nd ed. London and New York: Longman, 1999.

Shaw, William Arthur. *A History of the English Church during the Civil Wars and under the Commonwealth, 1640–1660*, vol. 2. New York: B. Franklin reprints, 1900.

Sheppard, William. *The Offices of Constables, Church-wardens, Overseers of the Poor, Supravisors of the High-wayes, Treasurers of the County-Stock; And some other Lesser Country Officers*. London: Ric. Hodgkinsonne, for E. Dod and N. Ekins, 1652.

_____. *The Whole Office of the Country Justice of Peace. Wherein is Plainly Set Down all their Power and Duty both in, and out of the Quarter Sessions*. 2nd ed. London: W. Lee, D. Pakeman, G. Bedell, 1652.

Simonova, Natasha. "New Evidence for the Reading of Sectarian Women's Prophecies." *Notes and Queries* 60, no.1 (2013): 66–70.

Simpson, Percy. *Shakespearean Punctuation.* Oxford: Clarendon Press, 1911.

Smith, Hilda L., Mihoko Suzuki, and Susan Wiseman, eds. *Women's Political Writings, 1610–1725.* London: Pickering and Chatto, 2007.

Smith, Horace. *Brambletye House; or, Cavaliers and Roundheads.* Rev. ed. London: H. Colburn, 1835.

Smith, Nigel. *Literature and Revolution in England, 1640–1660.* New Haven: Yale University Press, 1994.

_____. *Perfection Proclaimed: Language and Literature in English Radical Religion, 1640–1660.* Oxford: Clarendon Press, 1989.

_____. "The Rod and the Canon." *Women's Writing* 14, no. 2 (2007): 232–45.

Spargo, Tamsin. "The Father's Seductions: Improper Relations of Desire in Seventeenth-Century Nonconformist Communities." *Tulsa Studies in Women's Literature* 17, no. 2 (1998): 255–68.

Spooner, Barbara. *John Tregagle of Trevorder: Man and Ghost.* Truro: A. W. Jordan, 1935.

Stachniewski, John. *The Persecutory Imagination: English Puritanism and the Literature of Religious Despair.* Oxford: Clarendon Press, 1991.

Stow, John. *Survey of the Cities of London and Westminster, and the Borough of Southwark.* London: W. Innys and J. Richardson et al., 1754–55.

_____. *A Survey of the Cities of London and Westminster, Borough of Southwark, and Parts Adjacent.* Revised by Robert Seymour [pseudonym for John Mottley]. 2 vols. London: J. Read, 1733–35.

Stoyle, M. J. "'Pagans or Paragons?': Images of the Cornish in the English Civil War." *English Historical Review* 111, no. 441 (1996): 299–323.

Swarthmore Manuscripts MS VOL 354/116, Vol. 3. Library of the Religious Society of Friends, London.

Taylor, Joseph. *Antiquitates Curiosae: The Etymology of Many Remarkable Old Sayings, Proverbs, and Singular Customs.* London: T. and J. Allman, 1818.

Tenison, Thomas. *Of Idolatry a Discourse.* London: F. Tyton, 1678.

Thomas, Keith. *Religion and the Decline of Magic.* London: Weidenfeld and Nicolson, 1971.

_____. "Women and the Civil War Sects." *Past and Present* 13, no. 1 (1958): 42–62.

Thurley, Simon. "The Lost Palace of Whitehall." *History Today* 48, no.1 (1998): 47–52.

Tilley, Morris Palmer. *A Dictionary of the Proverbs in England in the Sixteenth and Seventeenth Centuries.* Ann Arbor: University of Michigan Press, 1950.

Tillinghast, John. *Generation-Work.* London: M. Simmons for Livewell Chapman, 1653.

Trapnel, Anna. *Anna Trapnel's Report and Plea; or, A Narrative of her Journey from London into Cornwall, the occasion of it, the Lord's encouragements to it, and signal presence with her in it.* London: Thomas Brewster, 1654.

_____. *The Cry of a Stone; or, A Relation of Something Spoken in Whitehall, by Anna Trapnel, being in the Visions of God*. London: s.n., 1654. New edition with introduction and notes by Hilary Hinds. Arizona: Arizona Center for Medieval and Renaissance Studies, 2000. Page references are to the 2000 edition.

_____. *A Legacy for Saints; Being Several Experiences of the Dealings of God with Anna Trapnel, In, and After her Conversion*. London: Thomas Brewster, 1654.

_____. "Poetical addresses or discourses delivered to a gathering of 'Companions' in 1657 and 1658." S.l.: s.n., 1659? In Bodleian Library, Oxford, UK.

_____. *Strange and Wonderful Newes from White-Hall*. London: Robert Sele, 1654.

_____. *A Voice for the King of Saints and Nations*. S.l.: s.n., 1657?

Turner, Jane. *Choice Experiences*. London: H. Hils, 1653.

Vann, Richard T. *The Social Development of English Quakerism, 1655–1755*. Cambridge, MA: Harvard University Press, 1969.

The Victoria History of the Counties of England. London and New York: Oxford University Press, 1911–.

Wallace, Dewey D., Jr. *Puritans and Predestination: Grace in English Protestant Theology, 1525–1695*. Chapel Hill: University of North Carolina Press, 1982.

Warren, Nancy Bradley. *The Embodied Word: Female Spiritualities, Contested Orthodoxies, and English Religious Cultures, 1350–1700*. Notre Dame, IN: University of Notre Dame Press, 2010.

The Weekly Intelligencer 243 (May 30–June 6, 1654).

Weinreb, Ben, and Christopher Hibbert, eds. *The London Encyclopædia*. London: Macmillan, 1983.

Wentworth, Anne. *A Vindication of Anne Wentworth*. London: s.n., 1677.

Westminster City Archives Research Group. *One on Every Corner: The History of Some Westminster Pubs*. London: Westminster City Archives, 2002.

Wheatley, Henry Benjamin, and Peter Cunningham. *London Past and Present: Its History, Associations, and Traditions*. London: John Murray, 1891.

Whetham, Catherine Durning, and William Cecil Dampier Whetham. *A History of the Life of the Colonel Nathaniel Whetham*. London: Longmans, Green and Co., 1907.

White, Paul. *The South-West Highway Atlas for 1675*. Launceston: Tamar Books, 2005.

Williams, Gordon. *A Dictionary of Sexual Language and Imagery in Shakespearean and Stuart Literature*. 2 vols. London: Athlone Press, 1994.

Wiseman, Sue. "Margaret Cavendish among the Prophets: Performance and Gender in and after the English Civil War." *Women's Writing* 6, no. 1 (1999): 95–111.

_____. "Unsilent Instruments and the Devil's Cushions: Authority in Seventeenth-Century Women's Prophetic Discourse." In *New Feminist Discourses: Critical Essays on Theories and Texts*, edited by Isobel Armstrong, 176–96. London: Routledge, 1992.

Woolrych, Austin. *Britain in Revolution, 1625–1660*. Oxford: Oxford University Press, 2002.

_____. *Commonwealth to Protectorate*. Oxford: Clarendon Press, 1982.

Worden, Blair. *Literature and Politics in Cromwellian England: John Milton, Andrew Marvell, Marchamont Nedham*. Oxford: Oxford University Press, 2007.

_____. "Providence and Politics in Cromwellian England." *Past and Present* 109 (1985): 55–99.

Worth, R. N. *History of Plymouth, From the Earliest Period to the Present Time*. Plymouth: W. Brendon & Son, 1871.

Wray, Ramona. "'What Say You to [This] Book? ... Is it Yours?' Oral and Collaborative Narrative Trajectories in the Mediated Writings of Anna Trapnel." *Women's Writing* 16, no. 3 (2009): 408–24.

Wrightson, Keith. "Two Concepts of Order: Justices, Constables, and Jurymen in Seventeenth-Century England." In *An Ungovernable People: The English and their Law in the Seventeenth and Eighteenth Centuries*, edited by John Brewer and John Styles, 21–46. London: Hutchinson, 1980.